KU-524-403

The History of Civilization
Edited by C. K. OGDEN, M.A.

Travel and Travellers of the
Middle Ages

CITY OF ST. ALBANS PUBLIC LIBRARY

The History of Civilization

In the Section of this Series devoted to PRE-HISTORY AND ANTIQUITY *are included the following volumes :—*

I. Introduction and Pre-History

II. The Early Empires

In the Section of this Series devoted to CHRISTIANITY AND THE MIDDLE AGES *are included the following volumes :—*

VI. Social and Economic Evolution

* An asterisk indicates that the volume does not form part of the French collection "L'Evolution de l'Humanité."

A full list of the SERIES *will be found at the end of this volume.*

CITY OF ST. ALBAN
PUBLIC
LIBRARY

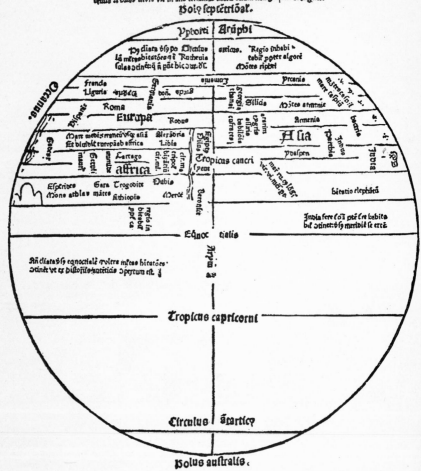

THE HABITABLE WORLD ACCORDING TO CARDINAL PIERRE D'AILLY, 1410.

TRANSLATION OF THE LEGENDS OF CARDINAL PIERRE D'AILLY'S DIAGRAM OR
MAP OF THE HABITABLE WORLD.

From *Trautatus de ymagine mundi, etc.*

Fol.   [Printed by John of Westphalia.   Louvain ?, 1480 ?.]

Seventh Figure.

This figure serves the xiiijth chapter and many others for the division of the earth into three parts and likewise for the distinguishing of the sea and of certain rivers and regions here set down by way of example because more particular distinction requires a larger figure. The Mediterranean Sea goes out from the ocean by the narrow strait of Hercules round Spain near Gades. The Red Sea indeed goes out from the ocean about the middle of the south-east, that is towards the south about midway between east and west. By the shore of which [sea] the end of the Indian ocean is scarcely reached in a year's sailing.

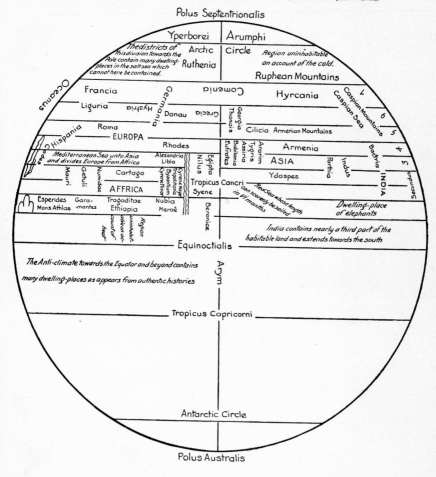

Travel and Travellers of the Middle Ages

Edited by

ARTHUR PERCIVAL NEWTON

M.A., D.Lit., B.Sc., F.S.A.

Rhodes Professor of Imperial History in the University of London

LONDON
KEGAN PAUL, TRENCH, TRUBNER & CO., LTD.
NEW YORK: ALFRED A. KNOPF
1926

910·9

RESERVE STOCK.

ST. ALBANS PUBLIC LIBRARY	
CLASS	B601
ACCESS	11929
SHELF	2164
DATE	5-10-26
BIND.	JAN. 1954

Printed in Great Britain by Stephen Austin & Sons, Ltd., Hertford.

CONTENTS

CONTENTS

LIST OF ILLUSTRATIONS

PREFACE

THE substance of the contributions here collected was comprised in a course of Public Lectures in the Departments of History and Geography in King's College, London, delivered in the Lent Term of 1925. Several of the contributions have been re-written and amplified with material that could not be included in the lectures, and I have added an entirely fresh chapter, but the book does not profess to be a complete survey of the fascinating field of which it treats. Those who are moved to explore further by the glimpses that alone are here revealed must betake themselves to the authorities that are mentioned in our footnotes and especially to the scholarly pages of Professor C. R. Beazley, Sir Henry Yule, M. Henri Cordier, and M. Ch. Schéfer. There they will find the full apparatus of maps and documents wherewith alone can justice be done to the ideas and achievements of medieval geographers. This brief conspectus of certain aspects of the subject may, however, be of interest to the general reader, summarizing as it does some of the more recent work done in the field, and it will be of value to the increasing number of students in English and American universities who, as a part of their geographical courses, are concerning themselves with the history of travel.

My warm thanks are due to the collaborators who have accepted so kindly my suggestions of subjects for treatment, and have facilitated my task in every way. For the planning and arrangement of the book I alone must accept responsibility.

ARTHUR PERCIVAL NEWTON.

UNIVERSITY OF LONDON,
   KING'S COLLEGE.
      3rd December, 1925.

CHAPTER I

INTRODUCTION : THE CONCEPTION OF THE WORLD IN THE MIDDLE AGES

By Professor ARTHUR PERCIVAL NEWTON, M.A., D.LIT., B.SC., F.S.A.

THE essays here collected have been arranged to show something of the way in which the men of the Latin West—in the course of a thousand years—gradually modified their conceptions of the physical world in which they lived. These conceptions differed widely from those of the Ancients, though they derived many of their components from the ideas of Classical times. They also differed from those formed on a wider base of knowledge in subsequent centuries, but they have contributed much to our everyday phraseology and to the imagery of our poets. While rejecting the ideas of medieval men, we have kept their names and phrases. Many of them are very persistent, but they have quite changed their meaning. At one time they were accurate descriptions of what men thought about the world, and might form the basis of argument. To-day they are mere poetic figures.

The contributions are arranged in roughly chronological order, and each discusses in some detail the concepts of the world and the conditions of travel and exploration of a particular period or associated with particular sources of ideas which have made material additions to the development of thought and knowledge.

The thousand years between the break-up of the ancient world and the period of the great discoveries of the late fifteenth and early sixteenth century falls in this, as in many other respects, into three main periods. The first stretches from the sixth to the eleventh century and is marked by the loss of the ancient scientific concepts of the world and their replacement by uncritical cosmogonies, based largely upon the crude ideas of the Hebrews as set out in the Scriptures. It can hardly be claimed that in this period there was any conception of the world generally held among educated and thinking men. Almost every writer who deals with cosmogony interprets the Scriptural phrases in his own way, and only the very ablest, like the Venerable Bede, who still were familiar with the remains of ancient learning, give us anything that remotely corresponds with reality. The second period includes the time from about A.D. 1000 to the beginning of the fourteenth century. It is the period of the Crusades, a time of rapid development in the realm of ideas and of critical power, as well as in material achievement. Men are no longer wholly dependent for their conceptions upon the Scriptures and a trickle of little understood survivals from the ancients. They can drink at the founts of Greek and Roman knowledge through new channels. Arabic thought and learning greatly influence them. Immense results flowed thence, and the time is marked not only by great advance in the sphere of thought and scientific criticism, but also by a large extension of exploration and a growth in practical knowledge of the landmass of Eurasia such as had never been possessed even in ancient times. Alongside, but flowing in a separate stream, were the achievements of the men of the North. Their practical accomplishment was astonishing, but its influence upon the development of European thought was comparatively slight and indirect. It was not until a very much later age that the travels of the Vikings became known throughout Western Europe, and their story is rather an appendix to our main theme than an integral part of it.

The third and culminating period of the Middle Age includes the fourteenth and fifteenth centuries, a period of great practical achievement. It was marked not only by a more systematic shaping of the typical medieval ideas, but also by immense improvements in navigation and the means of maritime exploration. These two lines of development, the theoretical and the practical, gradually approached one another, and the second absorbed or replaced the first.

For the earlier Middle Ages down to the middle of the thirteenth century material is comparatively scanty, but from thence onwards we have geographical treatises of a detailed and scholarly character, and we can summarize the ideas of the time with much more certainty. Possibly it was only in the period between the time of Roger

Bacon (*c.* 1270) and the recovery of Ptolemy's geographical work in the first half of the fifteenth century that there was formulated a conception of the world that was generally acceptable to educated men. The medieval point of view can thus be seen best in the ideas of the fourteenth century, for after its close other ideas came rapidly surging in, partly as has been said, from the results of exploration and partly from the recovery of the ancient learning and the rise of a new critical spirit, brought about in the geographical sphere especially by the study of the writings of Ptolemy.

Each of these three periods will be taken up in turn, and we shall endeavour to deal with the principal travels and travellers of the time, the motives that inspired and the circumstances that controlled them. Men in all ages are the creatures of their ideas, and it seems fitting, therefore, before entering upon the more detailed studies of our later chapters, to trace in outline some of the beliefs as to the nature of the world in which they lived that were familiar to the minds of the travellers of the Middle Age. Those beliefs pointed out the goals for which they sought, guided the direction they took, and coloured all their observations on the way. Hence, to understand aright the descriptions of travels that they penned, we should know something of the preconceptions with which they started.

The culminating work of ancient geography was that written in Greek about A.D. 150 by the Egyptian astronomer, Claudius Ptolomœus. By reason of his access to the stores of learning preserved in the great library of Alexandria, he was able to summarize in an orderly and complete way the work of earlier scientific thinkers like Hipparchus, Eratosthenes, and Marinus of Tyre. His point of view was that of a mathematician and his treatment orderly and systematic. His main work was devoted to Astronomy, and is contained in a book that had great influence on Arabic thought and is still known by the names the Arabs gave it, *Almagest.* His *Geography,* however, is not solely confined to the mathematical side of the subject, but is also descriptive, and it was provided with scientifically constructed maps which gave an elaborate picture of the world as known to the Greeks. For this work he was able to collect much

information from the traders and travellers who came to
Alexandria, then the greatest commercial centre of the world.
Ptolemy's *Almagest* was fairly well known to the thinkers
of the twelfth and thirteenth centuries through Arabic
versions, but his *Geography* was comparatively little known.
It was not until it was translated into Latin about A.D. 1410
that it began to exercise a gradually preponderating influence
upon geographical thought. The Middle Ages knew little
Greek, but in the fifteenth century this defect was remedied.
Ptolemy's *Geography*, which was at first circulated in poor Latin
translations, but by 1478, when a magnificent edition was
published at Rome with fine maps, it had become familiar
to scholars. It was printed in Greek in 1533. Between
1410 and 1478, therefore, the ancient view of the
world was revived, and profoundly modified the medieval
concepts and rapidly displaced them. The next half century
(1478–1528) saw increasing attempts to fit the facts of the
new oceanic discoveries of the sailors into the scientific
Ptolemaic framework, but ultimately it was realized that
the task was impossible. Ptolemy's system was bit by bit
abandoned, and the field was left for the modern conceptions
and the work of geographers and cartographers like Gerhard
Mercator and Abraham Ortelius, who used cartographical
apparatus and drew maps which differ little in essentials
from those in use to-day.

The geographical Renaissance may be dated roughly as
beginning, therefore, in the decade 1410–20, which also saw
the beginning of the first systematic efforts of the Portuguese
towards oceanic exploration. But the old ideas were
not abruptly abandoned. They were gradually modified
to fit the new knowledge, and many even of the greatest
discoverers, and above all Christopher Columbus, thought of
their work in a medieval way and sought in vain for the
fabulous wonders that had filled so many of the pages of
writers of earlier generations.

From the knowledge of the early Middle Ages true views of
the shape of the earth had almost disappeared and had given
place to fanciful ideas of symmetry based upon the speculations of Hebrew poets. The systematic thought of the great
writers of antiquity was almost forgotten, and only the
fables and marvels of compilers like Solinus (3rd c. A.D.)

remained in circulation. We may take as an example one of the BEATUS maps, so called from having been attached to a *Commentary on the Apocalypse* written by the Spanish priest Beatus at the end of the eighth century. The map he drew was intended to portray the spread of the Christian faith, as the kingdom of heaven is likened in the Gospel to a field sown with seed. The typical Beatus map contains a series of pictures of the Twelve Apostles, each in that part of the world where he is traditionally said to have preached. Jerusalem with St. James does not occupy the centre of the map, but Adam and Eve and the serpent are shown in a vignette at the top, which marks the East. The whole is surrounded by the ocean with pictures of fishes and sometimes row-boats.

But much sounder ideas of cosmogony than these were held by the leading thinkers of the time, the outstanding example of whom is the Venerable Bede in the early eighth century who, familiar as he was with many of the best writings of antiquity, still held fast to the ancient idea of a spherical globe. Much more cosmographical writing has been usually attributed to Bede than is now accepted as genuine by his editors. But there are certain passages in the authentic treatise *De Natura Rerum* which exhibit clearly his views of cosmogony. He tells us that the world is divided into five zones which are distinguished by differences of temperature, and herein he closely follows the system of the late Latin cosmographer Macrobius, whose influence was widely spread for many centuries :—

" The first is the northern, uninhabitable by reason of cold and whose stars never set for us. The second is the solstitial or summer zone, which is habitable and temperate ; the third the equinoctial covered by the burning orb of the sun, torrid and uninhabitable. The fourth zone is the brumal or winter zone (*brumalis*) on the lower side turned towards the southern pole, temperate and habitable. The fifth is the austral zone around the southern turning point (*verticem*), which is covered with land and is uninhabitable by reason of the cold. But the three middle zones are distinguished by inequalities of their seasons ; when the sun holds the first at the summer solstice, the second at the equinox, and the third in winter. The two extreme zones are always without the sun. Wherefore from the island of Thule with one day's sailing to the north the frozen sea is reached." [1]   In his *De Temporum Ratione*, a work relating to the astronomical calendar and undoubtedly genuine, Bede again touches on cosmogony and discusses the Antipodes, where he strongly denies that beings like ourselves can exist.

But other professedly scientific works have been ascribed to the historian that are now shown to be two or three centuries later in date, and it is from these credulous productions that what have been thought to be Bede's cosmogonical beliefs have usually been quoted, thus doing him serious injustice. The first of these, *De Elementis Philosophiæ*, possibly written by William de Conches about A.D. 1100, has been cited even by so erudite a scholar as the Visconde de Santarem [2] as exemplifying Bede's geographical ideas, though it commits itself to an elaborate symmetry of inventive detail that would be impossible for the rational thinking of the great scholar. An extract is worth quotation as showing something of medieval methods of geographical reasoning :—

" The earth is an element placed at the middle of the world ; it is at its middle as the yolk is in the egg ; about it there is water, as about the yolk there is the white. About the water the air like the skin containing the white of the egg. The earth is thus placed in the middle of the world and receives thence all heavy things, and although naturally it is congealed and dry in its divers parts, it comprises many different qualities by reason of happenings beyond itself. For the part that is subjected to the burning part of the air is torrid from the burning heat of the sun and inhabitable ; but the ends are frozen by reason of the two cold parts [of the air] and are uninhabitable, though the part subjected to the temperate part of the air is temperate and habitable. Since, as we have said before, there are two parts of this temperate sort, there are two parts of the earth that are temperate and suitable for habitation, one on this side of the torrid zone, the other on the further side. But although both are habitable yet we believe that only one of them is habited by men and even that not wholly. But philosophers make

---

[1] *De Natura Rerum*, cap. ix, Works (ed. Smith), vol. vi, p. 103.
[2] Barros e Sousa, Visconde de Santarem, *Essai sur l'histoire de la cosmographie*, i, 25.

mention of the inhabitants of both not because they are there, but because they say that they might be."

In another work, possibly a little later than Bede's time but falsely attributed to him, *De mundi cœlestis terrae que constitutione*, similar ideas are set forth, and it is implied that though there *may* be habitable regions beyond the torrid zone, yet their inhabitants, the Antichthones, cannot reach us and we cannot reach them. Again, the legend attached to a celebrated Turin map of the eleventh century describes a circumfluent ocean surrounding the torrid zone and says : " The ocean surrounding the coasts of the land almost at the height of the horizon divides it into two parts, of which we inhabit the upper and our antipodes the other, nevertheless none of us can come to them nor none of them to us." [1]

The most noticeable thing in these speculations and, perhaps, the most disconcerting to those who have thought of the men of the Middle Ages as believers in a flat earth, is that there is not a hint of such an idea. Its globular character is entirely accepted.

A typical scholar of the eleventh century, Adam of Bremen, who was canon and master of the school of the great cathedral there between 1060 and 1076, has left works of the greatest value for the history of Northern Europe in the early Middle Ages, but he also wrote geographical works of much interest. From his pages we glean the most nearly contemporary references to the explorations of the Vikings, and we may take him as fairly representing the thought of his age.

He clearly grasped the sphericity of the earth and refers to the axis around which the globe revolves, but he dealt little with abstract ideas and mainly devoted himself to geographical descriptions of Northern Europe derived from travellers. He considered that *terra firma* was entirely surrounded by the infinite and terrible ocean, the northern part of which was covered with ice and darkness. The sea was stiff with salt and covered with ice so ancient as to be black and tindery. Venturous sailors like Harold Hardrada, who had sailed north into those seas, had found terrible whirlpools like the Maelström at the " darkling end of the failing world ", which would suck in ships and disgorge them again like some gigantic monster.

[1] Santarem, *op. cit.* i, 27.

One of the most interesting representations of the globe
in medieval MSS. is to be found in the *Liber Floridus* of
Lambertus Audomarensis, a canon of St. Omer, written
in 1130. The work is an encylopædia of knowledge culled
from many earlier authors, and it had a considerable vogue
down to the end of the fourteenth century. Lambert
attempts to achieve two purposes, to give a symmetrical
conception of the whole globe, showing the relation of all its
parts, and to describe *terra firma*, the world inhabited by
man, which, according to him, fills only one quarter of the
whole. It cannot be claimed that any of his ideas were
original : they did not profess to be, but are in deference
to authority derived from the ancient philosophers, and
those recorded serve to show us the dim memories of the
learning of old times that alone remained among the men of the
twelfth century. In the most interesting of Lambert's several
mappemondes attached to the *Liber Floridus*, the east is at
the top and the earth is represented as a sphere round the
Equator of which flows a wide belt of sea. This mid-land sea
is said to be invisible to man, for the full strength of the sun,
" going just overhead by the Milky Way, raises it to torrid
heat," and prevents any human being from crossing it. *Terra
firma*, the great land mass of the habitable world, is thus
divided from the Land of the Fabled Antipods, the Australian
land, or *terra australis nondum cognita*. This is " temperate in
climate but unknown to the sons of Adam, having nothing
which is related to our race. . . . When we are scorched
with heat [the Antipods] are chilled with cold ; and the
northern stars which we are permitted to discern are entirely
hidden from them ". Many of Lambert's imaginings,
derived from ancient Greek science and also accepted by the
best writers of the later Middle Ages, are not widely removed
from reality, but he adds to them many impossible suggestions. He tells us that the Antipods have days and nights
of equal length, and that they suffer winter twice over,
while immediately to the south of them is a great region
entirely uninhabitable by reason of the perpetual cold and
darkness.

The Terrestrial Paradise, in which are Enoch and Elias,
is placed in a circle surrounded by rays and stars at the
extreme east, and the antipodes of Paradise in another circle

at the extreme west with the inscription " Here live our antipodes, but they have a different night, and days which are contrary to ours, and so for the setting of the stars." Lambert appears to conceive of this land of the antipodes as another world similar in form and size to *terra firma*.[1]

It is interesting to note how the idea of the antipodes appealed to the greatest of the poets of the Middle Ages. In the Thirty-fourth Canto of Dante's *Inferno*, written at the beginning of the fourteenth century, Virgil carries the poet by a secret path to the surface of the other hemisphere of the earth where once more they obtain a sight of the stars. In reply to Dante's inquiry of Virgil as to where they were :—

> " [He] answering spake. Thou deemest thou art still
> On the other side the centre, where I grasp'd
> The abhorred worm that boreth through the world.
> Thou wast on the other side, so long as I
> Descended, when I turn'd, thou didst o'erpass
> That point to which from every part is dragg'd
> All heavy substance. Thou art now arrived
> Under the hemisphere opposed to that
> Which the great continent doth overspread,
> And underneath whose canopy expired
> The Man, that was born sinless and so lived.
> Thy feet are planted on the smallest sphere
> Whose other aspect is Judecca. Morn
> Here rises, when there evening sets : and he
> Whose shaggy pile we scaled, yet standeth fix'd,
> As at first. On this part he [i.e. Lucifer] fell down
> From heaven ; and th' earth, here prominent before,
> Through fear of him did veil her with the sea,
> And to our hemisphere retired."

The Twenty-seventh Canto of the *Purgatorio*, too, begins with lines that show how Dante fully realized the sphericity of the earth and its effect upon differences of time in various parts of the world.

> " Now was the sun so stationed, as when
> His early radiance quivers on the heights
> Where streamed his Maker's blood ; while Libra hangs
> Above Hesperian Ebro ; and new fires
> Meridian, flush on Ganges' yellow tide.
> So day was sinking when the angel of God
> Appear'd before us."

[1] For a full analysis of the MS. of the *Liber Floridus* at Ghent, see J. P. Migne, *Patrologia*, vol. clxiii, pp. 1005–31. On fol. 19 of this MS. is the mappemonde entitled *Sphera triplicata gentium mundi. Gentes Asiae, Europe, Africe diverse*. For a discussion of all Lambert's maps, see Santarem, op. cit., ii, 194, etc.

Perhaps the most numerous class of medieval maps comprised those which are called from their form "T-O maps". The east is placed at the top of the map, and not as with us on the right. The continental mass is surrounded by the Ocean as an O, and through the middle of the lower or western half of the map is drawn the Mediterranean Sea stretching from the Pillars of Hercules (our Strait of Gibraltar) to the coast of Palestine. Into the inner end of the Mediterranean flows from the south on our right hand, a greatly exaggerated Nile, and from the north, on our left, a strip of water which represents our Black Sea, Marmora and the Ægean. Thus the inland seas form a rough T dividing the land (*terra firma*) into three unequal portions or continents, an idea that was universal in the Middle Ages and still sways us, though we know that it has little geographical value. Each continent was associated with one of the sons of Noah, Asia with Shem (hence our phrase "Semitic peoples"), Africa with Ham (hence negroes are called "sons of Ham"), and Europe, inhabited by men of white stock, with Japhet. Jerusalem is usually situated at the centre of the map after the Scriptural tradition, that it was a city set on a hill from which the Gospel light shone out to all mankind.

From fanciful conceptions such as these to the critical and systematic speculations of the scholars of the thirteenth century who had a knowledge of the work of the Arab astronomers is an immense stride forward. Two of the greatest writers of the Middle Ages, Albertus Magnus and Roger Bacon, each devoted attention to geographical study, and in the work of each we find valuable knowledge. Each gave much consideration to the extent of the habitable regions and the nature of the Antipodes.

Albertus Magnus in his *Liber cosmographicus de natura locorum* (written about 1260) discusses how difference in latitude causes a difference in climate. "All the torrid zone is habitable," he says, "and it is a popular error to believe that those whose feet are directed towards us must necessarily fall. The same climates are repeated in the lower hemisphere on the other side of the equator, and two races of Ethiopians exist, those of the northern tropic and the blacks of the southern tropic. The lower hemisphere, antipodal to our own, is not entirely watery; it is in great part inhabited, and if the men of those far-off regions do not come to us, it is because of the vast seas that are set between; perhaps also some magnetic power there holds back human flesh and blood (*carnes humanas*) as the magnet holds the iron. Besides, the peoples of the torrid zone, far from suffering in intelligence by reason of the heat of the climate, are very learned, as is proved by the books of philosophy and astronomy that have come to us from India."

Roger Bacon, who was contemporary with Albertus Magnus, before embarking in his *Opus Majus* upon an elaborate geographical description of the habitable world, devotes attention to a consideration of its extent and the possibility of other zones than the north temperate climate being habitable and inhabited. He shows that the sea necessarily must occupy less than three-quarters of the surface of the globe, although this conclusion conflicts with the ancient Hebrew idea as expressed in the fourth *Book of Esdras* (cap. vi, verse 42): "Upon the third day thou didst command that the waters should be gathered together in the seventh part of the earth; six parts didst thou dry up." In fact, he maintains that the eccentricity of the solar orbit is likely to produce even more dry land in the southern hemisphere than we know to exist in the mass of the northern continent. He explains clearly the effect of the sun's passage along the ecliptic on the climates of the world, and that it is the cause of the long days of summer and the long nights of winter in Scotland and beyond it towards the Pole. He considers with great interest the work done by the Arabs and the astronomers of Alfonso X of Castile in constructing astronomical tables for the determination of latitudes and longitudes, and claims that it is desirable that such work should be continued, and with greater accuracy, for obtaining the benefits that he enumerates. "For their place of birth is the principle of the generation of things," and so a knowledge of latitude and longitude is necessary for a proper understanding of man and of Nature, for the spiritual government of the world, and for a knowledge of the home of the lost ten tribes of the Jews and the place where Antichrist will arise.

By repeated touches such as these last we can perceive how, despite his seeming modernity, Bacon is still a friar of the

Middle Ages, and though the maps that almost certainly accompanied his copy of the *Opus Majus* when he sent it to Pope Clement have not come down to us, it is very possible that they would not have differed much from those that were being drawn by his contemporaries and by succeeding scholars in their studies for a century more. A new class of maps was certainly arising for practical use among seamen and merchants, but they were far beneath the lofty consideration of the learned cosmographers. The gradual development of a realistic representation of coast-lines in the seamen's charts runs a separate course and cannot here concern us. The scholastic conceptions of the world still continued to be elaborated throughout the fourteenth century and they received a wider circulation than ever before in the pages of one of the most popular books of the Middle Ages.

We shall say more of the spurious work called *Mandeville's Travels* in a later part of this book, but here we need only note the views therein expressed concerning the shape of the earth which are contained in the twenty-first chapter. The book was written about 1370 and was in constant circulation in Western Europe throughout the fifteenth century. It may fairly be claimed to represent the average ideas of cosmogony prevailing among educated men before the complete recovery of Ptolemy's work. A few extracts will suffice.

" How the Earth and the Sea be of round form and shape, by proof of the star that is yclept Antartyk, that is fixed in the south.

" In the land of Lamary [i.e. Sumatra] nor in many other beyond that no man may see the star Transmontane [i.e. the Pole Star] that is yclept the star of the sea, that is immovable, that is toward the north, that we clepe the lodestar. But men see another star the contrary to him, towards the south that is yclept Antartyk. . . . And this star that is toward the north that we clepe the lode-star appeareth not to them. For which cause men may well perceive that the land and the sea be of round shape and form, for the part of the firmament [that] sheweth in one country, sheweth not in another country. And men may well prove by experience and subtle compassment of wit that if a man found passages by ships that would go to search the world, men might go by ship all about the world above and beneath. . . . A man may environ all the earth of all the world as well under and above and turn again to his country that had company and shipping and conduct. And always he should find men, lands and isles as well as in this country. For we wit well that they that be toward the Antartyk they be straight feet against feet of them that dwell under the Transmontane also well as we and they that dwell under the Transmontane also well as we and they that dwell under us be feet against feet. . . . They have the night when we have the day, and [while] that men go upward to one coast, men go downward to another coast. But how it seemeth simple to simple men unlearned that men may not go under the earth, and also that men should fall toward the heaven from under. But that may not be upon less than we may fall toward heaven from the earth where we be. . . . For if a man might fall from the earth unto the firmament, by greater reason the earth and the sea that be so great and so heavy should fall to the firmament, but that may not be." [1] From these very sensible observations the author proceeds to a demonstration of the way in which astronomers apply mathematical reasoning to the mapping of the firmament and the earth which although it is beyond our present purpose is of considerable interest as showing that the geography of educated men at the end of the fourteenth century was by no means so entirely fabulous as has sometimes been imagined.

Before returning to Roger Bacon by an unexpected route it is necessary to say something of a scholar of immense reputation in his own day and of great influence for a century after. The cosmographical writings of Cardinal Pierre d'Ailly or Petrus de Aliaco, Archbishop of Cambrai (1330–1420) were almost forgotten after the great discoveries of the early sixteenth century, and it was not until Alexander von Humboldt again drew attention to them early in the nineteenth that their historical importance was once more recognized. D'Ailly's work relating to geographical and astronomical speculations and the reform of the calendar is contained in a series of short treatises which are bound up with some of the writings of Jean Gerson in the unique edition which

---

[1] *Mandeville's Travels*, ed. P. Hamelins (Early English Text Society, London, 1919), vol. i, pp. 120–4.

was printed at Louvain after 1480, but many MSS. copies of the treatises are extant showing how much they circulated in the fifteenth century. The most important treatise is the first in the published volume called *Tractatus de Imagine Mundi*. It was written in 1410 when d'Ailly knew the astronomical work of Ptolemy in his *Almagest*, but had not yet read his *Geography*, first translated into Latin in that year. Three years later in 1413 d'Ailly, having read the new translations, wrote another geographical work, the *Compendium Cosmographiæ*, especially to summarize the useful things contained in Ptolemy's *Geographiæ Syntaxis*, and he is therefore not only the last of the medieval geographers before the Ptolemaic revival, but also the first of the Western scholars who began that revival and thus had so great an influence on thought. Besides these two treatises d'Ailly also drew a mappemonde to illustrate his geographical ideas and wrote a short explanatory note, the *Epilogus Mappe Mundi*, to accompany it.

Into his general views concerning the arrangement of climate, and the sphericity of the earth we need not enter, because they very much resemble what we have already mentioned. His work is marked by great erudition, and not only are all the principal writers on geography, both Greek and Latin, quoted, but also many citations are given from Arab authors, Averroes, Hali, Alfragan, Avicenna, and so on. This display of wide reading is of interest, as will appear in a moment. Probably the most significant passages of d'Ailly's writings are those in which he discusses the extent of the habitable globe. Some extracts from these will enable us to see something of his ideas of cosmogony :—

" The earth is spherical," he writes in the seventh chapter of his *Imago Mundi*, " and the Western ocean is relatively small. Aristotle pretends, contrary to Ptolemy, that more than a quarter of the whole globe is inhabited, and Averroes sustains the same opinion. The Stagyrite affirms also that the extent of sea is small between the coast of Spain in the West and the shores of India in the East. We are not concerned here with the actual Spain, but with the Further Spain, which is Africa. Seneca asserts that one can traverse that sea in a few days if the wind is favourable. Again, Pliny teaches us that ships from the Gulf of Arabia can arrive in a

short time at Gades in the South of Spain. Whence we conclude that the sea is not big enough to cover three-quarters
of the globe. Esdras affirms in his fourth book that six
parts of the earth are habitable and inhabited and that the
seventh part alone is covered by the waters. The authority
of that work has been recognized by the saints, who have made
use of it for confirming the sacred verities. Beyond Thule,
the last island of the Ocean, after one day's sail the sea is
frozen and stiff. At the Poles there live great ghosts and
ferocious beasts, the enemies of man. Water abounds there,
because those places are cold, and cold multiplies humours
[or vapours]."

In the forty-eighth chapter he tells us : " Thus the water
runs from one Pole to the other forming a sea which extends
between the extremity of Spain and the beginning of India,
of small width, in such a way that the beginning of India
comes to beyond the half of the equinoctial line [i.e. in the
other hemisphere], a situation very near to that which the
end of our hemisphere occupies."

In the forty-ninth chapter he uses another argument
that he had borrowed from Aristotle : " The west coast of
Africa cannot be far removed from the east coast of India,
for in both those countries elephants are found."

Now the greatest interest of these and similar extracts
from d'Ailly is that they were of fundamental importance in
governing the ideas of the last of the medieval travellers,
Christopher Columbus. It has now been proved that practically the only books on cosmogony that were familiar to him
were two—the *Imago Mundi* of d'Ailly, published between
1480 and 1487, and the *Historia rerum ubique gestarum* of Æneas
Silvius (Pope Pius II), published at Venice in 1477. There
are still preserved in the Library of the Colombine at Seville
the original copies of these books that were used by Christopher
and his brother Bartholomew, and their margins are filled
from end to end with remarks and notes in their own hands.
Bitter controversy has raged over the nature of Columbus'
" Great Enterprise ", and it cannot be claimed that agreement
has yet been reached, but there can be no doubt that when
he set out upon his great voyage, and, in fact, long after,
it was with the geographical equipment of the later Middle
Ages. It is no paradox to include him in our survey.[1]

[1] See further on this point, Chapter VIII, of the concepts of that time.

On his return from his first voyage Columbus proclaimed loudly that the new lands he had discovered lay not far from the dominions of the Great Khan, of which Marco Polo had told. They were a part of the *India extra Gangem* of the ancients. He called his islands *las ylas indias*, or more usually *las indias*, a use of the plural that is not found at an earlier date. The term came into common usage, and to this day we are committed to the error and speak of " the West Indies " and " Red Indians ". But the best thinkers in Spain, and even the Catholic kings themselves, were incredulous, and rather believed that the Admiral had merely discovered another and larger group of oceanic islands like Madeira or the Azores. It is probable that it was only then that he and his brother Bartholomew began to attempt to support by geographical arguments the truth of their claims to have done more than all the celebrated captains of the King of Portugal. When the high hopes of the second voyage (September, 1493–June, 1496) faded into bitter disappointment and no signs whatever could be found of the rich lands of Cipangu and Cathay, scepticism of Columbus' theories deepened into certainty of their falsity. But he was obstinately determined to prove them true, and when he began his third voyage in May, 1498, he determined to sail further south in search of the eastern extremity of the habitable world. After a three months' voyage he sighted what was undoubtedly continental land, and hastily sailing on to Hispaniola he wrote home to give his news. He was quite certain that the new discovery was what he had been searching for, *India extra Gangem*, a part of the old ' habitable world ' and he therefore spoke of it by the old name as *terra firma* or in Spanish *tierra ferme*. The Elizabethans called it " the Spanish Main ". To confirm his statements to his sovereigns he entered, in his letter, on elaborate arguments from cosmogony that were either so fantastic or so obviously ill-digested that he very seriously damaged his reputation with the authorities. In his geographical ideas, as has been said, he was emphatically a man of the Middle Ages, and an uncritical one at that. He took his arguments ready-made from old-fashioned, handy compendia, but assumed an appearance of immense erudition by quoting passage after passage from classical authors, both Greek and Latin, to prove that the islands and mainland he had discovered are part of Asia. He refers incidentally to d'Ailly as an authority supporting his view, but he does not reveal the fact that almost every scrap of his classical learning is lifted bodily out of the Cardinal's pages. In a later chapter there will be occasion to refer again to the extraordinary cosmogonical ideas he expressed wherever d'Ailly's lead is not followed, but here we need only quote one passage.

" Pliny writes that the sea and land together form a sphere," says Columbus, " but that the ocean forms the greatest mass and lies uppermost, while the earth is below and supports the ocean, and that the two afford a mutual support to each other as the kernel of a nut is confined by its shell. The master of scholastic history,[1] in commenting upon *Genesis*, says that the waters are not very extensive ; and that although when they were first created they covered the earth, they were yet vaporous like a cloud, and that afterwards they became condensed, and occupied but a small space. In this notion Nicholas of Lira agrees. Aristotle says that the world is small and the water very limited in extent, and that it is easy to pass from Spain to the Indies ; and this is confirmed by Averroes, and by the Cardinal Pedro de Aliaco, who, in supporting this opinion, shows that it agrees with that of Seneca, and says that Aristotle had been enabled to gain information respecting the world by means of Alexander the Great, and Seneca by means of Nero, and Pliny through the Romans. The said Cardinal allows to these writers greater authority than to Ptolemy and other Greeks and Arabs ; and in confirmation of their opinion concerning the small quantity of water on the surface of the globe, and the limited amount of land covered by that water in comparison of what had been related on the authority of Ptolemy and his disciples, he finds a passage in the third book of Esdras, where that sacred writer says that of seven parts of the world six are uncovered, and the other is covered with water." [2] This reference to d'Ailly is to the passage in the Eighth Chapter of his *Tractatus de Imagine Mundi*.

The striking fact was first observed by Humboldt that the

---

[1] Petrus Comestor, author of the *Historia scolastica*.
[2] *Select Letters of Columbus*, ed. R. H. Major (Hakluyt Society), p. 140.

C

Cardinal had lifted this passage bodily and almost literally from Roger Bacon's treatise the *Opus Majus*. The demonstration is unmistakable and added to other evidence of a similar sort it shows us that the world of Columbus, who has long been credited in the popular view with a foremost position among the leaders of the Renaissance, was emphatically the world of the Middle Age. Columbus in 1498 cribbed his views from d'Ailly who wrote in 1410, d'Ailly cribbed from Roger Bacon whose work dates from 1267, Roger Bacon derives through the Arabs from the Greeks. The most famous of the explorers of the new age, in fact, drew none of his ideas directly from the newly recovered geographical literature of the Greeks as did the true Renaissance thinkers like Peter Martyr or Damian Goes. The discovery of a new world was accomplished not with Greek or modern geographical concepts but with medieval.

CHAPTER II

THE DECAY OF GEOGRAPHICAL KNOWLEDGE AND THE DECLINE OF EXPLORATION, A.D. 300–500

By M. L. W. LAISTNER, M.A.

THE question may be asked how an essay with the above title can be justifiably included in a volume dealing with the travel and exploration of the Middle Ages. A cognate query would be, at what chronological point should the beginning of the medieval period be fixed? Should it be dated from the reign of Constantine or from the fall of the Western Empire in A.D. 476? The truth, of course, is that it is impossible to fix any precise point at which Antiquity ends and the Middle Ages begin; the presence of such fixed points in examination syllabuses is, or should be, a mere convention. They certainly have no historical value, for the process of transition was gradual, and what may be called the 'water-tight compartment' theory of history is as scientific as solar myths or the postulate of the 'noble savage'. But there is, it may be suggested, adequate justification, first for introducing the topic of this essay in a book devoted to medieval travel, and, second, for fixing the period of two centuries from A.D. 300 to 500, though it may be added that the dates are only very rough. It is impossible to understand medieval conceptions of the inhabited world and to realize how very limited the geographical knowledge of even the most cultured men in the earlier Middle Ages was; impossible, too, to appreciate the full significance of that credulity which did not question the real existence immediately beyond the known parts of the earth, of dragons and Polyphemus-eyed men, without having assessed the knowledge possessed in earlier times and its gradual decline during the course of several centuries. And that is precisely the importance of our period in this connexion, for in it we can trace a more or less continuous deterioration both in the theory of geography and the practice of exploration from the glories of the Augustan and the Antonine ages.

The first century of our era was a very important epoch for the history of geographical exploration, and a brief review of the evidence for that period will serve two purposes : it will explain how Ptolemy, writing in the second century, was able to enrich his work with so much new information and, by way of contrast, the decline both in enterprise and in knowledge which characterizes the period of the later Empire will be the more apparent.

In the time of Nero we learn that a Roman expedition was officially sent to explore the Nile above Syene (Assouan). According to Pliny the elder, the explorers made their way a long distance up country as far as N. Æthiopia, and they found much desolation in those parts. " It was not Roman arms," he says, " that made that land deserted, but Æthiopia has been wasted by its wars with the Egyptians, having in turn ruled and been enslaved." [1] About the same time Suetonius Paulinus, better known as the conqueror of Boadicea, was in charge of an expedition which advanced some little way into the interior beyond Mt. Atlas. He crossed an expanse of desert and reached a river called Ger, which may be identified with the Ghir River which flows down from the eastern slopes of the Atlas range towards Beni Abbes. Paulinus brought back information of a people called the Canarii who dwelt in this region and of the abundance of elephants and snakes and other wild creatures there. Again, an enterprising knight explored the amber route from Italy to the Baltic ; we are not told the precise way followed, but only that he went by way of Carnuntum on the Danube, a site that lies about thirty-five miles east of the modern Vienna. The distance from Carnuntum to the shores of the Baltic was estimated at five hundred miles. Most of the way the route doubtless followed the valley of the Elbe, a highway for trade that was already in use in prehistoric times. Our explorer returned with large quantities of amber, which was prized not only as jewellery but for its supposed medicinal qualities. Further, there can be no doubt that after Agricola's governorship of Britain (A.D. 86–95) much new information about our island became available. But

[1] Pliny, *Nat. Hist.*, vi, 181.

perhaps the most interesting venture in this century was that of a certain Hippalus ; he had observed the periodicity of the monsoons in the Indian Ocean and he was the first to sail direct across that expanse of sea from Cape Fartaq in S.E. Arabia to the S.W. coast of India, instead of hugging the shores of E. Arabia and the Persian Gulf, as earlier navigators had been wont to do.

It is obvious that, even if the primary object of these various enterprises was either military or commercial, they also provided the scientific inquirer with a great deal of new material for the study of geography and ethnography. By using all the information to be obtained from such sources, together with the material amassed by Marinus of Tyre, Ptolemy was enabled to compile his work in the first half of the second century A.D. His geographical treatise, in spite of many imperfections, marks the zenith of achievement attained by the Ancients in this field. When treating of the Far East, Ptolemy tells us that he derived his knowledge " from those that had sailed from there and had spent a long time in traversing those parts ", which must mean native as well as Western travellers.[1] Now, nothing illustrates the advance made by Ptolemy's book upon previous geographical writers, as well as the faults of Ptolemy himself, better than the account he gives of the countries of the Far East. His erroneous system of longitude and latitude often leads him to put a wrong interpretation on information otherwise correct, while at times, in attempting to combine two different accounts, he is led into serious error. Yet he has very definite information about Chryse, the golden island or peninsula that is, undoubtedly, the modern Malaya ; and yet more distant is the city of Kattigara, the furthest point, so far as he knows, reached by any merchant coming from the West. Kattigara has been identified with considerable probability as on the site of Ha-noi near the coast of Annam. Ha-noi was once Kiau-tchi and is referred to more than a thousand years after Ptolemy's time by Marco Polo under the name of Caucigu. Ptolemy, however, had two accounts here which he has combined in such a way that he has introduced the Gulf of Siam twice over and, thereby getting his orientation wrong, placed Kattigara far away in the south-east,

[1] *Geog.*, i, 17, 4.

instead of to the north-east of Chryse. Ptolemy, in common
with other ancient geographers, believed that the unknown
land beyond ultimately joined the unknown parts of the East
African coast, thus making the Indian Ocean a vast inland sea.
Thus there can be no doubt that now and then adventurous
Roman and Greek traders had found their way even further
east than the mouths of the Ganges, and their general reports
and Ptolemy's remark already quoted suggest that natives
of Far Eastern countries also found their way westwards,
if not to Rome, at any rate to Syria and Egypt.

When we turn to Africa, it is also not easy to fix precise
limits to the knowledge acquired by the Ancients. On the
eastern side of that Continent the coast was reasonably
familiar as far as Cape Guardafui, but it is clear from Ptolemy
that enterprising merchants had occasionally made their
way much further south. He mentions several who had
sailed from Aromata, i.e. the Somali coast, past Cape
Guardafui, as far as Rhapta or Rhapton. This place has been
tentatively located near the modern Pangani opposite Pemba
island, that is to say at the northern end of what was till
1914 German East Africa and is now the Tanganyika
Territory. An Island, Menuthias, mentioned by the Greek
writer, has similarly been equated with Zanzibar. If these
identifications are correct—and they are given with all
reserve—then these intrepid sailors reached a point some
five degrees south of the equator.

For the western side of Africa our information is much more
scanty ; it is very doubtful whether any point beyond Sierra
Leone was ever visited, and in most cases it is likely that
traders got no further than the Arsinarian promontory,
which is probably the same as Cape Verde. Ptolemy has
preserved a record of another interesting expedition. In
this case one Julius Maternus pushed on from Garama in
the modern Fezzan, behind Tripoli, and after a four months'
journey reached " Agisymba, the land of the Ethiopians,
where the rhinoceroses gather together." [1] " Agisymba "
is a vague term, impossible to define exactly, and the term
" Ethiopians " was used generally to describe the black
peoples of the interior. Thus the whole vast stretch of
country from the northern Soudan to equatorial Africa was

---

[1] *Geog.*, i, 8.

vaguely designated as "Æthiopia" and Agisymba was the farthest point believed to have been reached by men. The Congress or Diet of Rhinoceroses is even more mysterious. Unimaginative scholars have asserted and doubtless will continue to assert, that the MS. reading is corrupt.

It has been necessary to say something of exploration in the first two centuries and of Ptolemy's work, because, as was suggested at the beginning, it is only by contrast with this earlier period that the retrogression in the succeeding centuries can be fully realized.

For this retrogression, which was most rapid during the period A.D. 300 to 500 political conditions are to blame first and foremost. Large tracts of country which had once formed part of the Empire were either wholly lost or occupied by half-civilized invaders, who even when they were nominally the vassals of the Roman Emperors were little to be relied upon. Thus gradually Dacia, much of Gaul, and Spain passed into barbarian hands ; and even within the shrunken empire there were many tracts occupied, with the forced consent of the Emperor, by kinsmen of those barbarians who had come there in the earlier years. Britain ceased to be part of the empire early in the fifth century and part of North Africa was seized by the Vandals ; for the next twenty years or so treaties and wars with Rome alternated, but the net result was the loss to Rome of the North African provinces. With this constant unrest, fighting and movement of peoples, necessary travel, even within the Empire, was hazardous ; to pass into the little known regions beyond was well nigh impossible. And, besides, exploration hardly comes under the head of necessary travel.

On the Eastern Frontier conditions were somewhat different ; after Julian's expedition to Persia in A.D. 363 that country and Rome were at peace, save for one or two insignificant episodes, for nearly a century and a half. Yet even here travel, and consequently knowledge, grew less ; for it would appear that while under the Early Empire, the Roman merchant himself not infrequently made his way to the Middle and Far East, in the later period the carrying trade passed almost entirely into other hands, Persian, Arab or Abyssinian. The northern overland route through the Dariel Pass by way of the Caspian to Central Asia was doubtless too insecure for even the most adventurous, and it is not till Justinian's time, in the middle of the sixth century, that some attempt at reopening this caravan route was made.

If political causes were responsible for a decrease in practical exploration, the decline in the theoretical study of geography was largely the fault of the Church. The attitude of most Christian writers at that time was not calculated to promote any form of scientific inquiry. A literal interpretation of *Genesis* could not be brought into harmony with the Ptolemaic system of the Universe and the postulate of a spherical earth, and so progress in knowledge was ruled out. A definite example will serve to illustrate how a truth stated in Ptolemy was lost for some twelve centuries : Herodotus in the fifth century B.C. knew the true nature of the Caspian Sea, that is to say he knew it to be a vast inland lake and not a gulf of the northern ocean. His successors adhered to the false view, but Marinus of Tyre and, following him, Ptolemy quite definitely stated the true facts. Marinus indeed seems to have known of a trade route running northwards from the River Don round the Caspian to Lake Aral, and he mentions rivers—e.g. the Volga and the Ural—not known before. This is the information found in Ptolemy ; in the early part of the fifth century A.D. one Marcianus of Heraclea composed a short geographical treatise which is a rehash of earlier authors, mainly Ptolemy. Yet when Marcianus says that the Persian Gulf is opposite to the Caspian Sea, and that by these two is formed the Isthmus of Asia, it is clear that he has reverted to the erroneous view about the Caspian. The Peutinger Table also perpetuates the error, which in the West lasted in fact till the fourteenth century, though the Arab geographers seem to have been aware of the true nature of that sea. It is a pleasure to find that one of the Christian Fathers, St. Basil, has the courage and fairmindedness to mention both the right and the wrong view, though he does not commit himself definitely to either. Elsewhere we also meet an ingenious attempt to combine both views—that at least is what it sounds like—for we are told that the Caspian was fed by the Northern, i.e. the Arctic Sea, through underground channels.

I have mentioned St. Basil ; he, in common with some of the other earlier Fathers, is well aware of the Greek scientific theory that the earth was spherical. There is a striking passage in one of his Homilies on the creation of the world in *Genesis* as follows : " Because those who write on cosmography have argued at length about the shape of the earth, namely whether it is a sphere or a cylinder, whether it resembles a quoit and is rounded off on the outside as with a potter's wheel, or whether it is shaped like a winnowing fan and is concave in the middle—for the writers on cosmography have been led to all these hypotheses, and each man sets out to destroy the views of the others—that is no reason why I should proceed to call our cosmography [i.e. that based on a literal interpretation of the *O.T.*] less valuable because Moses, the servant of God, has said nothing concerning the shape of the earth and not stated that the earth's circumference is 180,000 stades." [1] The last remark is a reference to the estimate of the Greek Poseidonios. Now this quotation is the utterance of one of the most enlightened of the Fathers, and it makes us understand why the truth was first suppressed and then forgotten by later ecclesiastical writers. In one or two secular authors of the fifth century —Macrobius and Martianus Capella for example—we still find something of a defence of the Ptolemaic theory on this point. But in the two ecclesiastical authors who exerted a paramount influence on later ages, Cassiodorus (early sixth century) and Isidore (early seventh century), the earth is described as a flat disc.

We may now consider some of the geographical treatises composed during the period under consideration. One of the few works written in Greek is the treatise of Marcianus of Heraclea, to which reference has already been made. It cannot be said to add anything to knowledge, though it has some value for correcting the text of Ptolemy that has come down to us. For instance, when Marcianus relates that east of the Seres (i.e. China) is an unknown land full of marshy lakes, in which great reeds grow so close together that you can cross the lakes by walking on top of the reeds, he is copying Ptolemy word for word. Supposing Ptolemy's text to be corrupt in some such passage as this, it is obvious that Marcianus may be useful to a modern editor for restoring the right reading in the older writer. Where Marcianus tries

[1] *Homil. in Hexaem.*, ix, 1 (= Migne, *Patr. Graec.*, xxix, 188 C–D).

to improve on his predecessors he fails miserably ; thus, in estimating the size of Ceylon, he attempts to correct Ptolemy and only makes matters very much worse. Ptolemy got the shape of the island fairly right, but he made it many times too large. In Marcianus' version the size of the island is even more exaggerated. Other Greek treatises of this period, like the *Outlines of Geography* by Agathemeros, have even less value than Marcianus.

The Latin treatises are no more helpful ; they repeat in abbreviated form what was to be found in the writers of the early empire. Thus Solinus (late third century) is mainly indebted to the elder Pliny and to Pomponius Mela ; nor does Orosius (early fifth century), who prefaces his history with a short geographical survey of the Ancient world, do more than excerpt his predecessors. Linguistically there are now and then points of interest in these writers ; for instance, Solinus is the first to use the word *mediterraneus*, though as an adjective, of what we now call the Mediterranean, while Orosius is the earliest writer to use the term *Asia Minor* in its modern sense. But the invariable practice of these later authors is to copy and abridge their predecessors, and from such work it is hopeless to expect much enlightenment. The chief interest of most of these compilations lies in the fact that their continued use can often be traced in the earlier Middle Ages. Thus, a little tract, dating perhaps from the fifth century, formed the basis of one section of a geographical treatise composed by the ninth century monk Dicuil. Another anonymous writer composed a work which bears the impressive title, by no means warranted by the contents, of *Description of the Whole World and its Races*, and this is even more instructive for our purpose.

What has come down to us is a Latin version of a Greek original compiled late in the fourth century. The Latin version is considerably later in date, and this version was in its turn worked over by a Christian writer. We fortunately possess both the earlier and the later Latin versions, and when they are compared it is seen that the Christian adapter has in a number of cases omitted sentences or sections that were too pagan in tone. He omits, for example, a section on the religions of Egypt, which is found in the earlier version. Elsewhere his methods are even more arbitrary. The original writer had given some account of the Indian Brahmins: in the Christian adaptation a remarkable story is superimposed of a people who once dwelt in the Garden of Eden, and this is fitted on to the description of the Brahmins, whose name is suppressed. As it is a good example of the mingling of fact and fiction the earlier part of the passage may be quoted : " In the regions of the East they tell us dwell the peoples of the Camarini, whose land Moses described by the name of Eden. From here a mighty river is said to flow forth and then to branch off into four streams named Geon, Phison, Tigris, and Euphrates. Now the men who dwell in the aforesaid land are extremely pious and good. No blemish is to be found in their bodies or in their minds. If you, reader, would wish to learn something more definite about them, it is said that they neither use bread such as is in common use amongst us, nor any similar food, nor yet do they use fire such as we use. Rather, we are assured that bread falls down like rain for their daily need, and that they drink honey and poppy.[1] The fire of their sun is of such intense heat that as soon as it is diffused from heaven on to the earth all of them would be burnt did they not quickly plunge into the river. There they tarry until the fire returns again to the place from whence it came." [2] It is easy to see how a few passages in the Old Testament could be the germs of this fantasy ; the noteworthy thing is that this passage is immediately followed by a rational account of the simple life and habits of the Brahmins. The regular immersions of these holy but amphibious dwellers in Eden remind one a little of the practice of the early Slavs who, we are told, " could elude a foe by diving under water and lying for hours on the bottom, breathing through a long reed, which only the most experienced pursuer could detect." [3]

Of far greater value than these treatises are the so-called *Antonine Itinerary*, composed about the year A.D. 300, and the *Peutinger Table*, the original form of which was slightly later in date. The *Antonine Itinerary* gives in tabulated form the distances between most of the towns and ports of the Empire. Hitherto the prevailing view has been that it was

---

[1] The MSS. reading is *pipere,* pepper. This is certainly a scribe's error for *papavere,* poppy.

[2] *Geogr. Graeci Minores,* ii, 513.

[3] J. B. Bury, *Hist. of the Later Rom. Emp.,* ii, 294.

in the nature of an official guide-book, but Kubitschek,[1] after an exhaustive inquiry, has shown conclusively that the *Itinerary* cannot have been compiled by any official having access to either civil or military records, nor yet by any trained geographer. The errors are too glaring for that, and the difficulties, that have up to now been unexplained, disappear if we regard the *Itinerary* as having been compiled from a map of the Empire, such as that of Agrippa, by some pupil or other inexperienced person. Even so, and for want of more reliable records, it has great value for showing the road system of the Empire and its administrative divisions after the reorganization of Diocletian.

The *Peutinger Table* has been aptly described as " a sort of panoramic chart on which towns, roads, mountains, forests, etc., are marked without any approach to delineating the outline of the countries, except in the vicinity of the Bosphorus and Constantinople." [2]   But, save for a few Christian additions, the map represents the Empire as it was in the first century A.D.

In the literature of this period other than the specialized treatises to which reference has already been made, it can be said that there is an advance in knowledge in one science closely allied to geography. Ammianus Marcellinus, writing in the second half of the fourth century, is for his geographical details primarily indebted to Ptolemy, and often he is less accurate than his authority. The advance in knowledge is in the sphere of ethnology or anthropology, not of geography. From Ammianus, from the surviving fragments of the fifth century historian Priscus, and from Jordanes, the Gothic writer of the sixth century, we get valuable information about the customs and mode of life of the nomad invaders of the Empire, Goths, Huns, and so forth. But the geographical data for the movements of these peoples are of the vaguest, making it at times singularly difficult to fix with precision the district which this tribe or that occupied within a narrow limit of time. That the spirit of inquiry, in so far as it is concerned with geography, was not wholly dead just before the time when Ammianus was composing his history,

---

[1] See his long articles, " Itinerarien " and " Karten " in Pauly-Wissowa-Kroll, *Realencyclopaedie d. klass. Alertums wisschenschaft.*

[2] W. G. Holmes, *The Age of Justinian and Theodora*, i, 141, note 1.

is illustrated by a reference which has apparently been ignored
or overlooked by modern scholars. When the future Emperor
Julian was governor of Gaul (A.D. 361–2) he corresponded
with his friend Alypius, who at the time held a high official
position in the neighbouring province of Britain. In the
particular letter to which I refer the following passage occurs:
" It happened that when you sent me your map I had just
recovered from my illness, but I was none the less glad on
that account to receive the drawing [or " chart "] that you
sent. For not only does it contain diagrams better than any
hitherto made, but you have embellished it by adding those
iambic verses. . . . In fact, the gift is such as no doubt it
well became you to give, while to me it is most agreeable to
receive it." [1] The reference is tantalizingly incomplete,
which is perhaps one of the reasons for its neglect by modern
writers ; but it does seem a not unreasonable hypothesis, in
view of Alypius' place of residence and official position,
that map and diagrams illustrated the geography of Britain.
Yet it is unlikely that Alypius' researches ever became known
to any but his immediate friends, for they have left no trace
in later authors ; and it was only fifty years later that Britain
was evacuated by the Roman Government. In the sixth
century Procopius could pen a description of Britain, which
made at least a part of this island a fabulous land and a home
for departed spirits !

One of the most cultured men of the fifth century was
undoubtedly, to give him his full name, Caius Solius
Apollinaris Sidonius. He held the highest civil offices and
later in life was consecrated bishop, and his letters are one of
the most valuable sources that we now possess for the history
of his age. Yet these letters give one the impression that
the man's interests were singularly narrow, centred very
largely on the city of Rome and still more on that part of Gaul
in which he spent most of his life. Still, Gaul was at that
period largely occupied, as well as surrounded, by the so-
called Barbarians, and Sidonius must have had unique
opportunities for learning something of their customs and
institutions, and something of the geography of the districts
beyond the Rhine and Danube, from which they had come.
What do we find ? Sidonius expresses the utmost surprise

---

[1] *Epistle* 30.

and admiration for his friend Syagrius for having "picked up
a knowledge of the German tongue " (probably Burgundian
is meant).   Where geographical references occur in Sidonius
they are mere literary adornment, echoes of older poets and
writers whom he had read.   When he speaks of "voyaging in
imagination with our citizen of Tyana to Caucasus and Ind,
among the Gymnosophists of Ethiopia and the Brahmins of
Hindustan,"[1] he merely shows us that he has read Philostratus'
life of Apollonius of Tyana, written more than two centuries
before ; when he writes " you come down to Langon harbour
with no less reluctance than one bound for the Danube
to resist the all-invading Massagetæ, or for the dull flood of
Nile with all its awful crocodiles ",[2] or when he refers to "the
Sigambri on their marshes or the Alans of the Caucasus or
the mare-milking Geloni ",[3] he is merely cramming his writing
with allusions to earlier literature and cultivating what his
age considered a fine literary style, though his modern readers
when struggling with his prolix periods will often give it a less
complimentary name.   At all events such passages have no
geographical or ethnographical value ; the Alans, or a large
portion of them, had long since moved from the Caucasus,
while the allusions to the Massagetæ and the rest are mere
echoes of Vergil, Horace or Lucan.

From such precious writing one turns with relief to actual
records of travel at this time.   Between A.D. 300 and 500
travelling within the Empire must often have been infinitely
more difficult and dangerous than in the earlier period,
and this is of course still more true of the districts beyond.
The records that have come down to us are not numerous,
though passing references to journeys undertaken, but with
no details given, are not rare.   The accounts that have
survived tell of travels that had a religious, not a commercial
purpose, with one notable exception, to which we shall
return.   The others are either narratives of pilgrimages to
holy places or expeditions for the conversion of the heathen.
One or two examples of each may with advantage be considered a little more in detail.

The so-called *Jerusalem Itinerary* preserves the record

---

[1] *Letters* (transl. Dalton), viii, 3.
[2] Ibid., viii, 12.
[3] Ibid., iv, 1.

of a pilgrimage undertaken in the year A.D. 333 from Bordeaux to Palestine. The route followed was via Milan to Aquileia and Sirmium, and thence, following the course of the Danube most of the way, to Constantinople; from there the pilgrims made their way through Asia Minor and Syria to the Holy Land. On the return journey they went by way of Macedonia, Epirus, and Rome. Unfortunately this record, apart from a more detailed description of Jerusalem and neighbourhood, contains practically nothing but the names of post stations and caravanserais on the route, with the distances in leagues or miles from point to point. Only rarely is there any further comment. Still this *Itinerary* is of considerable importance for the evidence it supplies regarding the Imperial road system at this date.

The narrative of the Abbess Etheria, is, however, of much more human interest.[1] In 386, or thereabouts, the Abbess started out from Southern Gaul to visit the Holy Land. The beginning of her story is lost, for when the account, as we now have it, opens she is already in the act of ascending Mount Sinai. After a considerable stay in the Sinai district, she made her way across a stretch of desert to Pelusium and thence she followed the coastal road to Palestine. She made some long distance excursions from Jerusalem, e.g. to the eastern side of the Dead Sea, and finally set out via Antioch to Edessa in Northern Mesopotamia. She then returned to Antioch and from there passed on through Asia Minor to Constantinople. As some of her narrative is lost, we do not know all that she saw, but we learn that she was away from home for four years. She proceeded in leisurely fashion and, being a person of importance, occasionally had a military escort. She received a friendly reception from the clergy and monastic communities wherever she went, and was keenly interested in all she saw. A modern reader can, however, but regret that the reverend lady's interests were so exclusively spiritual. A little more— we will not say profanity—but a little more interest in things secular is what we should like to find in her, for she could have told us so much of the condition of the countries through which she passed and of the people she saw, in a period about many aspects of which we know singularly little. It is no

---

[1] For a fuller reference to the Abbess Etheria see next chapter.

doubt improving to the mind to have a description of the cave where Moses rested before and after he received the Tables of the Law, or to learn the very place where he stood when the Lord appeared to him in the Burning Bush. Perhaps we are provoked to smile when she tells us that she saw the very spot, near the ancient Sodom, where the salt pillar stood that was once Lot's wife. She assures her fellow nuns, for whom her narrative was written, that the pillar was no longer to be seen, but the local bishop informed her that it had been standing there till a few years before. And yet, although Etheria commands our deep respect both for her intrepid enterprise and for a general saneness of outlook which, in spite of occasional lapses, is in striking contrast to the childish credulity of later pilgrims, nevertheless, we should give much to have an occasional remark about the conditions of life of the town and country dweller, or a passing judgment on the degree of material prosperity to be found, say in Palestine or Syria at that date, or even a stray comment on sites and buildings of purely secular interest. Only rarely she permits herself to comment on the beautiful scenery in some spot or on the fine vineyards and orchards that she saw on her journeys ; she also mentions that there was a small Roman garrison at Clysma, near the modern Suez, but such remarks are the exception in her tale ; the visiting of all possible sites mentioned in the Scriptures is her real purpose, and we can see that the inventiveness of her guides was fully equal to satisfying all her eager questions,

From pilgrims we pass easily to missionary journeys. There is a remarkable adventure, which is related by several ecclesiastical historians as occurring about the year A.D. 330. A certain philosopher of Tyre, Meropius by name, set out for "India", and was accompanied on his travels by two young boys Ædesius and Frumentius. What precisely is meant by " India " it is difficult to say for reasons which will be indicated hereafter. At any rate, on their way home the travellers' ship put in at a harbour for water and food somewhere on the coast of Ethiopia, that is to say, what we should now call Abyssinia. Meropius and the entire ship's crew were killed by the savage natives, but the two boys, in the words of the oldest historian who records these events, " were discovered beneath a tree in meditation and engaged in the preparation of their lessons." [1] Such virtuous diligence had its reward, for the natives had compassion on Ædesius' and Frumentius' youth, spared their lives and took them to the king of the country. They received employment at his court, rose high in the royal favour and began the teaching of Christianity there. On the death of the king, Frumentius was made tutor to the new king, who was still a child. Ultimately the two men were allowed to leave ; Ædesius returned to Tyre, but Frumentius made his way to Alexandria ; there he interviewed Athanasius, and was soon after made first bishop of Abyssinia. Here the historian ends his narrative, but it is known that some years later Frumentius was succeeded by an Arian bishop, Theophilus, since an Arian Emperor was now installed at Constantinople. Theophilus was a native of Diu island, off the Gujerat peninsula to the west of the Gulf of Cambay. He went on a mission to the Himyarites in South Arabia, visited the island of Dioscorides, now called Socotra, off the south Arabian coast, and thence went to Axum in Abyssinia. He does not appear to have been allowed to stay there very long. It is not till the very end of the fifth or the beginning of the sixth century that we hear of further missionary activities in those parts.

As in the itineraries of pilgrims, so in the accounts of the ecclesiastical historians, scarcely any geographical information is given. Early in the fourth century we further hear of the conversion of the Iberians of the Caucasus. The story of this conversion is full of the most miraculous particulars, but their embassy to the Emperor at Constantinople is doubtless an historic fact. They asked for alliance and treaty with the Empire, and also requested that priests be sent to them to propagate the Gospel. It is somewhat remarkable that no knowledge of Christianity had filtered through to them before, and it seems to confirm, what is made probable by other evidence, that the northern trade route to the Far East had practically fallen into disuse by this time. Again it is not till the sixth century that we get some more information about these people, and one writer who refers to them, Theophanes, adds the interesting comment that their chief city is Tiphilis. So far as I am aware, this is

[1] *Rufinus*, x, 9.

the earliest mention of Tiflis, the modern capital of the
Caucasus region, and the same historian is also the first
Westerner to refer to the Turks by that name.

It was hinted above that a difficulty often confronts the
modern inquirer when he meets with the name " India " or
" Indians " in writers of his time. " It is to be observed,"
says Professor Bury, " that the cessation of direct trade
with the East was reflected in the decline of geographical
knowledge illustrated by the misuse of ' India ' to designate
Æthiopia, which is frequent in Greek and Latin writers from
the fourth century." [1] Thus we cannot be sure that Meropius
and his boy companions really did visit India before they met
with disaster on their homeward voyage, or whether their
travels were confined to the Red Sea.   The fact is that all
the southern regions situated east of the Nile were commonly
referred to as India ; the Nile is referred to as the boundary
between Asia and Africa, and thus we find, for example, the
sixth century historian Procopius describing that river as
flowing from India to Egypt, and dividing the latter country
into two, till it reached the sea.

Here we may pause for a moment to consider that remarkable person, Cosmas, nicknamed " Indicopleustes " or the
Indian traveller. Chronologically he belongs to the sixth
century, but much of the information he gives is doubtless
true of the age immediately preceding his own, and we are
therefore justified in including him in our survey.   The main
purpose of his *Christian Topography*, written about A.D. 550 is,
in the words of Gibbon, " to confute the impious heresy of
those who maintain that the earth is a globe and not a flat
oblong table as it is represented in the Scriptures," but in
his earlier years Cosmas had himself travelled considerably,
and references to his experiences are scattered through the
earlier books of his work or collected in Book XI. This
book, though now attached to the *Christian Topography*, in
reality belonged to a lost work recording his travels. Cosmas
visited Ethiopia, i.e. Abyssinia, and voyaged in the Persian
Gulf ; he also went to Socotra, and he further quotes a
merchant, Sopatros, who had been to Ceylon. He speaks of
Christian Churches in that island and in several districts

---

[1] *History of the Later Roman Empire*, ii, 318, note 2.

on the West coast of India ; the bishop under whose care these Christians were had been ordained, he says, in Persia. Cosmas further has the distinction of being the first and the only ancient writer to enunciate the truth that beyond China on the east is the ocean. He speaks of " the land of Tzinista, beyond which is no other land. For the Ocean encircles it on the East". Ptolemy and earlier geographers had put *terra incognita* beyond the land of the Sinai and the Seres. And yet it is at least doubtful whether Cosmas ever himself visited India, though most modern writers state categorically that he did. There is really nothing in the information that he gives about that country or about Ceylon which he could not have learnt from Sopatros or other travellers. Thus, he describes the Indian ox in a delightful way : " This wild ox is a large Indian animal, and from it is got what is called toupha (i.e. a *chowry* or fly-flapper), with which commanders of armies decorate their horses and banners when taking the field. If his tail, it is said, catches in a tree, he does not seek to move off, but stands stock-still, having a strong aversion to lose even a single hair of his tail. So the people of the place come and cut off his tail, and then the beast, having lost it all, makes his escape. Such is the nature of this animal."[1] The words " it is said ", suggest that Cosmas had not seen the patient either before or after the operation ! In general it is to be noted that Cosmas on a number of occasions remarks that he had himself seen a particular thing, but he only does this when speaking of the lands bordering on the Red Sea. So perhaps " Indicopleustes " should really be rendered " Abyssinian " or " Red Sea navigator ". With South Arabia, and especially with Ethiopia or Abyssinia, he was clearly well acquainted. After describing a number of sights and occurrences he says, no doubt quite truthfully, " The facts which I have just recorded fell partly under my own observation and partly were told to me by traders who had been to those parts." He gives us a remarkable account of a great expedition of traders which was dispatched every other year by the orders of the king of Abyssinia from the capital, Axum, into the interior. The commodity for which the merchants were sent was gold ; in

---

[1] *Cosmas* (McCrindle's translation), p. 360.

exchange for it they gave the natives salt, iron, and cattle. Cosmas describes the very primitive methods of barter employed and tells us that the expedition was away six months. The return journey was made with all possible speed "lest", to quote him again, " they should be overtaken by winter and its rains. For the sources of the river Nile lie somewhere in these parts, and in winter, on account of the heavy rains, the numerous rivers which they generate obstruct the path of the traveller".[1]   The sources mentioned here are the sources of the Blue Nile, to which Ptolemy had also referred four centuries earlier. As regards the East Coast of Africa, Cosmas does not appear to have been further than the Somali coast. No attempt has been made here to discuss Cosmas' geographical theories, for two reasons : first, because they concern the theologian more than the geographer or the historian and, second, it is quite certain that, to use a colloquialism, they " did not catch on". That is to say, Cosmas' *Christian Topography* did not influence later writers in the field of geography.

An attempt has been made to show that in the period A.D. 300–500 the activities of Rome's attackers had virtually closed large tracts of country to the traveller, whatever his particular aims ; further, that what records of travel we possess for this age can only in a few instances be said to add anything to the geographical knowledge possessed in the preceding centuries, while, on the other hand, truths that had been known to Ptolemy or Marinus had been forgotten or condemned as impious ; and, last, that the geographical treatises composed in this period not only add nothing new, but merely repeat in a shortened, and often in a garbled form, what is to be found in writers like Pomponius Mela and Pliny, whose sum total of knowledge about the geography of the ancient world, the *oikoumene,* was less perfect than that of Marinus and Ptolemy. And here a word must be added about the geographical textbooks used in the earlier Middle Ages in the West. It has already been pointed out that some of the treatises composed between A.D. 300 and 500 continued to be used at a later date. Another little book which enjoyed great popularity was a sketchy geography

---

[1] Op. cit., p. 53.

put together by a certain Julius Honorius. It owed its large circulation mainly to the fact that Cassiodorus, the father of medieval scholarship, had recommended it to monastic students as a textbook. At the beginning of the seventh century Isidore of Seville composed a work in twenty sections which was a compendium of all the arts and sciences. To compile this book Isidore had recourse to older treatises of varying degrees of value dealing with the separate subjects, and his compilation very largely superseded the older works in the centuries that followed. The distinguished American scholar, Professor E. K. Rand, remarks in one of his most sprightly essays : " One of the most useful rules that I know for guiding the investigator in medieval fields is to inquire first ' what does St. Isidore say about it ? ' " [1] The universal use of Isidore in the Middle Ages implied in this sentence is not an exaggeration, and nothing illustrates this better than the subject with which this paper is concerned. Wherever you have a geographical treatise or a section on geography in a larger work during the next few centuries you are sure to find that Isidore is either the sole source, or at least one of the most important. Several anonymous geographical poems and treatises of the eight and ninth centuries depend mainly on him, and in the *Liber Glossarum*, that huge encyclopædia *cum* dictionary compiled early in the eighth century, the geographical sections are culled primarily from that author. The geographical sections in Orosius are also constantly used or reproduced, as for example in the *Liber Glossarum* and in the early part of the Venerable Bede's *Ecclesiastical History*. What then do we find ? Simply that the geographical treatises put together in these centuries bear little or no relation to the times in which they were composed. Dicuil's book has the distinction of being the first geographical work composed in the Frankish Kingdom ; the author used several sources besides Isidore, most of them earlier than the latter, but there are scarcely any references to the Frankish Kingdom and none at all to the remoter parts of Germany, for instance to Saxony or Bavaria. Instead he repeats vague statements about Germany from Pliny. In Pliny's day most of what we now call Germany was *terra incognita*, but

[1] *Philolog. Quarterly* (Iowa), 1922, i, 294.

that was not the case in Dicuil's time, when it should have been possible to obtain accurate information about the more easterly parts of that country. Dicuil had not even seen Tacitus' *Germania*, from which one may perhaps deduce that there was no manuscript of that work in the Frankish kingdom at that time.

It has seemed desirable to indicate, however inadequately, the sources from which in the age following the break up of the Western Empire geographical knowledge was acquired and books on that subject were composed. The work of Ptolemy might never have existed for all the influence it exerted in those centuries. As for our subject in the period of the later empire, one is, perhaps reluctantly, compelled to acquiesce in the severe judgment of a German scholar on this topic : "New countries were not discovered ; the empire became smaller not greater ; trade relations, thanks to the wars in the east, the south and the north, became more and more restricted ; besides, there was no longer any question of research in industry and of the spirit of discovery. Thus the only books that were put together were compilations from older works." [1]

[1] W. Schmid, *Gesch. d. griechisch. Liter.*, ii, 852.

CHAPTER III

CHRISTIAN PILGRIMAGES, A.D. 500–800

By The Rev. Prof. CLAUDE JENKINS, D.D., F.S.A.

THERE grows in the island of Madagascar a tree of which all have heard. Its long straight stem is crowned with leaves spread vertically, but like a fan. At its base collects water wherewith the wayfarer may slake his thirst and so pursue his road refreshed and comforted. The student of early medieval pilgrimages may often dream that he sees on the margin of his research a group of such travellers' trees in the figures known or anonymous of the chroniclers and writers of the times. But the stems of narrative have a symmetry only too often deceptive, the fan-like crown of travellers' tales soars beyond the reach of his perhaps too prosaic mind, and the moisture which trickles to the base affords a scanty draught for the thirst engendered by the sawdust of the modern scientific method. Yet there is more to win than discloses itself to the first view. The roots lie hid beneath the soil of many lands—Ireland and Britain, Gaul and the Teutonic regions, Italy, Spain, and many another yet further removed ; and a section of the stem discloses the rings of growth which tell the story of the years.

The period assigned to this chapter and the scope of its subject are alike limited ; but he would be a poor medievalist who should allow himself to be trammelled unduly by such considerations. Certainly the student who approaches a medieval writer of travels with the expectation of finding the information set forth with the succinct brevity of a Baedeker will not always be disappointed, and very precious may be the first part of the Itinerary of the Bordeaux Pilgrim of the fourth century to a man with an eye for country. But not less precious for other reasons are the apparent irrelevancies when a narrator halts in his description to tell a story which he has learnt from a fellow traveller by the way, or heard from the lips of a holy bishop or other unimpeachable authority, to introduce some marvel of what may seem to us very unnatural science, or to confirm a story by what we may regard as a piece of scriptural exegesis no less strange. Our copy of Herodotus may be studded thickly with the injurious reflexions of a modern commentator ; but the fame of the Father of History shines with a lustre quite undimmed by such criticisms ; and in the same way to stigmatize a medieval writer as credulous or superstitious is to throw away at the outset the key to the interpretation of what he writes, to falsify history through our own anachronisms, and to treat as negligible what may be the most valuable thing in the narrative before us—the disclosure of the man who wrote and of the age in which he lived.

How then shall we begin our own peregrinations through the literature ? We will remind ourselves that a peregrination is a journeying abroad, travelling through a foreign country far from one's own home ; but it is not therefore necessarily a pilgrimage, though it may be one. In other words many of the journeys of Celtic monks to the continent were peregrinations, but they were not, like those of Etheria, pilgrimages in the strict sense. Let us begin with one which purports perhaps to fall within the period with which we are mainly concerned and has some claim to both titles. It can be read conveniently in the new translation of the *Life of St. David* by Mr. Wade-Evans.[1]

St. David is bidden by an angel to go to Jerusalem, accompanied by two companions, also angelically warned, one of whom is Eiludd or Teilo, the other Padarn. 'When they had sailed over the Britannic sea and were come into the Gauls and were hearing the strange languages of diverse nations, father David was endowed with the gift of tongues like that apostolic gathering of old, lest when in need among foreign peoples they might want an interpreter, and also that they might confirm the faith of others with the word of truth. At length they arrive at the confines of the desired city, Jerusalem,' where they are received and placed in 'three most honourable seats' by the Patriarch who has been warned by an angel in a dream to expect them. 'Then, supported

[1] A. W. Wade-Evans, *Life of St. David* (S.P.C.K., 1923).

by the divine choice, he promotes holy David to the archiepiscopate,' and urges him and his companions to confute the Jews. ' They obey the command. They preach, each of them, every day. Their preaching becomes acceptable. Many come together to the faith. Others they strengthen.' When they set out to return ' the Patriarch presented father David with four gifts, to wit, a consecrated Altar, whereon he was wont to consecrate the Lord's Body, which, potent in innumerable miracles, has never been seen by men from the death of its pontiff but, covered with skin veils, lies hidden away. Also, a remarkable Bell, which too is renowned for miracles. A Bachall [i.e. pastoral staff] and a tunic woven with gold. The Bachall, resplendent with glorious miracles, is extolled throughout the whole of our country for its wonders. " But because," said the Patriarch, " they are a labour for you to carry on the journey, whilst going back to your country, return in peace. I shall send them over after you."' The gifts are accordingly transported by angels, David receiving his gift 'in the monastery called Llan Gyvelach', the others in their several monasteries. ' Therefore it is that the common people call them gifts from heaven.'

What inferences, if any, are we to draw from this story ? In the form here quoted it is not earlier than Rhygyvarch or Ricemarch who lived at the end of the eleventh century. He claims to have based it on ' very old writings . . . in the old style of the ancients ', and he connects the story with a subsequent synod directed against a revival of Pelagianism in which Dewi achieved recognition as archbishop with the consent of ' all the bishops, kings, princes, nobles, and all the grades of the whole Britannic race ' and ' his monastery too is declared the metropolis of the whole country '. If we accept as the old Welsh tradition [1] his account which places the birth of St. David thirty years after the arrival of St. Patrick in Ireland (c. 432), so that St. David would be born in 462, then Ricemarch himself is separated from St. David by more than five and a half centuries. If we accept the view of Bishop Basil Jones and Mr. Freeman, which places St. David's establishment of his see early in the seventh century,[2] he

[1] Wade-Evans, op. cit., pp. 2–3.
[2] W. B. Jones and E. A. Freeman, *History and Antiquities of St. Davids* (London : Parker, 1856), p. 257.

is separated by a century less, but still by 450 years. Everything then will depend upon the credit we attach to the mention of the ' old writings '. It is an argument in favour of their real existence that Ricemarch seems more than once to be reproducing statements the meaning of which he does not understand. But if they existed, and if they contained the association of Dewi with the Synod of Brevi and the Synod of Victory, which are fixed for other reasons about 569,[1] then did the writer realize that St. David if alive would have been 107 years of age ? The answer is that in any case Ricemarch, and perhaps the documents before him, made David's life extend to 147 years.[2] Now the earliest form of the ' Annales Cambriae ' that we have, a MS. of the tenth century, merely says that David died in 601.[3] It does not exclude the possibility of his association with the two Synods, nor does it confirm it. On the other hand such association would be impossible if we accepted the date given for David's death, viz. 546, by William of Malmesbury [4] a statement which is difficult to set aside so easily as is done by Mr. Henry Bradley [5]; and while it may seem rash to accept a fact from Geoffrey of Monmouth, it does not seem certain that he is not right in attributing David's burial to Maelgwyn king of Gwynedd,[6] who died probably in 547.

The story of Ricemarch and perhaps of his authority is a patent effort to establish the supremacy of St. David's see over the whole of the Church in Wales. We may venture to suggest that the substratum upon which the whole has been built is a tradition that David had visited Palestine. This was supposed to be confirmed by the existence of such relics as the portable bell mentioned later by Giraldus Cambrensis [7] as existing in his time in the church of Glascwm, a bell, he says, ' of very great virtue, which they call by its

---

[1] A. W. Haddan and W. Stubbs, *Councils and Eccl. Documents* (Clarendon Press, 1869), i, 116–17.

[2] Wade-Evans, op. cit., p. 29.

[3] *Y Cymmrodor*, ix, 156, cf. Wade-Evans, op. cit., pp. x, 114.

[4] *De Antiq. Glaston. Eccl.* in T. Gale, *Hist. Brit.*, etc., *Script. xv* (Oxford, 1691), i, 299.

[5] *Dict. Nat. Biog.*, s.v. ' David '.

[6] *Hist. Regum. Brit.*, xi, 3.

[7] *Itinerarium Kambriae*, i, 1 (Rolls Series, ed. J. F. Dimock, 1868, vi, 18).

proper name " Bangu " [i.e. " the dear, loud one " [1]], which also is said to have been St. David's.' That the tradition did not amount to more than a bare statement of a pilgrimage may be inferred from the fact that the story does not venture on an itinerary but transfers David and his companions straight from Gaul to Jerusalem. That it is early seems at least to be suggested by the further fact that Ricemarch does not mention as received from the Patriarch any relics connected with the sacred associations of Jerusalem itself, an omission which in the circumstances is noteworthy. Has the tradition itself any foundation in fact, or is it, as Mr. Bradley says, obviously an unmixed romance, as we may agree with him in holding the story of David's ' consecration as archbishop by the patriarch ' to be ? On the whole it would seem that the balance of probability does not justify us in wholly rejecting it. It may be said that we have pre- served very little of the good bishop's detailed story ; but at any rate we have not impeached his veracity, and have admitted the possibility that there may have been some vague foundation for what we hold him to have been sincere in believing.

Dom Gougaud, in his work on *Gaelic Pioneers of Christianity* has been at pains to collect descriptions of the motives which led men to leave their native land and flock to the continent in a voluntary exile ' for the love of God ', ' for the name of the Lord ', ' for the name of Christ ', ' pro remedio animae ', ' to gain a country in heaven ', and the like.[2] In some cases it may be difficult to distinguish such a motive from what we usually associate with a pilgrimage. Dom Gougaud, however, sees most of such travellers rather as voluntary exiles, ' for the real pilgrim betakes himself to the sanctuary which is the aim of his special devotion ; then, his pious journey over, he returns to his own land and resumes his usual life.' The distinction is perhaps sound and is certainly convenient.

The instinct for travel, or even for wandering, is innate in some natures in all ages, perhaps in far more than we often realize. But it was not universal. There is a story in the

---

[1] Wade-Evans, op. cit., pp. 82, 107.
[2] Dom. L. Gougaud, *Gaelic Pioneers of Christianity* (Dublin, M. H. Gill and Son, Ltd., 1923), pp. 5–8.

' Life of St. Columba ' of a wife who told the sixth century
saint that she did not refuse to undertake the whole care of a
house or even, if he bade her, go overseas (to which a later
editor adds,' to go on a journey to Jerusalem, if you bid me '),
and to continue in a monastery of young girls : the one thing
nothing would induce her to do was to live with her husband.[1]
It is clear that the preference is for the lesser of two evils.
But it is both devotion and enthusiasm for sacred antiquities
which inspires people like Etheria of Aquitaine, whose
' Peregrinatio ' was discovered by Giovanni Francesco
Gamurrini just over forty years ago. It was contained in
an eleventh century MS. at Arezzo, but it is to the fourth
century that the story belongs. The MS. is thus separated
from the journey by some 600 years, and though the narrative
was written for the benefit of other nuns at home it does not
seem to have acquired celebrity : at least we do not find it
quoted by others until much later. There are, however,
demonstrable, if unacknowledged, quotations from it in the
work of Peter the Deacon in the twelfth century. It is worth
while to remember this, for some of the most serious problems
both of historical and geographical writings of the Middle
Ages arise from the propensity of later writers to use, often
indeed without indication that they are doing so, the narratives and descriptions of their predecessors. Only too often
we think that we are reading, for example, the work of some
medieval author, and so indeed we are ; but what is before us
is, in fact, only an adaptation of Pliny the elder, or Solinus,
or some other writer of a far earlier age, and sometimes
we would give a good deal to be absolutely certain in the
case of a great story of travel like that of Cosmas Indicopleustes how much was the fruit of his own personal observation, how much borrowed from earlier sources.

Etheria belongs, as has been said, to the fourth century ;
but since her narrative contains features which illustrate
what follows some reference to it is excusable and even
necessary. It is a mere accident of transmission that her
' Peregrinatio', as we have it, opens with a sight of Sinai,
where the pilgrims were received ' humanely ' in the monastery. And whatever may be thought of some other writers,

[1] *Vita Sancti Columbae auctore Adamnano*, ii, 41.

she at least deserved to see the ' Tree of Truth ' of which she
tells us : it was a sycamore-tree said to have been planted
by Moses and Aaron ; it was very old and therefore very small,
but it still bore fruit.[1] The pilgrims travel at any rate in
some places under the protection of an armed guard, and as
they go Etheria gathers material in the way of stories. Her
narrative bears witness to a real passion for travel, for it is
the record not of one expedition but of several, and includes
a stay of three years at Jerusalem. She journeys to Mesopotamia, where she is impressed by the swiftness of Euphrates,
which is ' larger than the Rhone '. She visits the ' martyrdom ' of St. Thomas at Edessa, reads there some works with
which his name was associated, sees the marble portrait of
the great king ' Agbar ', who, unlike the Blessed Thomas,
believed though he had not seen, and sees too the famous letter
which he was said to have received from our Lord. There
are copies of it in her own land, ' but these are longer,' she
tells nuns for whose benefit she is writing, ' you shall read
them.'[2] At the shrine of St. Tecla in Cilicia she reads the
Acts of Tecla : it is characteristic of her whole attitude to do
so ; and in places of sacred associations she reads where-
ever possible the Biblical passages in which they are mentioned. What strikes us is the extraordinary humanness and
simplicity of it all, and also the amazing endurance, for the
narrative includes also a journey through Cappadocia,
Galatia, and Bithynia to the scene of the martyrdom of
St. Eufemia at Chalcedon, with the project at the end of a
new journey to Ephesus.

There is apparently a gap or dislocation in the MS. and
the preface to the long discription of Lent and the Holy Week
at Jerusalem is wanting. But what remains is of absorbing
interest. Some things must be noted for the sake of contrast
with the accounts of later pilgrims even if much has to be
omitted. We must pass over the description of the sermons
after Epiphany, when all the priests as well as the bishop
preached, in succession as it would seem, upon the same

---

[1] ' dendros alethiae,' *S. Siluiae Peregrinatio*, viii, §§ 3–4. [Corp.
Script Eccl. Lat. xxxviiii, *Itinera Hierosolymitana*, ed. P. Geyer
(Vindobonae : Tempsky, 1898), pp. 48–9.]
[2] Ibid., xix, § 19 (ed. Geyer, p. 64).

passage of Scripture,[1] and of the Lent which lasted for eight
weeks ; the account of what a fast means and of the instruction of candidates for baptism in the Scriptures and the
Creed, an instruction which occupied three hours a day for
seven weeks and was conducted by the bishop himself in the
presence of fathers and mothers and others. There is a
significant note that if anyone is a pilgrim (*peregrinus*) unless
he has testimonies of character from those who know him
he will not so easily attain to baptism.[2]

The Church of the Holy Sepulchre includes both ' Golgotha ' and the Sepulchre. Constantine's church there was
dedicated in 335, and destroyed by the Persians in 614. We
have to picture to ourselves one large building at the western
end of which is a round church, and in the centre of this again
is the Sepulchre. Such is the Church of the Holy Sepulchre,
or, as it is also called, the ' Anastasis ', or Church of the
Resurrection. Eastward of it is an atrium surrounded by a
colonnade, in one angle of which is ' Golgotha '. Still further
eastward is the basilica of Constantine, which is called the
' Martyrium'. This has its apse at the west end, and beneath
it is the crypt of St. Helena, the mother of Constantine, and
below that the crypt of the Invention of the Cross which she
discovered. Beyond the Martyrium and eastward of it again
is a rectangular court or atrium also with colonnades. The
whole of what we have been describing can thus be regarded,
as has been said, as one building with several divisions, each
with its sacred associations and each used for its appropriate
services. Most sacred of all is the reputed Sepulchre in the
centre of the round church, or, as Etheria calls it, the basilica.[3]
It is a cavern guarded by a railing and having a lamp burning
within.

We cannot stay to discuss the value of the authorities for
or against the traditional story of the Invention of the Cross
in 326 ; but there are two points which concern our present
purpose. First is the reference of St. Cyril of Jerusalem
twenty years later to pieces of the Cross as having been

---

[1] St. Lc. ii, 21–39 ; ibid. xxvi (ed. Geyer, p. 77).

[2] Ibid., xlv, § 4 (ed. Geyer, p. 97).

[3] Ibid., xxiv, § 10 ; xxv, § 2 (ed. Geyer, pp. 73, 75) ; but Etheria
distinguishes the basilica and the Anastasis, ibid., xxiv, § 8 (ed.
Geyer, p. 73). Cf. H. T. F. Duckworth, *The Church of the Holy
Sepulchre* (London : Hodder and Stoughton, n.d.), p. 96.

distributed throughout the world [1]; and second, Etheria's description of the Exposition of the Cross on Good Friday in the Chapel of Golgotha.[2] The bishop, she says, sat in a bishop's seat (*cathedra*), having in front of him a table with a wooden frame (*mensa sublinteata*). A silver-gilt box (*loculus*) is brought in which is the wood of the holy cross. It is opened, and the wood of the cross and the *titulus* or inscription are placed upon the table. The bishop, still seated, places the tips of his fingers upon the wood, and the deacons standing around keep guard. The people, both the faithful (i.e. the baptized) and the catechumens approach one by one. Bending down they touch the wood, first with forehead, then with eyes, kiss it, and pass on. The guard of deacons was established, so Etheria tells us, because on one occasion some one took the opportunity in venerating the wood to bite off a piece and carry it away in his mouth. As the people move on they pass a deacon who is holding Solomon's ring and the horn with which kings were anointed. The horn they kiss, but a lacuna in the MS. prevents us from saying what they did to the ring. We shall do well, for reasons which will appear, to bear these details in mind, and also that when it is said that people go to Sion to pray at the column at which our Lord was scourged, the bare fact is mentioned without further description of the column.

The date generally assigned to Etheria's narrative is about 385, i.e. some sixty years after the Invention of the Cross and half a century after the dedication of Constantine's great church at Jerusalem. No one who reads it can fail to be impressed with its historical value, and if so no apology is needed for the space given to it, since, if it can be relied upon, it affords a standard with which later narratives may be compared. We have to pass over nearly a century and a half till we come to the work known as the 'Situation' or 'Topography of the Holy Land'. Of its author, Theodosius, we know practically nothing save that he was in deacon's orders and was possibly an archdeacon; that he has an interest in describing distances and an evident taste for recording marvels; and that from internal evidence he appears to have written about A.D. 530. Bearing in mind what has

---

[1] Cyrill. Hierosol., *Catech.*, iv, 10; x, 19; xiii, 4; to him its genuineness was beyond question.

[2] *S. Siluiae Peregr.*, xxxvii, §§ 1–3 (ed. Geyer, p. 88).

been said about Etheria and quoted from her, let us look at Theodosius' description of the scene.[1]

'In the City of Jerusalem,' he says, 'at the Lord's Sepulchre there is the place of Calvary; there Abraham offered his own son as a whole burnt offering, and because the mountain is rocky, on the mountain itself, i.e. at the foot of the mountain itself, Abraham made an altar: above the altar the mountain rises, and to this mountain men climb by steps: there the Lord was crucified. From the Lord's Sepulchre to the place of Calvary are paces fifteen in number; it is under one roof. From the place of Calvary[2] as far as to Golgotha are paces fifteen in number, where the Lord's Cross was found. From Golgotha as far as to holy Sion, which is the mother of all churches, are paces in number 200: which Sion our Lord Christ together with His apostles founded: it was the house of St. Mark the Evangelist. From holy Sion to the house of Caiaphas, which is now the Church of St. Peter, are more or less paces in number fifty. From the house of Caiaphas to the Praetorium of Pilate are more or less paces in number 100: there is the Church of St. Sophia; near it St. Jeremiah was sent into the lake [or pit]. The column which was in the house of Caiaphas at which the Lord Christ was scourged is now in holy Sion: by the Lord's command the column itself followed, and even to-day it appears how while He was being scourged He embraced it: just as in wax, so His arms, His hands or fingers stuck into it, moreover His whole face, His chin, nose or eyes as though He marked them in wax.'

Two points in this account may be noticed. First, the writer is aware that the Column of Scourging is now in the Church of Sion. He has knowledge also that it was once in the house of Caiaphas. He solves the problem of its transfer by attributing this to a command of our Lord Himself. Further he describes it as bearing the marks of the Saviour's face and hands, of which Etheria says nothing, though she too speaks of the column as being at Sion.[3] Was she strangely unobservant or incurious (and one must admit that on a bare

[1] *Theodosii De Situ Terrae Sanctae* 7 (*Itinera Hierosolymitana*, ed. Geyer, pp. 140-1).

[2] The scribe or the author writes ' de Calvariae locum '.

[3] *S. Siluiae Peregr.*, xxxvii, § 1 (ed. Geyer, p. 88).

consideration of her narrative the inference might be that she had not seen it rather than that she had), or had Theodosius himself ever seen it ? Is his work a literary *tour de force*, or was he one of those whom local custodians thought it a pity to disappoint of the sights which he clearly wished to see ? The later Middle Ages had a different estimate of archidiaconal ingenuousness ; but we cannot help thinking on the whole that Theodosius had seen a good deal of what he describes, or if not is copying more or less faithfully the work of some one who had. ' From the house of Pilate,' he continues, 'as far as to the Sheep Pool are paces more or less in number 100. There the Lord Christ healed the paralytic, whose bed is there up to this day.' [1] 'In the place where the Lord was baptized there is a marble column, and on the column itself is made an iron cross ; there too is the church of St. John Baptist which the Emperor Anastasius constructed.' [2] ' On Mount Olivet the Lord placed His shoulders upon a stone, and in this rock both His shoulders descended as in soft wax.' [3] Or again, if it be not too threadbare an example, he quotes Psalm cxiv : ' O sea wherefore art thou troubled, and thou Jordan wherefore art thou driven backward, and ye mountains wherefore did ye skip like rams and ye hills like the lambs of sheep ? ' And he adds that in the neighbourhood of Jordan are many little mountains and when the Lord descended to baptism the mountains themselves ambled before Him dancing, ' and to-day they have the appearance of leaping.' [4] That is, of course, imagination, but is it the imagination of the study ? On the other hand there are not a few passages which look like notes from a commonplace book filled with scraps of more or less inaccurate geographical information collected from many sources, and the work as we have it may be a combination of observation and reading. In such a collection a person making notes might well record just barely : ' In the province Cilicia, the city Tarsus, thence was Apollonius,' [5] as an interesting fact, whereas in a note of an actual visit a man of Theodosius' turn of mind would never have omitted all

---

[1] Theodos., op. cit., viii (ed. Geyer, p. 142).
[2] Ibid., xx (ed. Geyer, p. 145).
[3] Ibid., xxi (ed. Geyer, p. 146).
[4] Ps. cxiii (cxiv), 5–6. Ibid., 22 (ed. Geyer, pp. 146–7).
[5] Ibid., 32 (ed. Geyer, p. 150).

E

reference to the most illustrious representative of no mean
city.   And the modern editor's suggestion that in Apollonius
or 'Apollius' we are to find a corruption of 'apostolus Paulus'
is perhaps best regarded as one of those emendations which
we all of us make sometimes, but which we do our best to
forget.

Let us return now to the little book by an unknown author
which is called the 'Breviarius', i.e. 'Short Description of
Jerusalem'.   It is very short, barely 62 lines in all, and the
date usually assigned to it is about the same as that of Theodosius, 527–30.   It was pointed out by Dr. Bernard when he
edited Theodosius for the 'Palestine Pilgrims' Text Society'
that the latter does not mention Justinian's building at
Jerusalem and that he was clearly used by Gregory of Tours.[1]
We cannot therefore date Theodosius much later than 530 ;
but this 'Short Description' may be a good deal earlier,
possibly as early as 500 or even a little before.   It would be
tempting to give it in full, for it is fascinating to read.   In
his book *The Dawn of Modern Geography*, which has laid
all students, whether they are always able to accept its
conclusions or not, under a heavy debt of obligation, Professor
Beazley summarizes one aspect of it by saying [2] :   'Short as
is the account, it is packed full of news for the relic seeker.
He is told of the " holy lance, made of the wood of the Cross,
which shines at night like the sun in the glory of the day " ;
of the " horn with which David and Solomon were anointed " ;
of the "ring of amber with which Solomon sealed his books";
of the "earth of which Adam was formed "; of the "reed and
sponge, and the cup of the Last Supper " ; of " *the* stone with
which Stephen was stoned " ;   of the crown of thorns, the
identical " lamp " of the upper chamber, and the " rod of
scourging enclosed in a silver column ".'   We will venture to
add one passage : ' Thence you go to the house of Caiaphas
where St. Peter made his denial : where there is a great
basilica of St. Peter.   Thence you go to the house of Pilate
where he handed over the Lord to the Jews to be scourged :
where there is a great basilica and there is there a chamber

[1] Palestine Pilgrims' Text Society, *Theodosius*, translated by
J. H. Bernard (London, 1893), p. 5.
[2] C. R. Beazley, *The Dawn of Modern Geography* (London : John
Murray, 1897), i, p. 98.

(*cubiculus*) where they stripped Him and He was scourged, and it is called St. Sophia.'[1] This is in Sir Charles Wilson's view the earliest reference to that church.[2]

It will be impossible not to have been struck by the increase in the number of relics associated with our Lord which this ' Short Description ' mentions. Two at least which are included as being then at Jerusalem became later, as we know, the subject of other stories in other places—the Lance and the Holy Grail. But the writer does *not* mention the earth out of which Adam was formed as being preserved as a relic : he identifies the place of Adam's creation, the place of the offering of Isaac, and the place of the Crucifixion as one and the same place—which is a very different thing.[3] One further point may be noted with a hope that even if the discussion may seem rather technical the result may not be uninteresting ; it relates to the ' ring of amber with which Solomon sealed his books '. It will be remembered that the horn of anointing and Solomon's ring are both mentioned by Etheria [4] ; but the ' Breviarius ' contains two very remarkable passages on the subject of the ring. We will take the second first. " There," says the unknown writer, ' is that horn wherewith David was anointed and Solomon, and that ring is there wherewith Solomon sealed '—what ? ' His books,' says Professor Beazley ; ' his writings,' according to Sir Charles Wilson. ' And it is of amber.' Now there are two MSS. of this little work, one at St. Gall, dated in 811; the other in the Ambrosian Library at Milan and belonging, apparently, though Geyer gives three different datings to it in different parts of his edition of the *Itinera Hierosolymitana*, to the twelfth century. The older MS., which is also the shorter, omits all reference to Solomon's ring : according to accepted custom we should therefore prefer it, unless some special reason can be shown for the omission. We look at the other MS. : what it says is not ' books ' or ' writings '—*sermones*— but ' demones ', demons, ' the ring with which Solomon sealed

---

[1] *Breviarius de Hierosolyma* (in *Itinera Hierosol.*, ed. Geyer, p. 155).
[2] Palestine Pilgrims' Text Society edition (London, 1890), p. v.
[3] Still less does the writer say that the Lance was ' made of the wood of the Cross ', but 'de ipsa facta est crux '.
[4] *Supra*, p. 47.

demons.' The emendation is ingenious, but does not explain the corruption. We turn now to the first passage to which reference has briefly been made. The writer is describing the apse of Constantine's basilica (we take the translation accepted by Sir Charles Wilson): ' The apse itself [has] twelve marble columns round about it, and [what is] altogether incredible [there are] twelve urns of silver on the top of these columns.' A reference to Eusebius' *Life of Constantine*,[1] shows that the columns with their great silver jars on the top are mentioned with special attention as the Emperor's gift, and we ask ourselves why in the world they should be described as ' altogether incredible ', for we see nothing strange about them. But when we look at the manuscript authority for the passage in the ' Breviarius ' we do find something strange. The older, and shorter, MS. has omitted the whole passage and other words as well, apparently by *homoesarcton*, i.e. because the next sentence begins with the same word and the scribe's eye skipped from the one to the other, as as has happened to most of us. But the later MS. reads: ' in the circuit [i.e. of the apse] are twelve marble columns, a thing altogether incredible, upon the columns themselves twelve water-pots, where Solomon sealed demons '. One secret at any rate is out. ' Omnino incredibile '—a thing altogether incredible—is the startled or scandalized observation of a reader of a MS. older than the Ambrosian, added when he came upon what looked like the introduction of an incident which to us suggests the Arabian Nights. In the Ambrosian MS. it has crept into the text itself. On the whole we venture to think that the genii or jinn may be retained.

We pass now to the Itinerary associated with the name of Antoninus of Placentia. Tradition has made him a martyr, and criticism has sometimes regarded him as a liar. Professor Beazley, who accepts the ordinary dating for his travels if genuine as A.D. 570, describes his work as sharing ' with Silvia's [i.e. Etheria's] peregrination the credit of being the most extensive, curious, and suggestive of all the pilgrim-records before the rise of Islam '.[2] He adds, however, that

---

[1] Eusebius. *Vita Constantini*, iii, 38.
[2] *Dawn of Modern Geography*, i, 109.

' in it we find the superstition and muddleheadedness of its class developed more fully than in any previous example '.[1] It may be suggested that this is not a very profitable method of treating an author if we are trying to understand him or the age in which he lived. The Itinerary exists in two recensions and is not by Antoninus but by one of his companions. If in what follows some things are stated without comment, it must not be inferred that we accept the genuineness of all that the narrator says that he saw, but merely that in our opinion he is probably truthful in stating that he saw these things and that he is honest even if he makes mistakes. It must be remembered that there is at least some evidence that in the second half of the sixth century there had developed in the West considerable interest in relics, and in this as in other directions it must be confessed that demand has been known to create the supply.

The motive of the journey is stated to be the following of the footsteps (*vestigia*) of Christ and beholding the scenes of the miracles of the holy prophets. As has been pointed out by Sir Charles Wilson and many others, the pilgrimage ' is remarkable for the extent of ground which it covers— Palestine, Sinai, Egypt, Syria and Mesopotamia '. It is hard to resist the temptation to discuss point by point the details of the journey and the writer's criticisms upon the characteristics of the cities and other places which he visited. We can, however, only call attention to the kind of things which the traveller saw, we may add, if we like, which he hoped to see. Thus at Sarepta he sees the chamber of Elijah and his couch and the kneading-trough in which the widow of Sarepta mixed her dough. In this place, he adds, many offerings are made and many works of power (*virtutes*) will be done there. Sarepta, he tells us, is a town of moderate size, but very Christian (*Christiana nimis*).[2] After visiting the monastery of Elisha he venerates at Diocæsarea the pail and basket of the Blessed Virgin : he is shown also the chair (*cathedra*) in which she was sitting at the time of the Visitation. The other recension calls the place Neocæsarea : it is the modern Seffûrieh where, according to Sir Charles Wilson,

---

[1] Ibid., p. 110.
[2] *Antonini Placentini Itinerarium* (in *Itinera Hierosol.*, ed. Geyer, pp. 160–61).

the birthplace of the Virgin is still shown.[1]   The party
proceeds to Cana, where they visit the scene of the Marriage-
feast.   The narrator tells us that he reclined on the seat, i.e.
the seat on which our Lord reclined, ' and there I unworthy
wrote the names of my parents ' [2] : some modern tourists,
one may fear, would have written their own.   In what follows
the two recensions present a curious variation which illustrates
very well what may often have happened in course of transmission.   The one says : ' Of these water-pots there are two
there, and I filled one of them with wine and lifted it full on my
shoulder and offered it at the altar.'   So stated, the incident
has at least verisimilitude ; but for the other recension it is too
commonplace.   It says : ' Of these water-pots there are
two there, I filled one of them with water and I brought
forth from it wine, and I lifted it full on my arm and offered
it at the altar.' [3] The story has been spoilt, but the redactor
has not understood why.   At the fountain, presumably that
from which the water came, the pilgrims bathed ' pro
benedictione '—for a blessing—a motive which determines
a good many of their actions.

At Nazareth the pilgrims see ' in the synagogue ' the
volume out of which our Lord learnt His A B C and the bench
on which He sat with the other children—a bench which
Christians can shake and lift but Jews cannot move, and which
does not let itself be taken out of doors.   The house of the
Virgin has become a basilica where many benefits are derived
from her garments ; and the beauty of the women of the place
is attributed to her intervention.   At Mount Tabor the
pilgrims find three basilicas where ' the disciple said
" Let us make three tabernacles ".'   It is at any rate more
reasonable than a list of relics belonging to a much later
period which purported to include some of the wood out of
which St. Peter had proposed to make them.   But here the
reader will observe a very curious thing : all the MSS. say
simply ' the disciple ', except one which says ' Peter '.
Nothing, we say to ourselves, is more natural : some scribe
has given an identification and has put it into the text ; the
vaguer reading is clearly to be preferred ; no one with ' Peter '
in the text before him would substitute the vaguer term

---

[1] Palestine Pilgrims' Text Society edition (London, 1896), p. 4.
[2] Itin., 4 (ed. Geyer, p. 161).
[3] Cf. Geyer, op. cit., pp. 161, 196.

' the disciple '. Clearly! But we may observe with a mixture
of malicious enjoyment and a note of self-warning that the
MS. which has the name ' Peter ' is a good deal older than
the others whose reading we are commending ; and we
remember what we are always in danger of forgetting, that a
later MS. sometimes preserves an earlier reading.

It is interesting to notice that the narrator does not vouch
for everything that is shown him. In a passage where he
makes a bad slip in confusing Samaria and Shechem he
mentions what *is said to be* the vessel out of which our Lord
drank at the well [1]. We smile when we find him mentioning
the two fountains Jor and Dan, the streams of which united to
form the River Jordan ; but it is wise to remember that even
so great a scholar as St. Jerome does not disdain to mention
the etymology, without however accepting it. [2]

The tendency which we noticed in Theodosius, and which
occurs in many other writers, to collect associations round
a single spot, e.g. Calvary, is seen in this Itinerary in regard
to the place of our Lord's Baptism. Here, says the writer,
was the scene of the passage of the Israelites, here the sons
of the prophets lost the axe, here Elijah was taken up to
heaven. [3] And here we in our turn pause to ask ourselves
the question To what extent did the language of Scripture
or an attempt to interpret it tend to create stories ? The
question is, as we know, of considerable interest in connexion
with St. Matthew's Gospel, but it has a far wider bearing.
At the risk of seeming obscurantist or worse we are bound to
say that we can find singularly few cases in which such an
explanation seems to have reasonable probability. An
example may be taken in regard to which judgment
is not likely to be affected by ulterior considerations.
Eucherius in the fifth century quotes apparently from
Josephus a statement that the city of Jerusalem in the midst
of Judaea was regarded by the learned as the navel of the
whole region. [4] We know that in later writers, as in some

[1] *Itin.* 6 (ed. Geyer, p. 162).
[2] Ibid., 7 (ed. Geyer, p. 163). Cf. *S. Hieronymi Comm. in Matt.* xvi, 13.
[3] *Itin.* 9 (ed. Geyer, p. 165).
[4] *Eucherii quae fertur De Situ Hierusolimitanae urbis atque
ipsius Iudaeae Epistola ad Faustum Presbyterum* (in *Itinera Hierosol.*,
ed. Geyer, p. 134), ' quasi umbilicus regionis totius, ut prudentibus
placuit, nuncupatur.' The passage is not contained in the Palestine
Pilgrims' Text Society edition.

earlier ones, Jerusalem and in Jerusalem Golgotha was regarded as the navel *of the world.* ' Two texts of Ezekiel,' says Professor Beazley, ' and two of the Psalms were supposed to prove that Jerusalem, where God had " worked salvation in the midst of the earth " was this central point. " For thus saith the Lord, This is Jerusalem ; I have set her *in the midst* of the nations and countries that are round about." ' [1] We are familiar with the consequences which the idea had in the drawing of primitive maps ; but even here, it may be thought, Scripture was cited to confirm an opinion which originated from other considerations but which it did not create. In any case it is absolutely certain that the passages quoted were not regarded as of coercive, nor even as of con- clusive, authority by every one.

We return now to the Itinerary of Antoninus at the point from which we digressed, and in doing so we observe the elaborate system of guest-houses or hospices, Xenodochia, for pilgrims and for those suffering from leprosy and other diseases, of which it affords evidence. Before the Persian and the Arab conquests Palestine must have contained a very large number of these 'inns', situated at natural halting places for travellers or at places to which by reason of their associations large bodies of people would be likely to congregate. In those at Jerusalem which are mentioned in the Itinerary the food was cooked, we are told, with dew from Hermon which descended there, and the statement is regarded as confirmed by the words of the Psalmist, ' Like as the dew from Hermon which descended on Mount Sion.' [2] What the words were regarded as supporting was the view that the dew which descended there and with which the food was cooked was dew from Hermon and not from elsewhere, and the narrator tells us that it was collected by doctors (*medici*) and was good for the healing of diseases.

The Itinerary is a perplexing work, for as we read it our opinion changes almost from page to page. The writer tells us that Scythopolis is on a mountain,[3] which is certainly not the case, and that nothing floats in the Dead Sea nor can a man swim in it [4]—a statement which is far more startling

[1] *Dawn of Modern Geography*, i, p. 338.
[2] Ps. xxxii (xxxiii), 3. *Itin.* 9 (ed. Geyer, p. 165).
[3] Ibid., 8 (ed. Geyer, p. 164).
[4] Ibid., 10 (ed. Geyer, p. 166).

and has given rise to injurious reflexions on his veracity
or the genuineness of his work as a record of observation.
It is not, however, clear that the inference drawn from the
blunder need be more unfavourable than that from the
famous story of the problem of the fish which Charles II
is said to have propounded to the Royal Society; though
we may be safe in conjecturing that the writer had not made
the necessary experiment. On the other hand the account
of the obelisk and the wooden cross at Jordan, where the
writer claims to have spent Epiphany, seems to represent
something that he had seen [1]; and we may count it as a point
to his credit that when he gets to Jericho, which he compares,
like Galilee, to Paradise, he does not claim to have been shown
then or later the two pence mentioned in the story of the
Good Samaritan, to whom indeed he does not refer. But
what are we to make of the story of the ' Ager Domini '—
the Lord's Field? [2] He did not originate it. Even in the
period with which we are dealing it is found in the narrative
of Theodosius, who says that ' the Field of the Lord in
Galgala is watered from the Fountain of Elisha ; it produces
six bushels more or less. In the month of August half of
the field is ploughed, and there is a crop at Easter from
which the oblation is taken for Holy Thursday and Easter
Day. And when that is cut, the other half is ploughed
and there is a second crop. There too is the vine which the
Lord planted, which vine bears fruit at Pentecost ; from this
the oblation [i.e. of wine] is taken. And so from the field
as from the vine the produce is transmitted at the proper
season to Constantinople.' [3] At the beginning of his treatise
Theodosius tells us what the Lord's Field is : ' there,' he says,
' the Lord Jesus Christ ploughed one furrow with His own hand.' [4]
To this, according to Dr. Bernard, one MS. adds : ' and sowed
it. And there is a monastery, and in the monastery 300
monks, who own the field ; and the field yields a crop every
third year, and every crop yields eight bushels.' [5] It is
clear that we have evidence of two different traditions, for

---

[1] *Itin.*, 11 (ed. Geyer, p. 166).
[2] Ibid., 13 (ed. Geyer, p. 168).
[3] Theodos., op. cit., 18 (ed. Geyer, p. 145).
[4] Ibid., 1 (ed. Geyer, p. 137).
[5] Palestine Pilgrims' Text Society edition, p. 7.

the reading is not one which can be dismissed as mere invention. Let us turn to the Itinerary. We learn there that before the basilica not far from Jordan, which contains the stones taken up from Jordan by the children of Israel, is a ' campus', the ' Ager Domini', in which ' the Lord sowed with His own hand, bearing seed up to three bushels : moreover it is reaped twice in the year ; it is never sown, but grows of itself. Further, it is gathered in February, and therefrom Communion is made at Easter. When it has been reaped it is ploughed and again reaped along with other harvests : it is subsequently ploughed again and left alone'.[1] The story is consistent enough to suggest the knowledge of a real field to which these stories attached, inconsistent enough to suggest doubts as to the original form of the story, but not as to the fact that there was a story.

We pass by the mention of the tomb of Absalom [2] which is a new feature here first introduced, of the tree into which Zacchæus climbed, and of the fig-tree on which Judas hanged himself. In Gethsemane is a basilica which, the narrator tells us, they say was the house of the Blessed Virgin and the place where she was taken (sublata) from the body.[3] Of the appearance of the Holy Sepulchre there is a most striking account. The rock of the Tomb has by this time been so much adorned with gold and precious stones that its colour cannot be distinguished. ' From iron rods hang armlets, bracelets, necklaces, rings, coronets, waist-bands, sword-belts, crowns of emperors made of gold or precious stones, and a great number of ornaments given by empresses.' ' The Tomb itself,' the writer adds, ' is like the winning-post of a course, covered with silver.' [4] This again may be regarded as a comparison suggested by personal observation. In the account of the Veneration of the Cross at Golgotha there is another note which suggests genuineness. The narrator says that he adored it and kissed it,[5] but not that he handled it : that, if the earlier description which we have mentioned represents a real custom, would not have been

---

[1] *Itin.*, 13 (ed. Geyer, pp. 168–9).
[2] Ibid., 10 (ed. Geyer, p. 166).
[3] *Itin.*, 17 (ed. Geyer, p. 170).
[4] Ibid., 18 (ed. Geyer, p. 171, cf. 203–4).
[5] ' adorauimus et osculauimus,' ibid., 20 (ed. Geyer, p. 172).

allowed. But if he did not do so, this may account for the
difficulty caused by his statement that the Cross was of
nut-wood, in regard to which Sir Charles Wilson notes that there
are no hazel-trees near Jerusalem and that the modern tradition
is that the Cross was of olive-wood, though it may have been
of oak.[1] The *titulus* or superscription, which the narrator
gives in the form ' Hic est rex Judaeorum ', he says that he
not only kissed but held in his hand. The story is, however,
embellished, though not improved, by an account of the star
which comes and stands over the place of the Cross when it
is brought out of its receptacle and of the effect upon flasks
of oil which are brought that the Cross may touch them and
which boil over in consequence.   The relics which the writer
mentions are the sponge, from which he says that he drank
water, the reed and the Holy Grail which was made, it would
seem, of onyx, a painting of the Blessed Virgin, her girdle
and her head band.

In the Basilica of Sion, which was the house of St. James,
he sees the ' lapis angularis ' or corner-stone and the Column
of the Flagellation. The latter shows the mark of our Lord's
breast, of His two hands, the palms, and the fingers. These
are measured and the measurements taken as a remedy for
various sicknesses,[2] a custom which was certainly common
in other connexions elsewhere in the later Middle Ages. It
will be noticed that the writer says nothing of the appearance
of the Face, of which we have found mention earlier. There
is seen also the ' horn with which kings were anointed and
David ', but nothing is said of Solomon's ring. Mention
is made of the crown of thorns, the lance, the stones (not, as
before, the stone) with which St. Stephen was stoned, a
little column on which was set the cross of St. Peter on which
he was crucified at Rome—which is in the circumstances a
strange relic to find here—the chalice used by the Apostles
at masses (*missae*) after the Resurrection and, the writer adds,
' many other marvels (*miracula*) which I do not recollect.'[3]
It seems hard that the frankness of this last remark should
have been used as an argument against his narrative.

---

[1] Palestine Pilgrims' Text Society edition, p. 17.
[2] ' Ita ut pro singulis languoribus mensura tollatur exinde,' *Itin.* 22
(ed. Geyer, p. 174).
[3] ' Et multa alia miracula, quae non recolo,' ibid.

Perhaps the most startling thing in the Itinerary is the mention a little later of a picture of our Lord in the Judgment Hall of Pilate, a picture which is said to have been painted from life. That such a picture, however, whatever its date, may have been there it is impossible to deny. The description given is of a person of ordinary height, a handsome face, hair inclined to curl, a beautiful hand with long fingers, a beautiful small delicate foot.[1] The absence of a beard is noteworthy for reasons which will at once suggest themselves to students of iconography; but the whole description is of importance, for if it is genuine it antedates by nearly two centuries what Mr. G. F. Hill describes [2] as the earliest literary representation of our Lord, that of John of Damascus, who died about 754.

It must be remembered in our judgment of such a writer as that of the Itinerary that we are dealing with a man who goes for example to a place where it was said that Samson slew 1,000 men with a jawbone of an ass : from that jawbone sprang forth a fountain which continues to this day : he has seen it.[3] He goes on to the place ' where Isaiah was sawn asunder or is buried ': the saw is preserved : he has seen it.[4] It is safer to assume that such a man has really seen the things that he says he has seen, whatever we may think of his credulity. But if so we can accept his evidence when he tells us of accommodation provided in hospices in his day for as many as 3,000 pilgrims at a time, though of course he may have been no better judge of large numbers than a modern speaker who believed himself to have addressed 6,000 people in a building of which the utmost capacity is 1,650. And with this we must leave him : it is not to his dispraise that we leave him with regret.

When we come to Bishop Arculf, almost exactly a century later (A.D. c. 670) we find ourselves confronted with a narrative not written nor purporting to be written by himself but by a man more famous—Adamnan, the biographer of St. Columba. Arculf's see is unknown, but Adamnan tells us that he was

---

[1] *Itin.*, 23 (ed. Geyer, p. 175).
[2] G. F. Hill, *The Medallic Portraits of Christ* (Clarendon Press, 1920), p. 9.
[3] *Itin.*, 32 (ed. Geyer, p. 179).
[4] Ibid. (ed. Geyer, p. 180).

of Gallic race, that he spent nine months in Jerusalem, and that he gave the account of what he had seen in response to a request, Adamnan acting as scribe.[1] The narrative which we have is divided into three books and covers a wide area, for Arculf would seem to have visited not only Jerusalem and the whole of Palestine but Damascus, Tyre, Constantinople, and Alexandria—a city so large that it takes a whole October day to traverse it—as well as the Nile Valley. About all these scenes he has many interesting details to relate as well as of the volcanoes of Lipari and other marvels. Adamnan describes him as ' uerax index ', a truthful guide, and, though there may not have been at Iona where the work was compiled great facilities for checking his statements, there is evidence that there were at any rate some, and there can be no doubt of the deepness of the impression which Arculf himself made upon Adamnan. For the later student the impression is enhanced as he looks at the plans of the Churches of the Holy Sepulchre and of Sion, of the Church of the Ascension on the Mount of Olives and of Jacob's Well which Arculf drew for his host with his own hand on a wax tablet and which Adamnan reproduced in his manuscript.[2] To the account of Jerusalem an additional importance is given by the fact that it is later than the attacks of the Persians and the Arabs. If in the narrative itself there are things that make us wonder, we must remember, as before, that the narrator is not therefore necessarily either dishonest or ridiculous. When, for example, he says that the noise of a volcano is louder on Fridays and Saturdays than on other days,[3] we shall infer, should we hesitate to accept the statement, not that he had never seen the volcano but that like many in a later age he had made a generalization based on the observation of insufficient instances. Probably everyone will concede so much, but it is fair to apply the same argument to the account of the yearly purification of the streets of Jerusalem on the night of September 15th by the fall of an abundance of rain from the clouds.[4] This is not mere trifling, for the credit attaching

---

[1] *Adamnani De Locis Sanctis*, i, Praef. (in *Itinera Hierosolym.*, ed. Geyer, p. 221).

[2] Reproduced in Geyer's edition, *Itin. Hierosolym.*, pp. 231, 250, 271.

[3] ' Maius sexta feria et sabbato intonare uidetur ', *Adamnani De Locis Sanctis*, iii, 6 (ed. Geyer, p. 296).

[4] Ibid., i, 1 (ed. Geyer, p. 225).

to the author's veracity, if not always to his judgment, is of the highest importance, since he gives detailed descriptions, e.g. as to the Round Church of the Holy Sepulchre based, as Adamnan states, on actual measurements. Thus he gives the length of the Sepulchre as seven feet : and he also corrects what he designates as false opinions, e.g. that the Sepulchre is not like a bed of rock but has a projection dividing the slab in two.[1]

As we have seen, Arculf's visit to Jerusalem was made subsequently to the conquests of 614 and 637. The Church of the Holy Sepulchre that he saw can therefore be only a restoration of Constantine's Church. There are real difficulties in the account which he gives, notably as to the three walls,[2] and there are discrepancies with the other stories, though some of them are not inexplicable in view of the course of events. At the time of the visit of Antoninus and his companions the stone which had closed the Sepulchre was, if the narrative be genuine, and we see no special reason to doubt it, in front of the entrance[3] : now, it is represented as having been cut in two and made into two altars.[4] In Antoninus' time the Sepulchre was covered with silver[5]; in Arculf's it was covered with choice marble[6]; at the present day it is also lined with marble. When Arculf saw it—if we may trust his statement, as it seems reasonable to do—the Sepulchre was entirely unadorned within : the natural rock of two colours, red and white, was visible and still bore the marks of tools,[7] whereas, in spite of the arguments of Mr. H. T. F. Duckworth to the contrary, we find it hard to believe from the description of it in the time of Antoninus that any part of it was then visible, though the passages to which Mr. Duckworth calls attention are difficult to explain if such a view be taken.[8] Our safest inference would seem to

[1] Adamn., i, 2 (ed. Geyer, p. 229).

[2] Ibid. (ed. Geyer, p. 227), cf. Duckworth, *Church of the Holy Sepulchre*, pp. 101–3.

[3] 'Ante os monumenti,' *Itin.*, 18 (ed. Geyer, p. 171).

[4] *Adamnani De Locis Sanctis*, i, 3 (ed. Geyer, p. 232).

[5] 'Ipsum monumentum sic quasi in modum metae coopertus ex argento sub solas aureos,' *Itin.*, 18 (ed. Geyer, p. 171).

[6] 'Totum extrinsecus electo tegitur marmore,' Adamn., op. cit., i, 2 (ed. Geyer, p. 228).

[7] Ibid., i, 3 (ed. Geyer, p. 232).

[8] *Church of the Holy Sepulchre*, p. 112.

HULAGU, CONQUEROR OF BAGHDAD AND FIRST ILKHAN OF PERSIA.

From an early Persian manuscript.   Brit. Mus., Add 18803, f.19

CITY OF ST. ALBAN
PUBLIC
LIBRARY

be that in Arculf's time the Sepulchre had not regained in the course of the restoration by Bishop Modestus all its former, perhaps rather garish, magnificence.

The place where the True Cross had stood is spoken of by Arculf as occupied by a great cross of silver. Among the relics which he saw was the Holy Grail, a cup of *silver* with two small handles, one on either side, and holding the measure of a Gallic sextiary i.e. a quart. It contained the sponge that was put to our Lord's lips and it is stated to be the same chalice that our Lord used with His disciples after the Resurrection. The cup was contained in a perforated case through which Arculf both touched and kissed it.[1] There, too, are the soldier's spear—the lance—and the sacred napkin placed on our Lord's Head in the Sepulchre : this ' sudarium ', of about eight feet long, is a new feature, and a story is told of its history for which the testimony of the whole people of Jerusalem is alleged.[2] Associated with it is a story of another linen cloth seen by Arculf. This was the work, as it is said (*ut fertur*), of the Blessed Virgin herself, and had inworked in it the image of our Lord and small representations of the twelve Apostles. It seems from the description to have been red on one side and green on the other, and it will be noticed that, while Arculf vouches for the fact that it is to be seen there, he does not commit himself to the story of its origin.[3]

We come now to a feature of which the interpretation is certainly wrong—the column in the midst of the city which is said to prove that Jerusalem is situated in the middle of the earth.[4] What will strike the reader, we think, with regard to it is the evidence that is adduced in support of this view. That evidence is the physical fact that at the summer solstice it casts no shadow : it is not merely the occurrence in Psalm lxxiii (lxxiv), 12, of the words : ' God our king before the ages has wrought salvation in the midst of the earth.' It is true that Arculf, or Adamnan, quotes that text ; but it is the confirmation of a fact which is deemed to be proved by the results of observation, however interpreted.

---

[1] Adamn., op. cit., i, 7 (ed. Geyer, pp. 234–5).
[2] Ibid., i, 9 (ed. Geyer, pp. 235–8).
[3] Ibid., i, 10 (ed. Geyer, p. 239).
[4] ' Quae mediterranea et umbilicus terrae dicitur,' Adamn., op. cit., i, 11 (ed. Geyer, pp. 239–40).

As in the account of the peregrination of Antoninus and his companions the tomb of the Virgin is mentioned, and mentioned as being empty—the body has been taken away (*sublata*). Arculf adds that the manner, the time, and the agents of its removal or in what place it awaits the Resurrection, no one, as it is said (*ut fertur*), can know for certain.[1] In the Itinerary of Antoninus again mention is made of the three ' resting-places ' (*accubita*) of our Lord at Gethsemane[2] : Arculf is shown the stone upon which our Lord knelt there to pray ; it was impressed with the marks of His knees as in very soft wax,[3] just as later in the round Church of the Ascension Arculf sees the marks of our Lord's feet, marks which refuse to let themselves be covered with marble, and although the faithful carry the earth away, i.e. as relics, the imprint still remains.[4] Arculf does not give this as tradition but as fact, and in relation to the Church of the Ascension itself he tells Adamnan that it is open to the sky because on Ascension Day at the hour of the Lord's Ascension there comes a wind there strong enough to carry away any covering: he has himself experienced its force.[5]

It will be obvious to anyone who knows the stories at first hand that we have been dealing only with quite a limited selection, and even that has had to be confined in the main to Jerusalem. Anyone who is tempted to pursue the subject further, as it deserves, will find most interesting food for reflexion in the successive stages of the story of Bethlehem as it appears in the several narratives, and also of the places specially connected with the lives of the patriarchs. Arculf saw the tombs of the four Patriarchs, Abraham, Isaac, Jacob, and Adam, buried with their feet towards the south, and the inferior memorials, ' uiliores et minores ' of three women [6]— a curiously Eastern touch, for the women are Sarah, Rebecca and Leah. Poor Mother Eve receives no mention, and Rachael, of course, is buried elsewhere with the ' titulus ' which her husband placed over her still to be seen.[7]   Arculf's

---

[1] Adamn., i, 12 (ed. Geyer, p. 240).
[2] *Itin.*, 17 (ed. Geyer, p. 170).
[3] Adamn., op. cit., i, 12 (ed. Geyer, pp. 240–1).
[4] Ibid., i, 23 (ed. Geyer, pp. 246–7).
[5] Ibid. (ed. Geyer, p. 249).
[6] Ibid., ii, 10 (ed. Geyer, pp. 260–1).
[7] Ibid., ii, 7 (ed. Geyer, pp. 258–9).

account of the ' oak ' of Mamre, under which Abraham received his angelic visitors, is really notable. He is talking about something which Adamnan, who in this as in several other instances shows himself an intelligent student of St. Jerome, regards as of considerable importance and about which he asks the Bishop numerous questions. Neither of them pledges himself to the statement that it is as old as the world, a statement which is quoted; but Adamnan ascertains by his questions what Arculf actually saw, the size of what remains of it, and the fact—in itself probable enough—that chips of it were carried away as relics.[1] It is true that, as has been pointed out, the Jewish and Christian traditions differed as to the situation of the tree,[2] and there is the same kind of difference of opinion as there is as to the site of Augustine's Oak ; but so far as Arculf's narrative is concerned our opinion of its value is enhanced rather than diminished by the character of the account that he gives here, as in other scenes which he describes.

The reader will perhaps have noticed that in his account of what he saw at Jerusalem Arculf is not represented as stating that he saw the True Cross. The reason of this is equally plain. Rightly or wrongly Arculf, if we accept his account as genuine, firmly believed that in his own time it was preserved at Constantinople and that he had himself seen it there : at least that seems to be a legitimate inference from Adamnan's narrative. It is said to be preserved in a magnificent round church there. In the church is an exceedingly large and very beautiful aumbry (*armarium*) which encloses a wooden box (*capsa*) which has a wooden cover. This shrine is exposed once a year for three days continuously, beginning on Maundy Thursday, on a golden altar two cubits long and one broad, and is then venerated on each day by a different class of persons, beginning with the Emperor. It is noted that there are not two but three short pieces of wood in the Cross, and that when the box is opened there is omitted a wonderful fragrance, as though all the flowers had been collected in it. The cause of this odour

---

[1] Adamn., op. cit., ii, 11 (ed. Geyer, pp. 261-2).
[2] *The Pilgrimage of Arculfus*, translated and annotated by J. R. Macpherson, ' Palestine Pilgrims' Text Society ' (London, 1895), pp. 33-4.

F

is a liquid that distils from the pieces of wood, one drop of which recovers the sick no matter what the disease from which they are suffering.[1] And here we must take leave of Arculf, however unwillingly, with the parting note that in the account of St. George, which follows, has been seen the first story of the English patron saint which can be regarded as having obtained circulation in England.

The eighth century yields much less than its predecessors to the student of narratives of pilgrim adventure. It was inevitable that this should be so, for with the advance of Moslem conquest the incentives no less than the facilities for Eastern travel were diminished. And though the modern historian looking back may feel justified in saying that ' from the government of the Isaurian emperors a new principle of life had sprung which was to enrich the world for ever ', the would-be pilgrim of the eighth century was more likely to have heard that the possibility of adequate protection was negligible, and that the Ummayaid Caliphate, which reached its period of crowning success under Walid (705–15) and had established its control over Spain in one direction and penetrated to Northern India and almost to China in another, had gained a firm hold on Syria and established a domination of which a great mosque at Damascus and the famous Mosque of Omar at Jerusalem were significant evidence. It is to the credit of the man who is perhaps the first, certainly the most famous, of early pilgrims of English race that with the enthusiasm of youth which alone could make the idea either conceivable in itself or possible of achievement he should have undertaken about 722 so formidable and hazardous a journey.

Willibald, later Bishop of Eichstadt but the nephew of St. Boniface, possibly of Kentish birth, certainly of English education, is the promoter of an adventure which may justly be called heroic, and his *Hodœporicon* is the record of his journey.[2] Like Arculf, he did not write it himself, but

---

[1] Adamn., op. cit., iii, 3 (ed. Geyer, pp. 286–8).

[2] Printed by D'Achery and Mabillon in *Acta Sanctorum Ordinis S. Benedicti*, Saec. III, pars. ii (Paris, 1672), pp. 367–83 ; (Venice, 1734), pp. 332–53 ; in the series of *Itinera Hierosolymitana*, published by the Societé de l'Orient Latin (Geneva, 1879) from the text of T. A. Tobler ; and in English, slightly abbreviated, by the Palestine Pilgrims' Text Society (London, 1895).

dictated it, only not in this case to a learned abbot of Iona but to one of the most ingenuous and delightful of nuns. She is, she assures us, an unworthy child of the Saxon race, a poor specimen of humanity (*quasi homuncula*) in character and attainments, a woman and tainted with the fragile helplessness of her sex (*fragili sexus imbecillitate corruptibilis*), and she is writing for the great Bishop's spiritual children, reverend priests, elegant deacons of distinguished ability, abbots and monks, plucking like a wilful uninstructed child a few flowers, etc. After telling the story of the saintly bishop's early life she relates the pilgrimage in which he persuaded his unwilling father and his brother to join. They set out from Hamelmouth, near the modern Southampton, and make their way to Rouen and thence through Liguria to Lucca, where the father dies.[1] The nun's knowledge of geography is a little vague or her mind confused, for she makes the pilgrims cross the Alps apparently after leaving Lucca. However, they reach Rome, escaping military violence, and after returning thanks at the Basilica of St. Peter proceed by sea from Naples to Reggio and so to Sicily where, she assures us, an eruption of Etna is wont to be stayed by placing the veil of St. Agatha upon it.[2] From Syracuse they cross the Adriatic to the south of the Morea and thence proceed by way of Chios and Samos to Ephesus. The places visited in Asia are not easy to identify, but they include Patara, and after much privation the pilgrims sail to Cyprus. After further journeyings they reach by sea the territory of the Saracens and find themselves at Emesa where the party of eight is cast into prison. Through the influence of a Spaniard they are at last set free and travel 100 miles to Damascus where they stay a week. Thence they proceed on foot to Nazareth and Cana, where is *one* of the six water-pots used at the Marriage-feast and where they partake of the wine which it contains.[3] The narrative as it brings them to Jerusalem is full of Scriptural references but singularly free from embellishments. At Galgala the pilgrims see the stones taken up by the Israelites when crossing the Jordan five miles away, and the spring of the

[1] *Vita S. Willibaldi*, c. 9 [8].
[2] Ibid., 12 [10].
[3] Ibid., 16 [13].

prophet Elisha. At Jerusalem it is really noteworthy that the narrative records that Calvary was once outside the walls and so continued till the time of Helena, who included it within the city.[1] A difficulty is thus solved which does not seem to have occurred to the other pilgrims we have been studying. The Sepulchre is described as cut out of the rock and having a ' lectus ' inside on which our Lord's Body lay. Nothing is said of its ornamentation save that over the Sepulchre is constructed a marvellous house. Willibald visits also the Church called Holy Sion, and mention is made of a cross before the gate of the city where the Jews had tried to deprive the Eleven Apostles of the Body of the Blessed Virgin after her death : she had died in Holy Sion, and angels came and took her from the hands of the Apostles and carried her to Paradise. Her memorial (not, it is stated, her resting-place) is in the Valley of Jehoshaphat. There is a striking description of the Church of the Ascension on the Mount of Olives, and another of a ' gloriosa domus '—the Church of the Nativity at Bethlehem. At Afframia they see the tombs of Abraham, Isaac and Jacob —Adam has disappeared from the list—and of their wives.

We cannot stay to trace the further wanderings ; but four visits in all are recorded as paid to Jerusalem. On the last the future Bishop bought himself some balsam and filled a calabash with it.[2] Into the calabash he inserted a hollow stem which he had filled with petroleum : he cut it level with the opening and then closed it. In consequence when they came to Tyre and the citizens searched their baggage to see if they had anything hidden (*aliquid absconditum*) in it, they found the calabash which Willibald had and smelt the petroleum ; but the balsam they did not find. Had they found anything, says the nun, they would speedily have punished them with martyrdom. But they did not find anything, and so let them go. We must confess that we do not know what would have been regarded as the appropriate comment upon this remarkable example of sanctified ingenuity ; for the good nun of Heidenheim makes no observation at all but merely goes on to record that it took the pilgrims from St. Andrew's Day to the week before

---

[1] *Vita.*, 18.   [2] Ibid., 23 [28].

the following Easter, i.e. over three months at the least, to sail from the coast of Palestine to Constantinople. There they saw the tombs of St. Andrew, St. Timothy and St. Luke, and also that of St. John Chrysostom. After a stay of two years they went to Nicæa, where the church was a round church like that of the Ascension on the Mount of Olives and where the great Council of 318 bishops had been held some four centuries before. In the church there were the pictures of the bishops who had been present at the Council. After returning to Constantinople the party made their way back to Italy two years later, i.e. apparently in 728, passing on the voyage the Island of Vulcan (Lipari)—the Hell of Theoderic—which furnishes the most vigorous piece of description in the whole narrative.[1] In Italy Willibald goes to Monte Cassino : it was seven years since he had left Rome and ten since he had first left his native land. After ten years more, spent in the observance of the Rule of St. Benedict, he was sent by Pope Gregory III to join St. Boniface in instructing the nation of the Franks,[2] and at last, at the age of 41, was consecrated to the episcopate at Salzburg,[3] to begin a new stage in a most eventful career.

It has been said of the Treatise upon the Holy Places compiled by the Venerable Bede that he traverses practically the whole range of the narrative of Arculf, but in about one-third of the space. As one looks back over the present study, one can but admire once more by comparison the marvellous skill of the Father of English History. And yet, in spite of all the omissions, and even it may be the misinterpretations as well as the defects, it is impossible not to hope that at least something of the glamour and fascination of these early narratives of Christian travel may survive even the clumsiness of our modern handling. If it tempts some at any rate to read for themselves in the pages of the *Itinera Hierosolymitana* or of the Palestine Pilgrims' Text Society the fuller story and in the work of Professor Beazley on ' The Dawn of Modern Geography ' a critical discussion from a somewhat different point of view, the labour will at any rate not have been expended in vain.

[1] *Vita*, 24 (30).   [2] Ibid., 27 (34).
[3] Ibid., 29 (37).

CHAPTER IV

THE VIKING AGE

By Professor ALLEN MAWER, M.A.

OF the great movements which have contributed to the making of modern Europe, the Viking movement, though certainly among the greatest, is probably the least familiar to the majority of historical students, professional and amateur alike. The Vikings can be shown to be pioneers in geographical discovery, chief among the founders of modern commerce, the possessors of a literature of unsurpassed value, men endowed with the highest technical and artistic skill, but all this is a discovery of the last fifty to a hundred years. How is it that the age of the Vikings has thus been neglected and its importance so long unrecognized?

The chief cause lies probably in the general misconception of the character and meaning of the movement. Our knowledge of the Vikings was, until the last half century or so, drawn almost entirely from the works of medieval Latin chroniclers, writing for the most part in monasteries and other kindred schools of learning which had only too often felt the devastating hand of the Viking raiders. They naturally regarded them as little better than pirates, and they were never tired of expatiating upon their cruelty, their violence, and their general love of anarchy. It is only during the last fifty years that we have been able to revise our ideas of the early Scandinavian peoples and to form a juster conception of the part which they played in European civilization. The change has come about chiefly in two ways. First, and chronologically the earlier, the literature of the Scandinavian peoples is no longer a sealed book to us. Northern literature has been a subject of interest to us ever since the days of the poet Gray with his *Descent of Odin* and *The Fatal Sisters*, but the general popularizing of the literature of the North belongs to the latter half of the nineteenth century when, to mention but a few names, we have the great work of William Morris in translation and adaptation of the old legends and sagas, of Sir George Dasent in renderings of such great stories as that of Burnt Njal, and lastly of such scholars as Vigfusson and York Powell who devoted themselves chiefly to the interpretation of the ancient language and its literature. Through the work of such writers as these we have come to recognize that Scandinavia, and more particularly Norway and Iceland, possesses a heroic literature which can on its own merits stand side by side with the great literatures of Greece and Rome and fear nothing from the comparison.

Secondly, and it is on this point that one would wish to lay special stress here, archæology has within the last half century become an exact science, and the work of archæologists, generally themselves of Scandinavian birth, upon the rich finds which have been brought to light during the last century or so in the Scandinavian kingdoms has given us a vast body of concrete fact with the aid of which we can reconstruct the civilization of the Viking period far more satisfactorily than we could from the sagas alone.

The period of Scandinavian history, and indeed of the history of Northern Europe generally, to which the term " Viking " has been applied extends roughly from the middle of the eighth century to the end of the first quarter of the eleventh century. The commencement of the period was marked by a series of piratical raids upon the coasts of England, Western Scotland, and Ireland, and upon Frankish territory. Its climax was reached when in the course of the ninth century Scandinavian kingdoms were established in Ireland, Man, and the Hebrides, and in the Northern, Midland, and Eastern districts of England, and its close was marked by the consolidation of the Scandinavian kingdoms in the tenth century under Olaf Tryggvason in Norway, Olaf Skötkonung in Sweden, and, greatest of all, King Knut in Denmark, who for a brief time held the whole of Scandinavia and the British Isles in one vast confederacy.

What were the causes which gave rise to this great Viking movement? There is an old belief among the Scandinavian peoples that at some early period in their history their country was overpopulated and that, as it could not support so large a number of people, the active youth of the nation were obliged to find fresh homes and possessions in foreign lands. The father himself often drove out his younger sons in order to provide for his eldest son. This over population is attributed to polygamy. It is doubtful if polygamy necessarily leads to overpopulation, and it was certainly not the universal practice in ancient Scandinavia, but it does seem probable that at one time that country was much more thickly populated than at present, and polygamy among the ruling classes would mean the presence of a large number of younger sons for whom it was necessary to make provision.

Other causes are not far to seek. The dwellers on the coast of the North Sea and the Baltic felt all that love of freedom and of enterprise which is the birthright of sea-girt nations, and when great kings or chieftains like Harold Fairhair in Norway endeavoured to consolidate the petty kingships under one sovereign their love of independence was outraged. Their nearest way of escape lay over the sea, and they straightway sought new homes in distant lands where they might lead a free and independent life.

More important than this is the relation in which the rise of the Viking power stood to the decline of the great trading empire which immediately preceded it, viz. the Frisian. Unfortunately we know only too little of this great power whose domination of the trade of Western Europe lasted from the end of the fifth or the beginning of the sixth century to the days when it fell before the power first of Charles Martel and then later of Charlemagne. According to Procopius, Frisians took part in the Saxon invasion of Britain. In Bede we hear of Frisian merchants in London, and there is mention in the *Life of St. Liudger* of the expulsion of Frisian merchants from York in the second half of the eighth century. Frisians and Scandinavians were already in conflict in the sixth century, for it was in a raid on Frisia that Hygelac, the sovereign and patron of Beowulf, fell somewhere about A.D. 512. When Alfred was at war with the Danes we find Frisian sailors in his service, and it is clear that Frisians and Vikings alike were now far ahead of the English in the art of shipbuilding. The extent of their travels westwards is illustrated by the name *Fresicum mare* given by Nennius to the Irish Sea. On the Continent there were important Frisian trading settlements at Mainz and Worms, and from North Frisia they made their way to the Eider, the old boundary of the Scandinavian North. From here they opened up trade with the Baltic and the North Sea. Their great trading centre was Dorestad, already mentioned in the seventh century, lying on an arm of the Rhine to the south of the Zuyder Zee. From here one trade route went south along the Lek, one of the outlets of the Rhine, towards England, while the Zuyder Zee itself gave an outlet to the North. When St. Anskar in A.D. 826 went on his first Christianizing mission to Sweden he went to Slesvik by Dorestad and thence made his way to Birka, later Björkö, the oldest of the great trading towns of Sweden, on the shores of Lake Mälar, a town which has now disappeared. The very name of this town is of intense interest, as it bears witness to the ancient importance of Frisian trade. The first element in this name is not, as one might think, *björk*, 'birch-tree,' but the word *birk*, still used in Danish to denote a district with its own special rights, privileges, and laws. This word in its turn is not of Scandinavian origin but a loan-word from Frisian, in which *birk* is used in the same sense, and the old trading city of *Birka* must have been founded, not by Swedes, but by Frisians who, from the special trading privileges accorded to them, gave the place this name. This particular place-name has been tracked down by Professor Wadstein over the whole of North-Western Europe, and he has shown that further examples of it may be found at the head of the gulf of Bothnia, in Pirkkiö on the Tornea, in the South of Finland, at Björkö near Viborg, in the North of Norway in the old district of Haalogaland, the home of Ohthere, at Bjarköy. In all these cases the early forms show that we have to do, not with birch-trees, but with this old word *birk*, and Professor Wadstein believes that we may well have further examples in Björköen at the entrance to Trondhjem Fjord, Bjerkeröen near Bergen, Bjerkö near Tunsberg, on Christiania Fjord, Björkö off Göteborg, near the ancient market of Kongaelf, and Björkö off the coast of Sweden opposite to the island of Gothland. It is noteworthy that all these places lie on the great trading routes of North-Western Europe, and they demonstrate clearly, when taken in conjunction with other evidence, that the Frisians had already opened up great trade-routes before the Vikings rose to power, and one can well understand that when the Frisian power was crushed under the heel of the Frankish empire the Vikings saw their chance. The overthrow of the Frisians and the Saxons brought the Danes and the Franks face to face along the Eider boundary, and henceforward there was no peace between them either on sea or land.

The great success of the Viking movement certainly depended to a large extent on their own military and naval prowess, their personal character, their instinct for organization, but it also rested largely on the weakness, division, and degeneracy of their contemporaries in Christian Europe at the time. The Carolingian Empire was in the throes of dissolution and the coasts of Western Europe began to swarm with heathen Northmen eager for devastation and plunder. They first visited England and Ireland about the year 780, and by 800 they were in full conflict with the Franks, where the divided counsels of the successors of Charlemagne gave them a ready opening. It was the Danes and Norwegians, as we might expect from their geographical position, who chiefly visited our shores, the Danes ultimately making their chief settlements in North-Eastern and Midland England, the Norsemen in Ireland, the Western Islands, the Isle of Man, and North-Western England generally. The Swedes found their outlet chiefly on the shores of the Baltic, though we must remember that much of what we now call Sweden then belonged to Denmark or Norway—including the provinces of Bohuslän, Halland, Skaane and Blekinge.

The story of these Scandinavian settlements in the British Isles and in Normandy is, or should be, familiar to us, but we must not forget that Scandinavian influences prevailed in other districts beside those of Western Europe. Already Finland and Lapland had largely been settled, and the Norse sagas tell of active trade with the shores of the White Sea and the ancient Bjarmaland, on the edge of the Ural Mountains, and behind the stories of the voyages of exploration of Ohthere and Wulfstan narrated to Alfred the Great there probably lies a long story of trade, first round the North Cape into the White Sea and second through the Baltic to the coast of Esthonia. Then too we must remember that the Swedes ruled the whole of the Baltic provinces of Russia and indeed founded the Russian Empire itself in the ninth century. ' Russ ' was a name given by the Finns to the Swedes, and in course of time this name of the alien rulers of the Slavs came to be applied to the whole people in much the same way as the name of the ' Frankish ' or ' French ' rulers of the Romance-speaking peoples of France came to be applied to the people themselves. The names of many Russian towns, such as Novgorod, are pure Scandinavian. Archæological finds of pure Northern origin are numerous.

Yet further south did the Viking influence extend. Adventurers made their way overland as far south as Constantinople or Miklagard, ' great enclosure ' as they called it, and there won honour and wealth in the service of the Byzantine emperors. Many Variags, as they were called, being discontended with their service under the Grand Duke Vladimir of Russia, journeyed to Constantinople, there to enter the service of the Emperor. These Variags, and others who had preceded them, became the emperors' well-known Varangian guard, and did them yeoman service. To be a Varangian was deemed a praiseworthy distinction, and men of the highest birth often enrolled themselves in the guard. Harold Sigurdsson, half-brother of St. Olaf, was for a long time captain of the Varangian guard, earned wealth and honour, and returned home to become king of Norway under the well-known name of Harold Hardrada, the Norse king who was defeated at the battle of Stamford Bridge. From Constantinople the Varangians were sent to all parts of the Byzantine Empire. Harold Hardrada himself visited the Greek Archipelago, Sicily, and North Africa. An interesting memorial of these journeys is still extant in the famous marble lion which the Venetians brought from Athens to Venice in 1687, and which now stands at the entrance to the Arsenal of that city. Formerly it stood on the shores of the Piræus, which from it bore the name of the ' Porto Leone.' The lion itself is of Greek workmanship, but it has a Scandinavian runic inscription on it, unfortunately too much worn away for us to be able to decipher it with certainty.

Enough has been said, perhaps, by way of introduction

as to the extent and importance of Viking activities. Let us now consider that side of their equipment which was the immediate cause of their contact with the peoples of Western Europe, whether in trade or warfare, viz. their ships. The art of shipbuilding was carried to a high level of excellence and the number of vessels was great. During the course of the Viking attacks on England and France we hear more than once of fleets of 250 or even 350 vessels, and when Knut the Great conquered Norway he had a fleet of some 1,200 vessels, which in modern reckoning is the equivalent of 1,440, as the Norwegians, like other Scandinavian peoples, used the long hundred in their reckoning, that is ten twelves instead of ten tens, a form of reckoning of which traces are still to be found in the parts of England most strongly affected by Scandinavian influence.

In vessels of the pre-Viking age in the North we find no sails. Now they have regularly a single mast and sail. The sail is usually of course woollen material, often with blue, red and green stripes. The magnificent sails were a source of much pride to their possessors. Thus we are told of Sigurd 'Jerusalem-farer' that on his way back from Jerusalem to Constantinople he lay for half a month off the coast of Greece and, though he had a favourable wind from the south to carry him through the Hellespont, he preferred to wait for a side wind so that his sails might be set lengthwise along the ship, for all his sails were trimmed with purple both fore and aft and could be admired by spectators on both sides of the straits. When the king entered Constantinople he sailed quite close to the shore so that from there one could see the whole expanse of the sails forming as it were one unbroken wall.

The size of a ship was reckoned according to the number of rowing benches two rowers being seated on every bench. Thus a 'fifteen' or 'twenty-seater' means a vessel having fifteen or twenty benches or pairs of oars.

Olaf Tryggvason's vessel, the *Long Serpent*, had thirty-four benches of oars, while Knut the Great had one of sixty-nine pairs of oars. The rudder was placed on the starboard side of the ship, hence called the *steer* or *starboard* side, while the gunwale was adorned with a row of shields painted alternately in different colours. The stem often ended in a dragon's

THE GOKSTAD SHIP.

As preserved in the Museum of Oslo (Christiania) University.

(Reproduced from a photograph kindly supplied by the Museum.)

CITY OF ST. ALBAN
PUBLIC
LIBRARY

head, done over with gold, whilst the stern was frequently shaped like a dragon's tail, so that the vessel itself was often called a "dragon". On going into action the ships were lashed together so that the fight resembled an engagement in the field. When at anchor, especially in harbour, tents and pavilions were erected on deck for the accommodation of the leaders.

The difference between a war and a trading-ship is well illustrated by Snorri's story of the escape of the Norwegian Harek of Thjotta through Copenhagen Sound after the battle of Helgeä in South Sweden. His king, St. Olaf, had returned to Norway overland, but Harek deemed himself too old for such a journey and determined to go back by sea. What happened may be told in the words of Morris in his translation of the passage :— "Harek did as he had said ; he abode a fair wind, and then sailed west about Skaney until he came east of the Knolls, and with a wind behind, blowing a breeze. Then he let strike sail and mast, and take down the vane, and wrap all the ship above the water in grey hangings, and let men row on a few benches fore and aft, but let most of the men sit low in the ship. Now King Knut's watch saw the ship, and spoke among themselves as to what ship it could be, and guessed that there would be flitted salt or herring, whereas they saw few men, and little rowing, and moreover the ship seemed grey and untarred, like a ship bleached by the sun, and withal they saw that the ship was much low in the water. But when Harek came forth into the Sound, he let raise the mast and hoist sail, and let set up gilded vanes, and the sail was white as snowdrift and done with red and blue bends." Naval camouflage is not an invention of the late war.

Fortunately we are not confined to written sources for our knowledge of the Viking ships. In Norway more than one Viking ship has been found, the most famous being those of Gokstad and Oseberg, both from burial mounds on the shores of Christiania or, as we must learn to say, Oslo Fjord. They owe their preservation to the fact that they were used as burial chambers for the persons to whom they belonged. The oldest of these vessels is the Gokstad find. It is clinker-built with seats for sixteen pairs of rowers and is 78 ft. long and 16 ft. broad amidships. In form and workmanship it is not surpassed by modern vessels of a similar kind and, to judge from the remains found in it, it must date from about A.D. 900.

The Oseberg ship is of a rather different type. The gunwale is lower and the whole vessel broader. The general impression it gives us is more of that type of vessel which Harek tried to turn his warship into, but the rich carving both of stem and stern, and also of the gunwale near the stern, suggest that it was probably not used for mere trade purposes. It was in the end used as the grave-chamber of a woman, and it is probable that it belonged to some wealthy king's daughter, or perhaps to a queen.

This account of the ships of the Vikings may serve to remind us that the relations between the Northmen and the rest of the world were by no means entirely of a warlike character. There was much peaceful intercourse, but its importance has as a rule been greatly underestimated by historians of the period.

One must in the first instance speak of the settlement of Iceland. The story is a simple one. It commenced about A.D. 870 when many Norse nobles sought there, for themselves and their followers, a freer life than they could obtain under the growing power of Harold Fairhair. It was greatly strengthened by settlers both from Norway and from Ireland and the Western islands when that power was firmly established by the Battle of Hafrsfjord, and by the year 930 the settlement was virtually complete. Iceland was more purely Scandinavian than any other settlement made during the Viking Age. Here we have, not the case of one civilization grafted on another and earlier one, as in England, Ireland, or the Frankish Empire, but the transference of the best and finest elements in a nation to new and virgin soil where, for good or ill, they were free to develop their civilization on almost entirely independent lines. Settlers from the Western islands and from Ireland may have brought Celtic elements, and Christianity was not without its influence when it was introduced from Norway at the close of the tenth century, but on the whole we can see in Iceland just what Viking civilization was capable of when left to itself.

At first the settlers lived in almost complete isolation, political and religious, from one another, but they soon found that some form of organization was necessary, and groups of settlers began by choosing from among their number a *goði*, or chieftain, half-priest, half leader, who was the speaker at their moot and their representative in negotiation with neighbouring groups. Then, continued disputes and the lack of a common law led to the establishment of a central moot or *alþing*, with a speaker to speak one single law for all. But the Norsemen were much better at making constitutions and enacting laws than they were at observing them when instituted, and the condition of Iceland has been vividly if roughly summarized as one of ' all law and no government '. The local *things* or the national *althing* might enact perfect laws, but there was no compelling force to make them obeyed.

The failure of the Icelandic Commonwealth is amply compensated for by the rich intellectual development of Icelandic literature, which owed many of its characteristic features to the fact that it was written in a land almost completely detached from the main currents of Western medieval thought and the general trend of European history, but in itself that failure is full of deepest import for a right understanding of the part played by Viking civilization in Europe. Powerful and highly developed as that civilization was in many ways, it only reached its highest and best expression when brought into fruitful contact with other and older civilizations. There it found the corrective for certain tendencies of too strongly individualistic character leading to political and intellectual anarchy, while at the same time by its own energy and vigour it quickened the life of the older civilizations where they were tending to become effete and outworn.

But Iceland was not their only peaceful settlement. From Iceland, Erik the Red when outlawed made his way to Greenland, and soon, in spite of the strenuous climate and the unceasing hardships, extensive Norse settlements were established, and by the end of the tenth century extensive trade in walrus tusks, whaleblubber, hides, and fish of various kinds had been set up.

There is a characteristic touch of Norse shrewdness and irony in the story that Erik the Red called the land *Green-land* for he said it would give people a desire to go there if it had a good name !

The Norsemen had first been drawn to Greenland, so the story went, because a certain Gunnbjörn, sailing west from Iceland, had caught sight of land. Now they were to venture yet further afield. Early navigation in the Mediterranean and elsewhere was almost entirely a question of hugging the coast. In the absence of any compass to steer by, it was but rarely that men ventured to sail straight across the open sea. It was one of the great triumphs of Norse sailors that they did not shrink from venturing boldly across the unknown, and there is no more striking example of it than the voyage which Leif, the son of Erik, made from Greenland in the spring of the year 1000, when he caught the first glimpse of a land which he called *Vinland*, or *Wine*-land, and gained the nickname of 'Leif the Lucky'. He had been driven far out of his course, and came upon a land with great forests, self-sown wheat, and vinestocks. A second expedition in which Leif's father and his brother Thorstein took part was less lucky, for they were driven back by contrary winds so far east that they caught sight of Iceland and so far to the south that they saw the seabirds off the coast of Ireland. In the spring of 1003 a fresh expedition under Thorfinn Karlsefne, with three ships and 140 men, set sail from Greenland. Two days' sail brought them to a land which they called *Helleland*, a land of great flat rocks and Arctic foxes, which has been identified with Labrador. A further day and a half's sail brought them to a well-wooded land which they called *Mark-land*, that is 'forest-land', which may well have been Newfoundland. Lured by the hope of finding Leif's *Vinland*, with its wine-grapes, they continued to sail south, passed a ship-shaped headland, but were still faced by a cold and inhospitable coast. Soon, however, the coast was broken by a succession of creeks, a landing was made up one of these, two Scottish runners who were of the party were sent to explore, and brought back news and examples of the long-sought grapes and wheat. The winter was spent a little further south in a pleasant grass-grown land, and in the spring, travelling yet further south, they reached a good and pleasant land which resembled Leif's own Vinland. Soon, however, the Norse settlers got on to bad terms with the natives, and so difficult did the situation become that in the summer of 1006 they sailed back home. Exactly how far south the Norsemen sailed will never be satisfactorily settled, the indications in the saga are too vague. They must however, have gone a good way south to find a climate which would grow grapes, where there was no frost in winter, and the cattle could remain out all night. Some of these details must be definitely historical, for as early as the second half of the eleventh century Adam of Bremen tells of an island called Vinland, so named because it produced self-grown vinestocks and the best wine. Whatever may have been the exact position of Vinland, it is clear that the Norsemen discovered America five hundred years before Columbus.

Voyages of Polar discovery were also started by them when, about the year 1050, Harold Hardrada sailed as far north in the Ice sea as he was able in the attempt to discover how far that sea stretched. Adam of Bremen, to whom we owe our knowledge of this expedition, tells us that Harold was driven back by storms, but from further details which he gives us Dr. Bugge has shown that there is good reason to believe that he also explored the White Sea in the hope of strengthening the trade in skins with the north of Russia.

Sweden was not behindhand in the expansion of trade and in the establishment of new settlements. At that time a great part of her coast-line was in Danish or Norwegian hands, but she had extensive relations with the countries to the south and east, which were easiest of access, and we find at the same time frequent traces of friendly intercourse between Sweden and Western Europe, and, more especially, between Sweden and England. Many memorial stones still standing in Sweden bear witness to the journeys of Swedes to England, their business or their death there. The Scandinavian countries are very rich in Anglo-Saxon coins, and though at first we might be inclined to attribute their frequency to that unhappy system whereby Ethelred the Unready and other English kings paid Danegeld to buy off the Viking raids, an examination of the places where these coins have been chiefly found shows that such is not the case. Most of the Viking raiders undoubtedly came from Denmark, Norway and Western Sweden, whereas the coins have been found chiefly in the eastern districts of Sweden, round Lake Mälar and in the neighbourhood of the great waterways connecting Sweden and the Baltic, but above all on the islands of Gothland and

G

Öland. Some of these coins must have come by way of trade from Norway and Denmark, the Vikings when they returned home spending as recklessly as they had plundered, but the majority must be due to direct intercourse with England. It is worthy of notice in this connexion that the Swedish National Museum at Stockholm is richer in Anglo-Saxon coins than is our own British Museum.

Eastwards their first settlement was on the shores of Lake Ladoga, at the place which they called Aldeigjuborg, established about 800. By the year 839 some of them had made their way overland to Constantinople, for there is a curious story from that year telling how an embassy from the Byzantine emperor visited the court of Louis the Pious, and how certain people among them, calling themselves *Ros*, i.e. Russian, asked to be allowed to return direct home instead of facing the perils of the journey back from Constantinople overland to their own home. Louis made inquiries as to their origin and found that they were really Swedes. The story of the intervention of Swedish nobles in the affairs of Russia, whereby they became its virtual rulers, is first recorded in the pages of the Russian monk Nestor, and its full significance has been explained by Vilhelm Thomsen in his masterly book on the founding of the Russian kingdom. By the year 882 they were as far south as Kieff, and soon they had their fleets on the Black Sea and the Sea of Marmora and were threatening Constantinople. From the political point of view it is easy to exaggerate the importance of this Swedish element in Russia, for the evidence is clear that these Swedish princes soon became completely Slavicized, lost all sense of their ultimate racial affinities, and became Slavonic princes pure and simple. But, however that may be, the story is remarkable for its giving yet further and striking proof of the expansive energy and initiative of the Scandinavian peoples, and, if it had few political results, it was all important in the development of trade and commerce.

Of that commerce there are various witnesses. Among the most interesting are the frequent finds of Oriental and especially of Arabian coins. These coins first made their way to Scandinavia about the beginning of the ninth century and are far more common in Sweden than in the rest of

Scandinavia, some 30,000 having been found in Sweden alone. Some of these coins may have been brought home by Viking raiders, who we know to have visited the Moorish kingdom of Spain in the ninth and tenth centuries, but there can be no doubt that the vast majority reached Scandinavia overland through Russia, where extensive finds of Arabian coins mark the route along which trade at that time travelled from Asia to the North. The greater number of these coins were minted at Samarcand, east of the Caspian Sea, others at Baghdad on the Euphrates. Further evidence of the importance of this trade is to be found in the fact that at the end of the Viking period the Persian weight-system was introduced into the North and that the earliest Swedish coinage is based on it. Olaf Skötkonung's coins, coined at Sigtuna, weigh half a Persian drachma.

Trading was a matter of great difficulty and many risks in those days. The line of division between merchant and Viking was a slender one, and more than once we read how, when merchants went on a trading expedition, they arranged a truce until their business was concluded and then agreed to treat each other as enemies. The trading was generally carried on in large market-centres, and these centres were generally to be found in places where numbers of people were accustomed to meet together for some religious or political purpose. Thus Uppsala, an ancient centre of worship in Sweden, had a large market, while one of the most famous of all Scandinavian markets was that held in Bohuslän on the Götaelv, at a spot where the boundaries of the three northern kingdoms met, and where periodical meetings were held for the settlement of business affecting the three countries. Other permanent centres were Skiringssalr on the S.W. coast of Norway, the lost Birka on Lake Mälar, to which reference has already been made, Visby on the Island of Gothland, later one of the Hanse towns, and Haddeby-Slesvik on the Eider, Denmark's chief channel of trade. The international character of much of this trade is well-illustrated by an incident which once occurred at the Götaelv market. On a certain occasion, a rich merchant named Gille (the name is Celtic), surnamed the Russian because of his numerous journeys to that country, set up his booth in the market and received a visit from the Icelander

Höskuldr, who was anxious to buy a female slave. Gille drew back a curtain dividing off the inner part of the tent and showed Höskuldr twelve female slaves. Höskuldr bought one and she proved to be an Irish king's daughter, who had been made captive by Viking raiders. This story serves also to illustrate what was one of the chief articles of trade at the time, viz. slaves, generally prisoners of war. Other exports included furs, horses, wool, and fish, while the chief articles of import would naturally be luxuries of clothing or ornament.

While the Scandinavian kings often had a coinage of their own in the lands which they conquered, in Scandinavia itself there was no coinage until the end of the Viking period, and foreign coins were used if prices were paid in coin at all. As a matter of fact, large payments were usually made in silver, whether in the forms of coins, ornaments, or ingots, and the required amount was weighed rather than counted out. The uncoined silver was often in the form of spirals, and we have preserved from the period several spirals which bear witness to the fact that trade was as full of tricks then as it is now. These spirals are made of copper with a thin coating only of silver. They must have been used in large payments where the spiral would not have to be cut and the fraud would not be detected. The weights used were generally of iron, with a thin coating of bronze. They were made thus so as to prevent trickery, for any attempt to diminish the weight by scraping its surface would at once reveal the iron beneath and the cheat would be exposed. Trading journeys were for the most part made by sea. Inland the lakes and rivers were used as far as was possible. There were no roads at that time, and such travelling as was done overland with goods had to be done with pack-horses. Carts were almost unknown.

There can be little doubt of the importance of Viking traders and settlers generally in developing the trade of the lands in which they made settlements. In England one cannot but feel that they must have done much in developing the trade of the Eastern coast towns. Unfortunately we have practically no contemporary evidence on this point, but there must be long history behind the close relationship between such English ports as Grimsby, Hull and King's

Lynn, and Scandinavia, which we find prevailing in post-conquest days, and which Dr. Alexander Bugge has done so much to illuminate. In Ireland we are very much luckier. Both from the Irish annals and from the Icelandic sagas we can glean a good deal about the influence of the Vikings on Irish trade. It was the Vikings who developed the great seaport towns, Dublin, Wexford, Waterford, Cork, and Limerick. The system whereby foreign merchants had to barter their goods at the various country fairs was largely done away with in favour of fixed markets at the important centres. The wealth of the trading centres is illustrated in more than one passage in the Irish chronicles and the Norse sagas. The spoils carried off by the Irish after a victory near Dublin in the year 1000 included "gold, silver, bronze, and precious stones, carbuncle gems, buffalo horns, and beautiful goblets, much also of various vestures of all colours", and similarly, a few years before, the Irish carried off from the Vikings in Limerick "their jewels and their best property, their saddles, beautiful and foreign, their gold and silver; their beautifully woven cloth of all colours and all kinds, their satins and their silken cloths, pleasing and variegated, both scarlet and green, and all sorts of cloth in like manner". In Erbyggjasaga we hear of a merchant ship that came from Dublin to Snæfellsness in Iceland in the year 1000. One of the passengers, a woman named Thorgunna, had a large chest containing beautifully embroidered bed-clothes, English sheets, a silken quilt, and other costly wares, the like of which were rare in Iceland.

These stories of the rich and varied possessions of the Vikings in Ireland may serve to introduce us to the last phase of our study of the Viking age, viz. the rich material civilization of the period and the high artistic worth of many of its products. The actual life and the houses of these Northmen may have been simple and even primitive, but even in their houses there was much rich carving of wood with incidents from the mythological and heroic sagas and the houses of great men were often hung with tapestry, and even the household vessels at times were things of great artistic beauty. It is, however, when we come to their dress and ornaments that we see this wealth in all its beauty and fullness. There can be little doubt that our Viking forefathers had attained a high standard of personal luxury and adornment. If we visit the museums of Copenhagen, Stockholm and Oslo-Christiania, we cannot but be impressed by the wealth of ornaments displayed before us, magnificent brooches of silver and bronze, massive silver neck rings and girdles, arm-rings and finger-rings, large beads of silver, glass, rock-crystal, cornelian, amber and other materials. The objects are not only evidence of the material wealth of the Vikings, but also of their high artistic skill. At one time it was usually thought that all antiquities showing artistic skill must have been brought from abroad as plunder, but patient research has shown clearly that the majority of the articles showing the best technical skill must have been wrought in Scandinavia itself, and there is a surprising scantiness of such objects which can be shown definitely to be of foreign manufacture.

The most characteristic of all these ornaments was undoubtedly the brooch. It is usually of bronze, oval in shape, with silver bosses. When found now the bronze is usually green with verdigris, but it must originally have had the brilliance of gold, and with their silver bosses and silver wire round the edges the brooches must have been of splendid appearance. The decorative art used in these various articles is interesting. It is in that style once known as 'dragon' style, but now commonly termed 'animal ornamentation'. There are no figures of dragons—fantastic creatures with wings or such-like—neither have we the full forms of any animal actually existing, but the ornamentation is built up from animal elements by an entirely unrestrained imagination. Thus we clearly have heads, limbs, and tails of animals interwoven with one another in fantastic designs, but it would be idle to try to find what particular animal the artist has in mind. This highly characteristic form of ornamentation is in fact based on that of a preceding period in the culture of the North Teutonic peoples, but at the same time it owes a great deal to foreign and, more especially, to Irish influence. Irish culture, art, and science played an important part in the civilization of Europe in the early Middle Ages, and one side of that culture, and indeed one of its most striking sides, was its decorative art. We have definite evidence that already early in the eighth century this influence was working with full force in Scandinavia.

The story of Viking ornament and Viking decorative design may in conclusion serve to remind us yet again of two marks characteristic of the Viking age which we must always bear in mind if we wish to understand it aright. The first is that it is an age of curious contrasts of barbarism and culture, direst cruelty and bloodthirstiness such as we find in the story of Ragnar Lothbrok, combined with a strong legal sense such as that which laid the foundations of what was ultimately to become the twelfth century 'jury by presentment'. The second is that the Vikings were a race capable of developing all that is best in civilization other than their own, whether it be Irish ornamentation, Romanesque architecture, or Frisian trade-routes.

CHAPTER V

ARAB TRAVELLERS AND MERCHANTS, A.D. 1000–1500

By Sir T. W. ARNOLD, C.I.E., Litt.D.

SINCE the great days of Imperial Rome, the Western world had not seen so vast an empire as that of the Arabs in the eighth century of the Christian era. We are accustomed to think of this great Muhammadan empire as belonging to the Orient; but if we remember that it stretched from the Atlantic Ocean, from the shores of Morocco and Portugal, all along the coast of North Africa and Egypt—that it included Palestine and Syria, and that even when we trace it on further east into Mesopotamia, we are still within territory that once formed part of a Roman province—it becomes clear that this new empire was a Mediterranean power. Closer examination reveals to us that this was not merely the case from a geographical point of view, but further that the Arabs were the heirs of that Hellenistic culture, for which a way was first opened by the conquests of Alexander and which became so widely diffused throughout the eastern provinces of the later Roman Empire. These Hellenistic influences, moreover, were not confined to the countries which once owed allegiance to Rome, but spread far eastward into lands that the Roman armies never succeeded in reaching, for the Oriental Christian Churches had cherished the inheritance of Greek thought—philosophy, medicine, mathematics, physical science—and had diffused its stimulating influences through the channels of those Oriental languages into which the works of Greek authors were translated, and thus it spread among the Arabic-speaking peoples.

Western Europe is apt to view the Muhammadan world as something entirely remote from itself; such a judgment leaves out of consideration the fact that both the Christian West and the Muhammadan East are in many respects heirs of the same vivifying cultural influences, and that Islam in the ultimate analysis of its civilization reveals itself as the aftermath of Hellenism in the East. In our estimate of the culture of the Muhammadan world we are apt to forget that the population of the Arab Empire included the races from which sprang St. John of Damascus and many another great theologian of the Christian Church, and that the revelation of Greek literature, to which in Europe the intellectual movement of the Renaissance was largely due, wrought a similar and even more profound influence on the intellectual outlook of the Muslim world. The first translators from the Greek into Arabic were members of the Jacobite and Nestorian Churches, and their translation of Ptolemy laid the foundation of that geographical science which the Muhammadans were to carry so far. The very word for "geography" in Arabic—a mere transcription of the Greek into Arabic letters—indicates its origin, and it is to this origin that Muhammadan geographical science owes much of its sanity, its careful observation of actual facts, its unceasing prosecution of the cognate studies of mathematics and astronomy. We accordingly find a serious pursuit of geographical science among the Arabs from the ninth century onward; it was often cultivated for its own sake, and the geographical literature in the Arabic language is a very creditable outcome of the Greek sources from which it grew.

A further stimulus to geographical research was given by the very immensity of the Arab empire, so long as it was still undivided. There was a period during which the traveller could pass from the confines of China to the pillars of Hercules, from the banks of the Indus to the Cilician Gates, from the Oxus to the shores of the Atlantic, without stepping outside the boundaries of the territory ruled over by the Caliph in Damascus or Baghdad. Even after this vast empire broke up into separate principalities, the journey of the Muslim traveller was facilitated by that brotherhood of Islam which gives to the Muhammadan world its cosmopolitan character, and enables community of faith to wipe out all differences of race and origin. However many hundreds of miles the Muslim might journey from his native town, he could confidently hope for a welcome and generous hospitality at the hands of his co-religionists, especially if he had any reputation for piety or religious knowledge, and he might even chance to come across a fellow townsman, even though his wanderings had

carried him into the land of the infidels, far beyond the
boundaries of the Muslim empire ; thus Ibn Baṭṭūṭah, an
energetic traveller of the fourteenth century, to whom reference
will be made later, tell us how on his arrival in a town in
China, which he calls Kanjanfu, the Muhammadan merchants
there came out to receive him with flags and a band of
musicians with trumpets, drums and horns, bringing horses
for him and his party, so that they rode into the city in a
triumphal procession.   During his stay there he heard of the
arrival of a highly respected doctor of the law among the
Muhammadans of that part.   His friends asked leave to
introduce this person to him, and he was announced as
Mawlānā Qiwām ud-Dīn of Ceuta.   As Ceuta was near his
own birthplace, Tangier, Ibn Baṭṭūṭah was naturally struck
by the name and scanned his face eagerly.   After they had
been talking awhile, the visitor said, " You seem to be looking
at me as though you knew me."   "From what country do you
come ? " asked Ibn Baṭṭūṭah.   "From Ceuta."   "And I am
from Tangier," replied the traveller, and they wept together
at the thought of this strange meeting at the other end of
the world, so far from their distant home in the West.   After
some further conversation Ibn Baṭṭūṭah realized that they
had met before in India, in the capital, Delhi, which
Qiwām ud-Dīn had visited as a young man with his uncle,
a Spanish Muhammadan.   The Sultan of Delhi had tried
to induce the young man to settle in India, but he refused
to stay as he had set his heart on visiting China ; and there
he soon acquired a high position and considerable wealth.
Some years later, after his return home, Ibn Baṭṭūṭah started
off to explore Central Africa and met a brother of this same
man in a town in the Western Sudan.[1]   Ibn Baṭṭūṭah quite
naturally remarks on the enormous distance that separated
these two brothers from one another.   This incident is
characteristic of Muhammadan society during the Middle
Ages ; it reveals the enterprise that merchants and travellers
showed in journeying such enormous distances, and the
facilities which their co-religionists provided for those who
braved the perils of such arduous journeys.

[1] *Ibn Baṭṭūṭah*, ed. Defrémery and Sanguinetti (Paris, 1858), iv,
pp. 281-2.

Under such circumstances it is not surprising to find that there is a very considerable mass of geographical literature in the Arabic languages. The earliest examples of it derive their origin from the administrative necessities connected with the vast empire over which the Caliphs held sway. In order that there might be rapid communication between the capital and the outlying provinces, an elaborate system of posts was kept up ; at intervals of every few miles there was a postal station where the official messenger could get a fresh relay of horses, or pass on his despatch to another member of the same service ; and for the benefit of such messengers, and for the passage of troops, a network of roads was kept in good order so as to render possible rapid transit from one administrative centre or one strategic point to another. This postal system was one of the many administrative arrangements that the new Arab Government took over from the Roman Empire whose provinces on the southern and eastern shores of the Mediterranean it had annexed. The very Arabic word for this postal system *barīd* derived from the late Latin word for a post-horse, *veredus*, is an abiding acknowledgment of this indebtedness. At present we are concerned with it only in its connexion with the growth of geographical literature in the Arabic language, for we possess some of the handbooks in which a list of the postal stations was set down with the distances between each, a description of the principal routes and of the taxes levied in the various provinces they traversed.

Besides this feature of the administrative organization of the Arab Empire, there was another circumstance—in this instance connected with the religion of the conquerors— that served to stimulate interest in geography and to induce many persons to undertake lengthy journeys. This was the pilgrimage. Among the duties incumbent upon every Muslim, provided only that he had health and sufficient money for the expenses of the journey, was that of making the pilgrimage to Mecca once at least in his lifetime. Consequently throughout the whole of the Muhammadan era, except on the few occasions when political disturbance has prevented, there has been a stream of pilgrims setting their faces towards the Holy City in which their religion first had its origin, from every part of the Muhammadan world—Egypt, Syria,

Mesopotamia, and Persia, the inhabitants of which enjoyed
a certain proximity to Arabia—but also from more distant
countries such as Turkistan, India, China, and the Malay
Archipelago in the east, and Spain, Morocco and the Sudan in
the west, the inhabitants of which had, in early times, to face
great risks and undergo much toil and trouble in order to
attain the fulfilment of their pious aim.   Religion thus came
in to stir up any latent desire there might be for travel,
and that to a still greater extent than was the case in medieval
Christendom, because the Muhammadan pilgrimage to Mecca
was not regarded, as was the pilgrimage to Jerusalem in
Christendom, as an exceptional experience in the life of the
devout believer, for it was one of the five pillars of the
practical observance of the faith of Islam, and though
theologians recognized circumstances that absolved the
faithful from the fulfilment of this pious duty, so that it was
not an act of universal obligation, still in practice these
indulgences have been disregarded by thousands of devout
persons who have undertaken the journey despite all obstacles
of age, poverty and ill-health.

There is still a third circumstance that stimulated travelling
in the Muhammadan world—one common to almost every
community in the world—and that is commerce.   In
Muhammadan society the merchant enjoys a respect and
consideration that is closely connected with the origin of his
faith ; for Muḥammad, the Prophet, the founder of Islam,
had been himself a merchant, and thus conferred upon the
profession of the trader an elevation and a dignity which has
gained for him an entrance into the highest society.   Several
sayings traditionally ascribed to the Prophet assigned an
honourable position to the merchant in the Muslim hierarchy,
e.g. " In the Day of Judgment the honest truthful Muslim
merchant will take rank with the martyrs of the faith ",[1]
and in another tradition the Prophet says that the truthful
merchant will sit under the shadow of the throne of God on the
Day of Judgment.[2]   The Prophet commends the merchants to
his successors, for " they are the couriers of the world and the
trusty servants of God upon earth ".[3]   Consequently, trade has

---

[1] *Kanz al-'Ummāl* (Haydarābād, A.H. 1312–15), ii, No. 4084.
[2] Ibid., No. 4086.
[3] Ibid., No. 4112.

never implied any disparagement in Muhammadan eyes, for are not the market-places the table of God and whosoever comes to them partakes thereof ? The greatest of the early Caliphs, 'Umar, said, " There is no place where I would be more gladly overtaken by death than in the market-place, buying and selling for my family." [1] This same great ruler is reported to have set honesty in the commercial life above the punctual fulfilment of religious duties, as a test of the worth and excellence of a man. There was a case brought before him in which it was of importance to decide whether confidence could be placed in the testimony of a certain witness, and before 'Umar would allow the man to bear testimony, he said " Bring me a man who knows you ". So the witness brought forward a friend, who vouched for the excellence of his character. But 'Umar asked, " Are you his near neighbour ? Do you know his goings out and comings in ? " " No," he replied. Then 'Umar asked again, " Have you been his companion on a journey so as to have had opportunities of recognizing his true character ? " Again the answer was " No ". Then 'Umar asked, " Have you done business with him, for it is when money passes from hand to hand that the true piety of a man is learned ? " Again the answer was " No ". " Then I presume you have seen him standing in the mosque, repeating the Qur'ān and bowing down in prayer." This time the answer was " Yes "; whereupon 'Umar drove the man away, saying, " You know him not," and turning to the witness said, " Bring me a man who really knows you, for trading is the true test of a man, and it is in the operations of trade that his piety and religious worth become known." [2] It is in the same spirit that one of the greatest thinkers of the Muhammadan world, Ghazālī, who flourished towards the end of the eleventh century, draws a picture of the ideal merchant : he must begin his business with a pure intention, be content with gains that can be got by lawful methods, and spend these gains on his family and pious purposes ; justice and benevolence are to be the guiding principles of his commercial activity, and in the market he must promote righteousness and check iniquity. He must not come into the market full of greed, and should leave it

---

[1] *Al-Ghazālī, Iḥyā al-'Ulūm* (Cairo, A.H. 1289), ii, p. 53, 20.
[2] Ibid., ii, p. 73.

when he has gained sufficient profit for his wants. He must
not neglect the market of the next world, i.e. the mosque, for
the market of this life, and in all his actions he must observe
the prescriptions of the religious law, remembering that he
has to give account of his doings in the Day of Judgment.[1]
Into all the details of this picture it is impossible to enter here,
but it is of significance as having been drawn by one of the
greatest theologians that the Muslim world has produced
and as implying the expectation that the trader would serve
as an exemplar of the devout life, and would be a model of
righteousness for others to follow.

So much for the ideal presentation of the Muhammadan
merchant. As for the actual business with which he was
concerned, a manual for traders,[2] composed possibly about
the same period as that of Ghazālī—though the exact date
is uncertain—gives us a list of the various articles in which
the medieval trader was interested. First come precious
stones—pearls, diamonds, turquoise, cornelian, onyx, coral,
etc.—then scents, such as musk, amber, camphor, sandalwood,
and cloves. The best amber comes from south-east Arabia,
the next best from Spain or Morocco; the best aloes come from
India. These geographical references show how wide the
medieval merchant threw his net. Of spices there is naturally
a long list : pepper and cinnamon and ginger and many others.
Paper was an important object of commerce ; the best kind
is described as heavy, well polished, pleasant to the touch,
and free from worm holes, which can be prevented by means
of a species of Indian mint. Many kinds of silk and woollen
stuffs, furs and carpets are mentioned, and then follows a
large group of metals ; iron, copper, lead, tin, etc., and another
group of various articles of food. Of any one of these various
articles it would be possible to speak in detail, but for
our consideration here I will select only furs and skins.

Unexpected evidence as to the extent of the fur trade between
Muhammadan countries and the north of Europe before the
beginning of the eleventh century, had been obtained from
the enormous finds of Muhammadan coins in various parts
of northern Europe, especially on the shores of the Baltic.
These coins were obtained from Muhammadan traders in

---

[1] Ibid., ii, pp. 73–5.
[2] *Kitāb al-ishārati ilà maḥāsini 't-tijāra* (Cairo, A.H. 1318).

exchange for skins and furs, and some estimate may be formed
of the development which this trade attained from the fact
that upwards of ten millions of such coins have been discovered,
and even these do not represent the total number once in
circulation, because there is direct evidence that in some
instances the discoverers of a hoard of precious coins have melted
them down, and such destruction has doubtless happened
in cases that have escaped record.   As many as ten or twelve
thousand of such coins have been found in a single locality,
and in Sweden alone there is a record of such finds in as many
as 169 different places.[1]   How far north the Muhammadans
went in search of furs it is difficult to determine, but the
observation made by an Arab geographer that, at one of the
emporia in which the Muhammadan traders purchased these
wares, the night was shorter than an hour shows that some
of them at least must have journeyed a very considerable
distance to the north of their native country.[2]

Such trade was of course carried on by land, but equally
adventurous was the sea traffic, and there are some manuals
for mariners that have come down to us, dealing especially
with the Red Sea, and the journey thence to the Persian
Gulf, to India, and to China.   The author of one of these
handbooks for pilots tells us that his father and grandfather
had both been pilots on the Red Sea, and that after he had
himself gained experience for forty years he embodied in
his book what he had learnt from them, as well as the fruit
of his own experience.[3]   It was such bold seamen as these
who brought back the stories which we find in the later
compilations upon geography, and their adventures served as
the basis for the well known story of *Sindbad the Sailor*.
Much that they reported we know now to be true, such as the
waterspouts that endangered the safety of their frail vessels,
the flying fish, and other marvels, that seemed incredible
to some of their contemporaries ; but many of their stories
were obviously exaggerations, or misunderstandings, or sheer
inventions of a lively fancy.   The compiler had no means of
testing the accuracy of such reports : even what we now

[1] Cf. Chapter IV.

[2] Georg Jacob, *Der nordisch-baltische Handel der Araber im Mittelalter*
(Leipzig, 1887), pp. 26, 40, 122.

[3] Ibn Mājid, *Instructions nautiques et routiers arabes des XVe et
XVIe siècles*, ed. G. Ferrand (Paris, 1921).

know to have been entirely false probably did not appear to him more marvellous than some of the narrations that were really based on accurate observation ; and though he sets it all down, he cannot from time to time refrain from an expression of mild scepticism in the phrase, "But God knows best." [1] Still, apart from the audacious mendacity and the romantic picturesqueness of some of these stories, we cannot but admire the splendid courage and intrepidity of these Muhammadan seamen who set out on such perilous enterprises.

These sea captains in the Middle Ages not only possessed a very considerable knowledge of the art of navigation, but they had a high ideal of the responsibilities attached to their profession.　One of the earliest of such collections of mariners' tales that has come down to us from the tenth century gives us some little insight into the character of these sea captains, in the record of a conversation that one of them had with a terrified passenger, who for three nights and days had suffered agonies during a violent tempest. "You must know," he said, "that travellers and merchants have to put up with terrible dangers, compared with which these experiences are pleasant and agreeable ; but we who are members of the company of pilots are under oath and covenant not to let a vessel perish so long as there is anything left of it and the decree of fate has not fallen upon it ; we who belong to the company of ships' pilots never go on board a vessel without linking our own life and fate to it ; so long as it is safe, we live ; but if it perishes, we die with it ; so have patience and commend yourself to the Lord of the wind and of the sea, who disposes of men's lives as He will." [2]

Let us now turn to the scientific writers on geography, who pursued their investigations on rigid lines of scientific inquiry, in several instances undertaking extensive journeys and collecting materials on the spot.　The number of such Arab geographers is so extensive that it is only possible here to refer to a few of them.　One of the most remarkable of them, of whose personality we know something from the account that he himself has given of the labours he underwent in compiling his book, is al-Muqaddasī.　Born in Jerusalem about the middle of the tenth century, he spent twenty

[1] Cf. Chapter VIII, p. 160.

[2] Buzurj b. Shahriyār, *'Ajā'ib al-Hind*, ed. P. A. Van der Lith. (Leiden, 1883), p. 22.

years in travelling throughout the various Muslim dominions of his time, for, unlike other geographers of a later date, he made no attempt to describe the countries of the unbelievers. He speaks slightingly of the work of some of his predecessors as being based upon mere hearsay ; he himself took infinite pains to obtain in each locality accurate information as to the climate, the products, the state of trade, the coinage, weights and measures, and the general characteristics of the inhabitants. He mixed with persons of every class, and tells us how he had audience with princes and mixed familiarly with the great, while at other times he had to gain a scanty livelihood by hawking in the bazaar, or make his living by bookbinding. Sometimes he could afford to ride or be carried in a palanquin, at other time he had to tramp on foot in the blazing sun or in the snow. His caravan was plundered again and again by highway robbers, and once he nearly lost his life by drowning. He was thrown into prison as a spy, was falsely accused of heresy, suffered shame and humiliation of all kinds, and had many unpleasant encounters with highwaymen and cut-purses. He never actually had to beg his bread, but he must often have come near to being reduced to such an extremity. He supped with Sufis, and shared the scanty meal of ascetics. He led the public worship in the mosque, preached from the pulpit, and gave the call to prayer from the minaret. He watched the Byzantine galleys engaged in a sea fight, and attached himself to military expeditions to other frontiers. During these travels al-Muqaddisī tells us that he received as many as thirty different designations, such as pilgrim, ascetic, reciter of the Qur'ān, teacher, lawyer, merchant, bookbinder, paper-maker, doctor, messenger, and the like.[1] The book he produced, ranks as one of the most accurate descriptions of the territories of Islam during the Middle Ages, and in spite of the long account that al-Muqaddisī gives of himself and of his efforts to secure accuracy, he modestly disclaims any assumption of completeness, and frankly says that he does not consider his book to be above criticism or free from possible error. But whatever defects there may be in his work, they are certainly not due to any failure on the part of the

---

[1] *Aḥsan al-taqāsīm*, ed. De Goeje, 2nd ed. (Leiden, 1906), pp. 43–5.

author to make every effort within his power to obtain the fullest and most trustworthy information.

About two centuries later, another great geographer, Yāqūt, who died in the first half of the thirteenth century, was likewise an energetic traveller. His parents were Greeks, but while he was still a little boy he was carried off as a slave and sold to a merchant in Baghdad. His master gave him a careful education and sent him on long journeys connected with his business. In this way Yāqūt acquired an extensive knowledge of various parts of the Muhammadan world, and he continued his journeys even after the death of his patron. His chief work is a great Geographical Dictionary, largely compiled from the writings of earlier geographers, but enriched by materials he had himself collected during his travels. Muqaddisī and Yāqūt may be taken as good examples of the Arab geographers who approached the subject of their study from a scientific point of view, and composed works aiming at a certain degree of completeness.

To a different category belong the travellers whose purpose was to leave behind an account of their own personal experiences. Of these we may select for consideration two only : Ibn Jubayr in the twelfth century and Ibn Baṭṭūṭah in the fourteenth. Ibn Jubayr was a Spaniard who, after a successful career as a student, was appointed secretary to the then Prince of Granada. One day his master gave him a cup of wine, bidding him drink it. "I never drink wine," replied Ibn Jubayr. "By Allāh, you are going to drink it now and seven times over," and the unfortunate secretary dared protest no longer, but after he had drunk the seven cups the Prince gave them to him again, this time full of gold. When Ibn Jubayr returned to his home he made a vow that he would spend the money upon making the pilgrimage to Mecca in order to atone for his involuntary breach of the religious law. Of this journey, which lasted for two years, from 1183 to 1185, he wrote a full account, of great interest from many points of view ; all the observances of the pilgrimage to Mecca at that period are minutely described, the measurements of the sacred buildings are given in detail, and they serve as valuable material for comparison with present conditions.

Saladin was at that time engaged in his struggle with the

Crusaders, and Ibn Jubayr frequently mentions his great
contemporary with enthusiastic admiration. When he
describes the pilgrims in prayer around the Ka'bah, he makes
reference to the profound emotion that stirred the vast
congregation when prayers were offered for this great
champion of the faith : " At the name of Saladin all tongues
quivered as they cried ' Amen ', for when God loveth one of
His servants, He inspires the love of him in the hearts of
men." Such an enthusiasm did he feel for his hero that when
the news arrived of Saladin's conquest of Jerusalem in 1187,
it stirred Ibn Jubayr to undertake this long journey to the
East once more, though at the time, when there was so much
hostility between Christians and Muslims, a journey from
one end of the Mediterranean to another was not without
peril of its own. One of the most interesting parts of Ibn
Jubayr's travels is the account he gives of the condition
of the Muhammadan population under Christian rule in
Sicily. William II was reigning at Palermo when he reached
that island, and Sicily had been for about a century under the
rule of the Norman kings. Though the Muslims seemed
to have lived in some apprehension, and to have practised
the religious observances of their faith to some extent in
secret, the king appears to have treated them with much
consideration and to have employed many Muhammadans
about his person, and given them positions of responsibility
as ministers and chamberlains. His chief cook, too, was a
Muhammadan, and he had also a Muhammadan bodyguard.
There were so many Muhammadan maidservants in the
palace that Ibn Jubayr was assured by one of the officials
that they had succeeded in converting to Islam the Christian
women there. William II himself could both read and write
Arabic, and the superscription on royal documents was
written in the same language.[1]

The other traveller, Ibn Baṭṭūṭah, to whom attention may
be drawn, was a man of quite a different type. Ibn Jubayr
had been a true scholar, exact, even meticulous, a close
observer, with a sound judgment of men and manners ;
his elegant and attractive style, together with the justness
of his descriptions, caused late writers to incorporate whole

[1] *Travels of Ibn Jubayr*, ed. W. Wright and M. J. De Goeje (London,
1907), pp. 97, 325.

passages of his narrative into their own works often without acknowledgment.   On the other hand, Ibn Baṭṭūṭah did not himself write the work that passes under his name, for it was taken down from dictation and embellished by one of the secretaries of his master, the Sultan of Fez.   He is certainly at times guilty of inaccuracies, and his account of China, in particular, is so confused that some of his critics have doubted whether he ever went there at all; others, on the contrary, in spite of these faults, have strongly upheld his general veracity.   His narrative is lively and often entertaining, and reveals him as a man of restless energy and curiosity, clearsightedness, and a determination to enjoy life ; at the same time he was a devout observer of the practices of his religion, with a particular devotion for the saints.   His travels extended over a period of twenty-eight years ; starting from his home in Tangier, he made his way across the north of Africa to Egypt, then spent several years in visiting various Muhammadan countries—Palestine, Syria, Arabia, Persia ; after living for three years in Mecca he went to Aden and travelled down the east coast of Africa to Quiloa ; having got so far south, he made his way north till he reached the Crimea, and went as far up the Volga as he could in the hope of seeing what he called " the land of darkness ".   After a visit to Constantinople, where he received as kindly a welcome from the Christian Emperor as he was accustomed to receive from Muhammadan princes, he returned to the Crimea, and turning east made his way through Khwarizm, Bukhara, Turkistan, and Afghanistan into India, where he remained for about eight years in the service of the Sultan of Delhi.   In A.D. 1342 he attached himself to an embassy that was being sent to the Emperor of China ; but the vessel carrying the envoy and the presents was wrecked off the coast of Malabar, and Ibn Baṭṭūṭah, after some unpleasant adventures, went to the Maldive Islands, where he held the post of a judge for a year and a half. Thence, after a visit to Ceylon, he went by way of Bengal and the Malay Archipelago to China.   From China he returned to his native country in 1349, after an absence of twenty-four years.   Still he was not satisfied, but soon started off again on a visit to Spain, and later into Central Africa, where he visited Timbuktu and sailed up the Niger, returning through the Sahara to Fez. According to one computation, his wanderings had extended over a length of 75,000 miles.

This chapter may conclude with two extracts from Ibn Baṭṭūṭah's travels as typical of the risks this adventurous traveller had to run. The first is his account of the departure from Calicut of the embassy intended for China. The Zamorin of Calicut had fitted out for the use of this embassy one of a fleet of thirteen Chinese junks that were then in the harbour. Ibn Baṭṭūṭah said to the captain, a day before the vessel was to sail, " I want a cabin to myself, because of the slave girls that are travelling with me." The captain replied, " The Chinese merchants have taken return tickets and have occupied all the cabins, but my son-in-law has one which I can let you have ; it has no bathroom, but you may be able to exchange it for another during the voyage." Accordingly Ibn Baṭṭūṭah had his luggage taken on board and made his slaves embark. This was on a Thursday ; he himself remained on land so as to take part in the Friday prayer. Early on the Friday morning one of his servants came to tell him that the cabin they had got was very uncomfortable and small. So he spoke to the captain about it, who said, " I can't help it, but if you care to go on board one of the smaller vessels you will find plenty of cabins to choose from." So the change was made, and all his goods and slaves were transferred to the other ship before the Friday prayer began. But in the afternoon the sea became very rough ; all the other vessels had started except three—the junk carrying the presents for the Emperor of China, another whose owners intended to spend the winter on the Malabar coast, and Ibn Baṭṭūṭah's little vessel. " I had to sleep on shore that night with nothing but a rug to lie on, as I could not get on board the vessel, nor could those in it come to me." By Saturday morning the three vessels had been carried far out to sea ; one of them was dashed to pieces on the rocks and only a few of the passengers escaped with their lives. One of the merchants who was saved had with him a slave girl who clung on to a board at the stern of the junk. The merchant offered a reward of ten pieces of gold to anyone who would rescue her, and one of the sailors—a man from Hormuz—succeeded in bringing

her safe to land ; but he refused the proffered reward, saying,
" I did it only for the sake of God." The same night the vessel
with the presents was thrown up on shore and all the
passengers drowned, and Ibn Baṭṭūṭah had the melancholy
task of burying the members of the embassy with whom he
had left Delhi and reciting over them the prayers for the dead.
Ibn Baṭṭūṭah's vessel got safely away to sea and he heard
no news of it, until some months later he fell in with two
of his missing slaves, who told him that all his belongings
were scattered, without chance of recovery. For some time
he debated in his mind whether or not he should return to
Delhi and inform the Sultan of the fate of the embassy,
but he wisely decided against running the risk of putting
himself again in the power of this irascible monarch. But
he was much perplexed, and spent the greater part of his
time in the mosque reading the Qur'ān ; at first he read it all
through once a day, but later read the whole of the sacred
volume through twice each day, and so he continued for three
months. Finally he made his way to the Maldive Islands
where he was invested with the office of judge, already
referred to.[1]

The other extract is interesting as showing the kind of
misapprehension that might give rise to some of the marvellous
stories the Muhammadan travellers related on their return
home. Ibn Baṭṭūṭah tells how he was caught in the monsoon
somewhere in the China or Java Sea ; for forty-two days his
vessel was driven by the storm, till the sailors lost their
reckoning and had no idea of where they were ; the rain fell
in torrents and for ten whole days they could not see the sun.
Very early one morning the clouds lifted, and twenty miles
off they sighted a mountain rising out of the sea, and the
wind carried them rapidly towards it. The sailors were
terrified, saying, " We are nowhere near dry land and we
know of no mountain in this sea ; if the wind dashes us against
it, we are all lost men." Then all those on board humbled
themselves before God and renewed their vows of repentance,
offered fervent supplications to Allah, and sought the
intercession of the Prophet. The merchants vowed to
bestow alms in abundance, and Ibn Baṭṭūṭah wrote their
vows down for them in a note-book. The wind dropped

[1] Op. cit., iv, pp. 94–6, 105.

a little, and when the sun rose they saw the mountain high up in the air, with clear sky between it and the sea. All the passengers were amazed ; but Ibn Baṭṭūṭah noticed that the sailors were weeping and bidding one another farewell ; and when he asked them what was the matter, they replied, "What we thought was a mountain, is a roc ; if it catch sight of us it will certainly destroy us." It was then less than ten miles off from them. But by the grace of God, a favourable wind arose and carried them in the opposite direction ; so they saw no more of the roc, and had no opportunity of finding out its real shape.[1]

[1] Ibid., iv, pp. 305–6.

CHAPTER VI

TRADE AND COMMUNICATION IN EASTERN EUROPE
A.D. 800–1200

By BARON A. MEYENDORFF

IN an earlier chapter the most prominent features of travel in the Dark Ages, the Christian pilgrimages, were considered down to about the end of the eighth century and we then turned to consider two special aspects of the succeeding period, the travels of the Vikings and the Arabs. Our last chapter carried us right down to the end of the Middle Ages, and we must now return to examine another aspect of travel at the beginning of the ninth century. The main motive of the travellers whose narratives have come down to us from the period A.D. 800-1200 is still, as before, that of pilgrimage.

Two quotations from the oldest monument of Russian travels [1]—the pilgrimage of the Abbot Daniel of Kiev to the Holy Land about 1106–7 will suffice to illustrate this and also both the moral and national assets of European development still prevailing, or at least surviving, in our times. 'Many virtuous people,' so we read in the introduction of the narrative, ' practising good works and charity to the poor, reach the holy places without leaving their homes . . . Others . . . after having visited them . . . boast as if they had done something meritorious and thus lose the fruit of their labour . . .' A still more fervent feeling of national consciousness, at a time when no political unity existed among the Russian people, strikes our ear when we read the following words addressed by the Abbot Daniel to Prince Baldwin : ' My prince . . . for the love of God and out of regard for the Russian Princes . . . allow me to place my lamps on the Holy Sepulchre in the name of the whole land of Russia.' . . . And what a joy when the

[1] Palestine Pilgrims' Text Society, London, 1897, vol. iv, C. R. Beazley, *Dawn of Modern Geography*, and R. Histor. Soc. Transactions, vol. xiv.

lamps of the Russians kindled and the miracle of the fire from Heaven had thus been accomplished, whereas the lamps placed by the Latins did not shine. The satisfaction which this neglect of the Latin worshippers on the part of the Divine Power caused to our abbot indicates clearly enough another momentous element, that of religious rivalry, which tends to prove more resistent against the action of time than anything else in the East of Europe to-day.

Besides the travels of the pilgrims, the Vikings, and the Arabs in our period, there were two other types of travellers who added considerably to the knowledge of the world among the Western peoples, namely the Jews, among whom Benjamin of Tudela [1] may be considered the most prominent, and the German merchants and warriors in the Baltic,[2] a category of travellers which is not mentioned in Professor C. R. Beazley's *Dawn of Modern Geography*, otherwise so rich in information and so stimulating for further research.

Alongside them we may place the narratives of diplomatic missions such as the two missions of Luitprand to Byzantium in A.D. 957 and A.D. 968, the early commercial enterprises of the Frisian, Italian and German towns. Our attention here will be mainly directed to an examination of the bases of our knowledge of the east of Europe.

The beginning of our period, as Marquardt puts it in his *East European and East Asiatic Rambles*,[3] referring to the ninth and tenth centuries, coincides with the formation of the ethnological body of Europe. The modern independence of the minor nationalities, like the Finns, Esthonians, Letts and Lithuanians, and the aggrandisement of territory allotted to some others were not only due to their demands for national emancipation from alien rule but also to a doctrine of restoration of the ethnological border supposed to comprise a homogeneous racial organization. Hence the specific form of East European land reform, dispossessing or despoiling the racial or legal successors of the conquering minorities.

[1] The latest English version from a thirteenth century MS. by M. N. Adler, London, 1907.

[2] The famous edition of the *Origines Livoniae sacrae et civilis seu Chronicon Livonicum vetus* was dedicated by J. D. Gruber (1740) to George II with reference to his ancestor : Henrici Leonis, Slavorum domitoris.

[3] *Osteuropaeische und Ostasiatische Streifzuge.*

The latter were sometimes the representatives and often the unpleasant agents of the two universal principles of the European community, the Empire and the Papacy, of which the latter has remained an important component of European civilization. The beginning of modern Europe has been traced back to the partition of Verdun, A.D. 843, to the progress of the Christian missions, to the competing influence of the Muhammadan culture, to the zenith of Scandinavian activity—exploring, raiding, conquering, colonizing—to the decisive breach between the Eastern and Western parts of the Church, to the new national formations in the East, including the political growth of various principalities and towns in the Russian plain. Such were the features of the ninth century, followed by some symptoms of fresh life in nationality, language, literature, Christian philosophy, Christian political ambition, and the commercial expansion of the Italian cities. Towards the end of our period the Christian world of Europe was chequered with disaster. The destruction of the Levantine outposts of Latin Christendom, the paralysis of the Byzantine power, the Mongol rule in Asia and all over the Russian plain were already imminent (1240). It is difficult to find a clue among the vague and confused movements of these obscure centuries, and the historian often tries to operate with a very few general and preconceived assumptions derived from his own experience and immediate observation. Thus Heyd, the historian of the trade of the time, makes the rather surprising assumption that the Jews during the internecine wars among the Christians, were circulating freely amid the warring peoples without arousing suspicion and were consequently making large profits.[1] This estimate of the advantages of the almost extra-territorial position of the Jew, Heyd derives apparently from his observation of modern, even of very recent and apparently temporary and sporadic conditions of toleration. Again in another instance Professor Golubinsky, who ranks first among the historians of the Russian Church, examines the narrative of the Russian Chronicle, known as the Chronicle of Nestor, showing the Kiev Prince Vladimir making his choice from among the various teachings of the Christian Churches and giving the preference to the Greek or Byzantine Rite, adopting

---

[1] W. Heyd, *Histoire du Commerce du Levant*, i, 125.

the same method of competitive examination (A.D. 988) as the Prince of the Khozars some time earlier is reported to have followed in selecting the Hebrew doctrine. It is not the composite origin of the Chronicle with its multifarious layers of various authorship and age, nor the two centuries which separate the supposed author of the Chronicle from the event described, nor the fact that the earliest existing MS. belongs to the year 1377, that determines the more critical attitude adopted by Professor Golubinsky towards the relevant tale, as compared with many of his predecessors, among whom he mentions Professor Soloviev. It is the assumption of the universal and permanent value of a psychological observation which he thus raises to the level of a psychological law. Professor Golubinsky understands that the human mind does not admit of a vacuum, that therefore Prince Vladimir must have given up his heathen faith before the new concepts could have penetrated into his mind. Hence, the picture of a detached selective process being excluded, the whole story must be discarded as psychologically improbable. We see here how the real and deep learning of a first class historian is dependent upon the assumption of an untrained psychologist, and it is the latter which in the given case conducts and supervises the historical research, though it is outside our present scope to examine the validity of the psychological law referred to by Golubinsky.[1]

In dealing with a period so obscure as the one here treated and one concerning which our information is so scattered, it is essential for us to avoid as far as possible the use of preconceived assumptions and the reading back of modern conditions into medieval times. We certainly distinguish between economic, political, and military activities in our modern definitions of human conduct, but as we actually meet them in the practice of the Middle Ages, those branches may occasionally blend, or combine, or replace one another in a remarkable manner, so as to give rise to varieties intermediate between those which are commonly regarded as typical, when we say 'travel', 'trade', 'war'. It might sound paradoxical, but we are almost led to assume that in the

---

[1] In his work on *Canonization* (Moscow, 1903) Golubinsky bases his negative attitude on another psychological fact, namely that at the age of 30 men of excessive sensuality 'do not come to repentance'.

Middle Ages between A.D. 800 and 1200 peace and war were undifferentiated.

The common basis of travel and intercourse is the road or route ; the mere existence of a route as a fairly constant or permanent link between distant parts of the inhabited globe is an important indication of a complex social, economic and political system, the expression of varied supra-tribal interests and of an extensive interdependence between groups scattered over large sections of the known world. The Roman Empire was one of such systems, and the roads were one of its expressions.

The first question which arises is that of the Roman trade routes. Which of them survived down to our period, which were the new routes corresponding to the regrouping of the populations, connecting the new and old centres of civilization and maintaining the exchange of goods ? This exchange had already become an essential of social life in the countries surrounding the Mediterranean and large tracts of the Hinterland with its developed provincial life ? After the fall of the Empire we still hear of trade in skins, hides, wool, leather, feathers, whalebone, honey, wax, timber, ships, various kinds of textiles as linen, muslin, silk, brocades, dye stuffs like purple, scents, ornaments, glassware, pearls, precious stones, metal goods, arms, coins, and last, but not least, foodstuffs, fish, oil, spices, cereals (which require special attention as to their mode of distribution), beverages (wine, beer, spirits), earthenware.

This list of commodities covers a great part of the goods mentioned incidentally in narratives of medieval travel. It would be interesting to draw up a list comprising the sources whence the goods were drawn, their destination, and the route which they are reported to have followed. This would help us to understand the commercial geography of our period, and would indicate the changes caused by political events bringing about the breakdown of one trade route and the formation of new ones, just as it was in our days with regard to the countries engaged in the great war, when the one main requisite of the trade route, the security of traffic, could not be maintained, or when the communication ceased to be possible owing to internal disorder. Thus cotton-growing Turkestan reverted after 1917 to wheat cultivation.

Spruner and Menke in their *Atlas of Medieval Geography*
(1880) have tried to project on their maps among other
information relating to ethnology, political boundaries, etc.,
indications relating to the routes found in medieval
sources and compiled by the respective experts. On one
of their maps (pl. 63) under the heading ' The States and
Travels of the Northmen' (Staaten und Fahrten der
Normannen) we see a yellow line running from Gothland to
the estuary of the Neva and Lake Ladoga, thence southward
across the Russian plain as far as Cherson, and from
Cherson across the Black Sea direct to Constantinople.
Westward from Gothland a line shows the overland and sea
communication to the Mediterranean centres and thence to
Constantinople, thus completing the circular route. This
circular route at different points on the Atlantic in Spain,
at Venice and Genoa, at Constantinople, on the Dnieper
from Bolgar on the Volga through Novgorod, is connected
with the routes coming from Baghdad, the principal city
trading eastward with India and China. What was the
meaning of this colossal network ?   To what extent would
it be an instrument of world trade and world travel under
the conditions of universal warfare, prevailing between
800–1200 especially in the Eastern half of Europe ?   It
is striking that there existed a comparatively wide knowledge
of the possibility of a circular travel route from Constantinople through Russia,[1] Scandinavia, around Western Europe or
by land to Rome and back to the point of departure, without
it being practicable to traverse it otherwise than by means
of a military expedition.

The only mention of any one having attempted the route
we find, if we are not mistaken, in the Russian Chronicle
referring to the Apostle Andrew's journey from Cherson to
Rome ' where he told about the wonders observed on his way
through the Russian lands and the steam baths delighted
in by the natives'. The chronicle asserts the existence of the
route as a means of communication and intercourse and
gives for our epoch a number of instances as to the use of the
section between Scandinavia and Constantinople favoured by
Varangian commercial and military enterprise, a section of

[1] Professor M. I. Rostovtsev lifts the veil from an obscure past in his
Iranians and Greeks in South Russia (Oxford Press), 1922.

intermittent land and water traffic of necessarily limited tonnage, demanding more than one season, complicated means of transport, boat building and package, and victualling, especially for the slaves who were one of the most important commodities transported. The trade has not yet been sufficiently analysed on the basis of Byzantine and Russian sources. The Scandinavian sources apparently speak more of the glory of their kinsmen on the *Austrweger*, the Eastway, than of the actual practicability of the route across the Russian plain, which had probably been as well, if not better, exploited by the Greeks before the Christian era. Adam of Bremen had only a vague notion of the possibility of getting from Scandinavia to Constantinople and he did not know that it involved river navigation. He calls Kiev the finest jewel of Greece, thus mixing the Scandinavian term for Russia, *Gardarika* (the country of the towns), with *Grikland*.[1] Only one Scandinavian merchant can be named at Constantinople about the year 1000. The Emperor Constantine VII's[2] description of the visit annually paid to the port of Constantinople by the Russo-Varangian Princes and their hosts deserves to be quoted. The goods brought to Constantinople must have been chiefly *res sese moventes*, to use the term of the Roman law, namely slaves, and in addition some wax and furs such as later reached Venice. Everything was collected at home as tribute during the previous season. The goods must have been in a poor condition owing to their transport in canoes, μονόξυλα, probably simply trunks hollowed by fire, unless the martial tradesmen helped themselves to better vessels such as those owned by the Greeks of Cherson and arrived before Constantinople as a threatening fleet, though as a rule they reached only Mesembria. This commerce and the description of the Russian invasions a century earlier in the ornamented homilies of the Patriarch Photius (A.D. 865) certainly do not impress the reader as a manifestation of international trade. The Eastern section of the great circular route turns into a comparatively secondary, almost local, approach to the luxuries of the East by rather primitive savages who provide chiefly slaves, probably an illgotten gain, to the more advanced

[1] Heyd, op. cit., pp. 73 and 77.
[2] A.D. 911–59.

Easterners through the Greeks as middlemen. The Arabs also were then manifesting their high business morality in this branch of commerce. The Russo-Byzantine treaties of 907, 911, 945 and 971, mentioned by the Russian chronicle, of which three are indirectly referred to and even those unacknowledged as treaties by the Byzantine sources,[1] have until late served to represent the Russian trader in a more cultured attitude. The description of the Russian Prince Svyatoslav on the Danube near Dorystolon (modern Silistria), A.D. 972, gives a vivid picture of the primitive chieftain and his army of 22,000 men, each of whom received one μεδίμνος (nearly 12 gallons) of wheat for victuals on their return homeward. At the same time a special mention is made of maintaining the ancient ' friendly ' trade relations with Constantinople.

The Byzantine-Scandinavo-Russian road shows a series of phenomena where invasion alternates with trade in rapid succession. The irregularities and risks were obviously considerable. The development of Greek influence in Kiev, crowned in A.D. 988 by the triumph of the Greek Christian mission, nevertheless gave to this centre the brilliant appearance of an important and rich town, where according to a German description (in the chronicle of Thitmarus, Bishop of Magdeburg, referring to the year A.D. 1018), forty churches, eight market places, and a multitude of fugitive slaves and ' Dani veloces ' were equally striking. And, in the north, Novgorod gains already the social characteristics of a commercial commonwealth, later affiliated to the German Hansa. Let us add to these few points the Arab trade along the Volga to the town of Bolgar [2] where the traders from Novgorod are met, if they have not been down the river as far as Itil, the capital of the Khozars, near the Caspian Sea, and we get a puzzling picture of contradictory elements standing for what may be called travel and travellers, but fluctuating from piracy, pillage and invasion, conquest, military

---

[1] Professor V. I. Sergeyevich, *Lectures and Researches* (St. Petersburg, 1910, p. 627), writes : The Byzantine sources ignore the four treaties mentioned by the Russian chronicle.

[2] J. Marquardt has recently tried to discover new indications for the location of this and other places along the Volga route. *Ungarische Jahrbücher*, pp. 261–334, December, 1924, Ein Arabischer Bericht über die arktischen (uralischen) Laender aus dem X Jhdt.

organization, tribute and tax collecting to trade and missionary work.

The circular road with its subsidiaries—White Sea-Volga, Novgorod-Volga (Bolgar), Novgorod-Dnieper — does not appear, as has been too readily assumed by some writers, to be the economic breathing canal of Europe ; it appears as an aggregate of independent sectors of unequal importance with occasional intermittent intercommunication leading to the exchange of goods from one end of the road to the other only through a succession of semi-fiscal and semi-military commercial acts. The finds of Arabic coins in the North of Europe, without very clear evidence of a corresponding delivery of goods by these countries to the middlemen dealing with the Arabs, does not indicate what we call trade in the usual sense ; nor are we certain that the Scandinavians, even the Swedes who according to Adam of Bremen (A.D. 1076) were rich in cereals and honey, were really exporting any goods that after a succession of exchanges could bring wealth to Constantinople.

The trading capacities of the Scandinavians at this early date are hard to credit, and indeed according to the Norwegian scholar, Dr. A. Bugge, his countrymen were nothing but seafaring agriculturists in constant need of cereals. The only regular export from Sweden was the fighting host, which until the ninth century levied blackmail from Novgorod. Probably this tribute was paid in Arabic coins and local furs, hides, tools, and other goods of the kind which in the fifteenth century formed the peasants' dues[1] in that part of Northern Russia, as the contemporary surveys show.

The political adjustment along the Eastern as well as along the Western half of the circular road was obviously lagging behind the economic needs to such a degree that the latter either became extinct or had to find new routes of communication. Of these the Western Dvina route became an important trunk road at the close of our period. The more ambitious Eastern seaway of the late sixteenth century, from England to the White Sea and thence to the Caspian,

---

[1] Sergeyevich in vol. iii of his *Russian Antiquities* (St. Petersburg, 1911), p. 108. C. Brinkmann, *Die Aeltesten Grundbücher von Novgorod*, in *Vierteljahrsschrift für Soc. u. Wirtschaftsgeschichte*, 1911.

which had only a shortlived importance, will give us an adequate idea of the importance in trade and politics of the river routes, for a long time the only means by which the inner parts of a continent were accessible from outside.

Going back to the crucial question of the meaning of the colossal network of assumed trade routes, we must refer to the appreciation of its value by the Belgian historian, Professor Pirenne. His main proposition is based upon the assumption that some economic interdependence of nations still survived at the fall of the Roman Empire. Marseilles, Professor Pirenne states, maintained its position as a port long after the Germanic invasion. The latest written papyrus which has been identified comes from A.D. 787, and this date corresponds to the period of the hostile Arab rule on the southern shores of the Mediterranean extending from Syria to Spain. The golden coin *solidus aureus* obtained from Byzantium still continues to circulate as a currency in the West between the eighth and ninth centuries but is tending to disappear. Islam having blocked the western part of the Mediterranean in the seventh and eighth centuries, the European continent is bound to rely for its requirements from Constantinople and the East in general upon two lines of communications only. The one passes through the Levant from Venice to Constantinople, the other from Flanders via Russia down the Dnieper to Constantinople, or down the Volga to Baghdad. At the same time Professor Pirenne does not surprise us when he stresses with insistence the fact that external trade was less important than under the Roman Empire, so that the towns of Gaul fell into decay, while international trade was hampered by strict regulations in accordance with the requirements of the self-supporting natural economy of the rural estate, which then became the main organization of production. What there could be of external trade was due to the achievements of the martial adventurers who, like St. Godric, were breaking the rules in a spirit of freedom and risk, until international commerce was later captured by the large trading communities, such as Venice, Pisa and Genoa.[1]   But this process was already

[1] The lectures delivered by Professor Pirenne at University College, London, have since been published in book form—*Medieval Cities : Their Origin and the Revival of Trade* (Oxford Press, 1925).

beginning during our period, though it was subject to many irregularities and accidents, forming, as we believe, the very essence of medieval travel in the broadest sense of the word.

Before we attempt to trace its articulation, which indicates the movements of the growing organization of travel, let us contrast the above sketch with the generally accepted view.[1] The Eastern part of the circular route is treated thus : "Northmen of Denmark and Norway were the terror of all the coasts of Europe, and established themselves in England and Ireland, in France and Sicily. From the eighth to the eleventh century a commercial route from India passed through Kharism and Novgorod to the Baltic, and immense quantities of Arabian coins have been found in Sweden, and particularly in the island of Gothland, and are preserved at Stockholm." The wording of a more recent passage on the Northmen sounds less confident. "The coins . . . prove how closely the enterprise of Northmen and of the Arabs intertwined." The expression 'enterprise' seems an especially happy one for its vagueness. To characterize the predominant view one could quote popular textbooks on history with passages such as this : 'What do you bring us ? ' the merchant is asked, in an old English dialogue. ' I bring skins, silks, costly gems and gold,' he answers, ' besides garments, pigments, wine, oil and ivory, with brass and copper, and tin, silver and gold, and such like.' We are unable to check the exact value of the old English dialogue.

Let us remember that the Northern shore of the Black Sea was successively occupied by more or less ephemeral nomads : Goths, Avars, Turks, Uzes, Huns, Bulgars, Pechenegs, the tolerant Khozars and Kumans, this list being probably incomplete, while Bosphoros or Panticapeum (modern Kerch), Olbia (on the mouth of the Bug), Odessos (near the present Varna), Cherson (the Russian Sebastopol), called by the Russian Chronicles Korsun, perpetuated the memory of the past and retained to the end of the twelfth century the aspect of Greek settlements. Trade had to accommodate itself to the

---

[1] Such a view is shortly expressed in the article " Geography " in the *Encyclopaedia Britannica*, ed. 1897, and may be compared with the edition of 1910, vol. xi.

respective conditions of domination or subjection among the
intermediate tribes in the historical mosaic of races along the
trade route converging to the Black Sea or to the Caspian, and to
their material culture, which was conditioned by slave raiding,
hunting in general, and agriculture.   The following utterance
taken from the Russian Chronicle [1] throws a sidelight on the
situation.   The young Prince Svyatoslav, the same whom
Leo Diaconus described, declares to his mother and the
host, 'I do not like to stay in Kiev; I want to live at
Pereyaslav [2] on the Danube, because that is the centre of
my land, as all goods go there : from Greece gold, brocade,
wine, and various fruits or spices; from the land of the Czechs
and Hungarians silver and horses; from Rus hides, wax,
honey, and slaves.'   These words suggest a special aspect
of trade, perhaps its utilization as a basis for raising toll.
Svyatoslav apparently intended to secure various advantages
by his subsequent nefarious expedition, to which reference
has already been made.   During the retreat he was captured
with his army and put to death by the Pechenegs
(Patzinaciti), who controlled a part of the trade route and
who acted either under dictation from Byzantium in return
for advantages amounting to a tribute paid to them, or at
their own discretion.

There is just one more trait which is at first sight surprising
in the Russian Chronicle.   Describing the military expedition
of Prince Oleg (A.D. 907), the semi-legendary basis of Russian
claims on Constantinople, the writer speaks with disgust
of the sufferings inflicted upon the Greek population, saying
'and many other things did the Rus, as warriors usually
(or often) do'.   A tribute is exacted from the Byzantines
amounting to 12 grivna per head, and in each of the 2,000
ships there were 40 men, for later the Chronicle speaks of
forty oars.   Furthermore the expedition returns with new
sails, bread, wine, meat, fish, spices and anchors.   This booty,
should the text stand the test, serves as an indication of
the goods appreciated by the invaders.   The goods mentioned
are not fit for further exportation to the North; on the

---

[1] Laurentian MS. a. 6477.
[2] Formerly called Martianopolis, the modern village Preslava on
the right bank of the St. George arm of the Danube.

contrary all were for immediate consumption or use. A handful of precious stones, some yards of silk or brocade, would not alter the position substantially; the expedition would still not indicate a commercial war. This throws a light on the value of the great route to Scandinavia as a commercial thoroughfare and would appear to show that its value has been much exaggerated.

The northern portion of the route was controlled by the Norsemen, to whom Novgorod then paid a tribute in order to secure peace. The Arabs knew the lower Volga only and nothing beyond the town of Bolgar. It might be noticed here that Professor C. R. Beazley, describing the trade between Russia and Constantinople as barter, enumerates as Greek export goods : silks, stuffs, gold, wine, and fruit which were exchanged for Russian furs, honey, wax, corn and slaves. The corn item seems exceedingly dubious, for about a thousand years had passed since the Black Sea had been bordered by wheat-growing districts,[1] and Russian agriculture was yet in its infancy. Oleg's booty, supposing that the whole passage is among those parts of the Chronicle which may be admitted as a true record, is the more suggestive as this same Prince Oleg, when taking possession of Kiev, was admitted into the town as a ' merchant '. This would mean that there were traders along the Dnieper River eager to secure the right to pass through the various territories, which were under the control of several conflicting powers ; but this is but slight evidence as to trade relations between Constantinople and Scandinavia. We can glean here and there an indication of the nature of the protection of river traffic in this remote past. The Russian Chronicle [2] mentions an expedition of the Kiev Prince Mstislav to protect against the pillaging Polvtsy the trade route used by Greek merchants for the supply of salt and another commodity, the nature of which the unintelligible term *zalozhny* (the merchant being called *zalozhnik*) does not disclose to us. It may be assumed that this trade was a dutiable occupation and hence

[1] Max Ebert, *Südrussland in Altertum*, Bonn, 1921. J. W. Pratt on A. M. Shepard's *Sea Power in Ancient History*, Boston, 1924, and Rostovtsev, op. cit.

[2] For the year A.M. 6675, i.e. A.D. 1165–6.

was protected by the respective territorial authorities interested in the gathering of the toll.

With regard to the eastern part of the circular route, i.e. the route across Russia, during the period covering the eighth to the twelfth centuries, one may say on behalf of Central and Western Europe that the remote parts of the East had no direct commerce with Europe,[1] but only through many intermediaries at a costly rate and with infinite risk from pirates and enemies, and the trade there was to a great extent dependent on booty.

Let us try to understand the connexion and transitions from booty through tribute to trade and travel. It might be reasonable to assume that at the beginning of our period the force which actuated the removal of individuals and groups beyond the region of settlement was chiefly the necessity or desire to acquire goods by force, or in return for goods and services rendered. The cynic might add that commercial and military enterprise are fused almost more intimately than in our days. The evolution thus to our days would be : from war to trade and from trade back to war. From the eighth to the twelfth century we can find distinct traces of the formation of a trading class, and travel becomes chiefly an accompaniment of commerce. The evolution of the Arabs and Northmen from pirates into traders was observed long since at a time when the encouragement of trade became a principle of politics.[2]

The mere spoliation of the invaded country may contain a variety of economic phenomena and does not exclude acts of generosity. The consequences of the act of depredation depend upon the nature of the goods seized, such as land, slaves, women, foodstuffs, etc. Some require a more permanent cultivation like cereals, others maintenance like slaves; compulsory labour requires organization and a number of objects that presuppose the existence of artisans producing arms and tools, ornaments, textiles, and furs. The accumulation of the booty by the individual

---

[1] See expressions found in an early seventeenth century document published by Mme. Lubimenko in *The English Historical Review*, 1914. *A Project for the Acquisition of Russia by James I in* 1612, a striking illustration of the organization of trade through foreign lands along a river system from the White Sea to the Caspian.

[2] A. L. Schlözer, *History of Commerce*, 1761.

invader and its appropriation are different from the accumulation under a chief or a constituted authority, and so is the subsequent complicated rationing of the output or result of the expedition. In case of seizure of specie (coins, metal, and other mediums of exchange), especially if it has been designed, individual smuggling and hoarding is made easier, and this might serve as a fund for trade ; rationing will be laborious, it will be difficult to counter open or latent resistence by 'vested interests'. Accidental or casual yield, correlated with the respective forms of social and political organization, with a distributive authority of some sort even in the occupation of new land, may and will tend, together with the preparing of a periodical or frequent repetition of the same expedition, to secure a permanent or recurrent yield by means of the application of more sophisticated forms of ransom and probably later tribute. The organization of the *entrepreneur* or aggressor adjusts itself to needs of production. The exaction of a permanent tribute and its distribution is an exceedingly complicated economic task, as could be illustrated by the only communistic state we know, where there is a main source of provision.

The periodical raising of a tribute in kind, which was apparently peculiar to the Mongol rule in Russia,[1] presupposes together with the organization of pressure, if not the organization at least the toleration and growth of crafts among the tributary population. The beginnings of our period are rich in instances of more or less organized annual tributes and ransom. Novgorod paid annually till the tenth century 300 *grivny* tribute to the Varangians to have peace. Svyatoslav in A.D. 901 exacted ransoms.[2] The various

---

[1] Beazley, *Dawn of Modern Geography*, ii, 291 and 323. Those who resisted were made slaves, individually or the whole family, or the women only—we do not know. Nor do we know anything about the fate of the slaves : were they sold in their native land or exported ? These and similar questions arise when the Mongol rule is to be considered. In Professor Vinogradov's *Outline of Historical Jurisprudence*, i, 259, he contrasts slavery in Muhammadan countries with primitive agricultural slavery and serfdom.

[2] Professor Klyuchevsky remarks that the names of the traders mentioned in the Russo-Byzantine trade agreements are the names of the agents of the Kiev prince. They are received as allies, not as traders (*Kurs*, i, 173, 4th Russ. ed.).

northern neighbours of the Byzantine Empire obtained
a fairly regular income by blackmail, fluctuating between
tribute for keeping quiet and ' wages ' for troubling some
third party.

Among the various kinds of tribute we can distinguish
the fluctuating tribute casually obtained by the Rus from
the neighbouring Baltic tribes from the fixed and almost
assessed tribute such as is mentioned in the interesting
passage referring to Ohthere's tale to King Alfred (about
A.D. 890) : " The principal wealth of the people of Helgaland
consists in the tribute the Fynnes pay them . . . skins
of wild beasts, feathers of birds, whalebones, cables, and
tacklings for shippes made of whales' or seales' skinnes.
Every man payeth according to his ability. The richest pay
ordinarily 15 cases of Marterns, 5 Rane deere skinnes and
one beare, ten bushels of feathers, a coat of a beare's skinne,
two cables three score elles long a piece, the one made of
whales' skin the other of seale's." [1] Another instance of
assessed tribute we find in the Russian Chronicle. The
Khozars claim a sword from each Polyan hearth and are
frightened as by a bad omen when they get swords with
double-edged blades. The dues payable for free passage
are also a kind of tribute more or less regulated, stipulated,
or exacted *ad hoc*. It was the favourite profit of the nomads
threatening the communication between Kiev and
Constantinople.

It seems clear that the regular booty and more so the
tribute presupposes the organization of forces (hosts) and,
if permanently arranged, the security of production. The
oppressors often have to become organizers of supply, and
the consent or submission of the subject races becomes
an important element of stability.[2] The organizing capacity
of the masters is one of the requirements of progress which
it is most difficult to appreciate correctly. A rationalistic
interpretation of history will simply reject it as a stage of
unjustifiable oppression. One of the transitory stages

---

[1] Hakluyt, ed. 1903, pp. 11–14.
[2] Th. Talbot, *The Manorial Roll of the Isle of Man*, 1511–15. ' At
the end of the eighth century the Scandinavian conquerors imposed
upon the Celtic population a new division of land into six *shedyngs*
or ship districts.'

from tribute to trade is the farming out of the tribute. As
the tax farmer works for the ruling power and commerce
appears as a subsidiary branch in the tax collector's enterprise,
the system is the reverse of the military slave-hunting
organization, where the ruling power works for private,
mostly foreign, traders. This latter institution was still
surviving, and perhaps even developing, at the beginning
of our period, whereas the farming out of tribute and taxation
belongs to a later time, reviving very ancient devices of
administration. An unlimited exploitation appears only
possible if there is no escape for the tributary tribe. The
taxation of hunting tribes or individual hunters will
necessarily be closely related with some form of trading and
consent, because a regular return is only obtainable when the
hunters have food and equipment. Ohthere's tale ought to be
examined from this point of view. The comparatively
rapid Slavicization of the Swedes who controlled the Russian
tribes and the survival of the national assemblies may have
something to do with that type of taxation. Here then
trade and primarily barter appear as a semi-private undertaking. The tribute collector might in some respect act
as a *publicanus* or tribute farmer, with public authority and
responsibility backed by his national organization, or else
he merges with the tributary community and becomes
one of its chiefs and organizers. This kind of transformation
appears in the political career of the Scandinavian (Varangian)
Princes on Russian soil. Under such conditions tribute,
trade, and truce are interwoven with travel and exploration.
The increase of output, the discovery of shorter and less
endangered communications and means of transport are
more a matter for political than private concern. Our modern
terminology is hardly fitted to represent the state of things we
find described in the Byzantine or Russian sources.

A succession of trade agreements was required to secure
the conditions of transit, the remedies against injuries and
damage, the protection of the trade route and of the traders
and foreigners in general along the line leading from Gothland
to Novgorod,[1] from Cherson to the Danube, from the Danube

---

[1] Professor C. R. Beazley in his introduction to Professor Nevill
Forbes's translation of the *Chronicle of Novgorod*, 1016–1471 (London,

to Mesembria, the final port for the Russian ' vessels ', according to Constantine VII, and from Mesembria for the 130 miles to Constantinople.

There was the same pressing need in the case of the still longer line leading from Novgorod to the Caspian, or from Novgorod to the estuary of the Western Dvina, where Riga was gradually becoming an important centre. The sources from which we derive our scanty knowledge refer to fragments of those large and ambitious schemes of trade organization which haunted the peoples of the day but which hardly formed anything but shortlived, incomplete settlements. When the ports only, without the hinterland, were occupied by foreigners, we have perhaps the least oppressive form of obtaining goods, as long as the goods are being brought to the ports instead of being fetched and collected by the occupant of the port. From this initial period down to the formation of large territorial Empires one can hardly expect the travellers of the time to be much concerned with the advance of geographical knowledge.

During our period there seems to have been a queer coexistence of general and vague notions of the possible lines of communication with very remote countries, together with legendary information slavishly repeated by generations of authors without any attempt to check the fateful traditions by contemporary experience. If Adam of Bremen and the Russian Chronicler at Kiev, who were presumably closely contemporary, both repeat the same details about the *Amazones* in what is now Finland, and if the same tale is told two centuries earlier by the Byzantine, Georgius Amartolus, who in his turn has borrowed it from older sources, such survival of legend seems to confirm that there was very little travel indeed in the time when they were writing. The maps of so late a period as the sixteenth century bear similar evidence of the very slow advance of geographical knowledge. If among the geographical tradition there were surviving indications of routes between the remotest parts of the world, this tends to show and to

1914), gives a summary of the growth of the Republic, its empire, and its foreign relations. L. K. Goetz, *Deutsch-Russische Handelsvertraege des Mittelalters*, Hamburg, 1916, is also an important contribution for the non-Russian student of Russian history.

confirm what recent writers seem to assume, namely the frequentation of such routes at a much earlier date when there was apparently more trade and travel and less fighting. The renaissance of the routes was not accomplished during the period under consideration. This general view however ought not to obscure certain features of international life even during the dark ages. These features are especially fascinating amidst the general insecurity. The hostage in enemy's land, the intermarriage between the reigning princely families, the diplomatic negotiation, the hired warrior from foreign land, offer so many occasions for mutual observations of intense interest to the widely differing Christian and non-Christian peoples.

The religious, non-political and non-material travel—the pilgrimage, with its spirit of otherworldliness, adds a peculiar charm to the epoch by the very contrast with its roughness. The immense variety of types, races and degrees of culture, to be overshadowed by a few, possibly by one system of religious and political thought, manifests perhaps for the first time the common basis of a still latent humanism, but still a mere dream, at the very eve of its failure.

The conflux of people of various nationality at Alexandria, Baghdad, Damascus, in the Italian cities Amalfi, Genoa, Venice, at Constantinople, in comparatively out of the way places like Kiev, Novgorod, Wisby, at Itil and Bolgar on the Volga, at Prague and Ratisbon (Regensburg) on the Danube, and Jumna on the Oder, seems to indicate a considerable intensity of international life between the eighth and the twelfth centuries. This is, as it were, confirmed by the growing uniformity of international religious life, in the vast domains of the Patriarchate of the Western and Eastern Churches, and in the territories gained by Islam, as well as by the variety of countries where the Jews were domiciled. Does the difficulty resolve itself into the coexistence of a small number of world-centres keeping up the intercommunion of races inherited from the Roman Empire, some vanishing while new ones take their place, whereas the numbers of people engaged in this international life and the intensity of this life were very much on the ebb ? Is not Constantinople during our period more remote from

Western Europe than in Roman times ? Is there not a disruption of the forces which tend towards a renewed unity and fail because the international communion has no actual basis ; the political disruption is too great, the religious unity not sufficient to restore the *pax Romana*, the process of consolidation of the larger nationalities too slow to facilitate travel and restore to the travellers the prominence which they once possessed and which is reserved to them in a later age.

CHAPTER VII

The Opening of the Land Routes to Cathay

By Eileen Power, M.A., D.Lit.

THE century lying between 1245 and 1345 is of unique importance in the history of medieval travel, because for a brief period it brought into contact the East and the West, the two centres of the civilized world; for during the Middle Ages it is true enough to say that the world had two centres, each of which thought that it was the only one, the great civilizations of India and China, proud and immemorially old, and the budding civilization of Christendom, then in all the vigour of its lusty youth.

In a sense, of course, they had always been in contact. Once before they had met and mingled, when Alexander took his Hellenism westward and left an ineffaceable mark upon the faces of the Buddhas of Northern India. Once again they had, as it were, looked at each other without meeting, when Chinese traders met the agents of Rome at the craggy city of Tashkurgan, called 'the Stone Tower', and unrolled their bales of silk on the banks of the Yarkand River.[1] And although all this had become a fairy tale to the men of the Middle Ages, they were still in contact with the East in the sense that they seasoned their dishes with spices from Ceylon and Java, set diamonds from Golconda in their rings, and carpets from Persia on their thrones, went splendidly clad in silks from China and played their interminable games of chess with ebony chessmen from

[1] See M. B. Charlesworth, *The Trade Routes of the Roman Empire* (Cambridge, 1924), pp. 99–109. 'Here, indeed, these merchants, though they little knew it, stood at what is the very head and centre of all commerce for the Old World and the most ancient meeting-place on the whole earth; at this lonely point three civilizations, those of China, of India, and of the Hellenized Orient, met and gave in exchange their products, their wares, and their painting and art.' But Sir Aurel Stein places 'the Stone Tower' at Daraut-Kurgan in the Karategin valley.

Siam. But for all that a black and heavy curtain shut the East and the West from each other's sight.

For although the thriving merchants of Venice and Genoa and Pisa grew rich upon the Eastern trade, they knew it only at its termini, the ports of the Levant. From China and India merchandise could take two roads to the West. One was a land route across Central Asia, ending upon the shores of the Black Sea, or passing southward to Baghdad. But though the Greeks of Constantinople and Trebizond did an active trade in Eastern merchandise coming by this route, and though Italians were already beginning to frequent the Black Sea ports, it was impossible for them to go further along the trade routes, for all across Central Asia lay the Turks, blocking the road to the East. The other road was a sea road, separated from the Mediterranean by two land-vestibules, the vestibule of Persia and Syria, and the vestibule of Egypt. In Palestine and Syria the Christians still held a remnant of the Crusading States, with a valuable row of ports, and by treaty with the sultans at their backdoor they were allowed to journey a few miles inland to the busy cities of Aleppo and Damascus. But beyond this, to the great mart of Baghdad, the centre for the whole district, and along the trade routes to the Persian Gulf, they might not go. Here again the Turks stood in their path. In Egypt, too, their galleys came to Alexandria and did a great trade, but by what road the camels brought their loads and where the Nile boats took on board their cargoes, the Frankish merchants did not know, for once more the Turks blocked them. Islam, the hereditary foe of Christendom, lay like a wall between Europe and all the trade routes to the East.

But in the period which we have now to consider all this was changed. Italian merchants chaffered and Italian friars said Mass in the ports and cities of India and China, moved unhampered with their caravans on the great silk route across Central Asia, or passed through Persia to take ship on the long sea road. The East and the West for the first time came into direct contact from end to end. And if it be asked how this came about, the answer is an unexpected one—that it was the result of the conquests of a nomadic Mongol people from Central Asia of the same stock as the Turks, a people, moreover, which has come down in history with a reputation for unintelligent destruction equalled only by that of the Vandals. That people is best known under its medieval name of the Tartars.

The Tartar conquests began at the beginning of the thirteenth century, when Chinghiz Khan and his hordes came down from Mongolia and attacked the Chinese Empire, taking Peking in 1214 and by degrees, in the course of the next fifty years, extending their sway until they ruled almost the whole of Eastern Asia. They first turned westward in 1218 and the flood of conquest slowly spread right across Asia, over a large part of Russia, into Poland and Hungary, and all over Persia and part of Asia Minor, until by the death of Mangu Khan in 1259 one empire stretched from the Yellow River to the banks of the Danube, and from the Persian Gulf to Siberia. Nothing like it had ever been known in history before, for the Roman Empire was a mere midget in comparison, and nothing like it was to be known again until the great land empire of Russia in the nineteenth century. In the last half of the thirteenth century it broke up into four khanates. The Great Khan himself ruled from Cambaluc or Khanbalik (Peking) over the whole of China, Corea, Mongolia, Manchuria and Tibet, taking tribute also from Indo-China, Burma and Java. The Chagatai Khanate, with its capital at Almalik (Kulja), stretched over Central Asia, Turkestan and Afghanistan. The Kipchak Khanate, or the Golden Horde, with its capital at Sarai on the Volga, covered the country north of the Caucasus, Russia, and part of Siberia. The Persian Ilkhanate, with its capital at Tauris (Tabriz) held sway over Persia, Georgia, Armenia, and part of Asia Minor. Nevertheless, although thus divided, the Tartars were essentially one people, acknowledging the sway of the Great Khan at Peking and communicating with each other by messengers across the length and breadth of Asia.

The appearance of these wild horsemen, swift and savage beyond description, coming like an irresistible flood, a sort of terrible and overwhelming tidal wave, from the East at first struck horror into the soul of Europe, for it seemed as though they would continue their triumphant progress westward and ravage all Christendom to the sea. Twice they appeared, in 1222–3 and again in 1241. In 1238 Matthew

Paris tells how fear of them kept the people of Gothland
and Friesland away from the Yarmouth herring fishery,
and in 1241, when the Christian host was heavily defeated
at Lignitz and they ravaged Poland, Silesia, and Hungary,
the Emperor Frederick II called upon Henry III of England
and other princes for common action against this new
' Scourge of God '.[1] Horror and disgust and fear were the
sentiments which they aroused.

But after 1241 the flood of conquest rolled back, and when
next it rolled West again, it was seen to overwhelm not
Christian kingdoms but the caliphates of Baghdad and Syria,
establishing in the '50s Tartar for Muslim rule there, sacking
Baghdad and extinguishing the Caliphate in 1258. For this
reason this attitude of Europe began to undergo a change,
and men saw in the Tartars not a menace to Christendom
but a possible ally against a common enemy. As Europeans
got to know more about the Tartars, they learned that they
were tolerant to all creeds, Buddhist, Muhammadan, Jewish
and Christian, having no very strongly marked beliefs
of their own. They began also to learn that there were
large groups of Nestorian Christians still scattered throughout
Asia. Europeans who visited the Tartar camp at Karakorum
brought back news of ladies of high rank, wives and mothers
of khans, who professed the Christian faith. Rumours
of the conversion now of the Great Khan himself in Cathay,
now of one or other of the lesser khans in Persia or Russia,
kept rising, and men repeated also the famous legend
of Prester John. All these things, together with the
indisputable fact that the Tartars had laid the Muslim power
low all over Asia, began to present them to Western rulers
in a totally new light. Gradually there took shape the
dream of converting the Tartars to Christianity and then
forming a great Tartar-Christian alliance which should
smite Islam hip and thigh, reconquer Palestine and Egypt,
and succeed where crusades from the West alone had failed.

From the middle of the thirteenth century, therefore,

---

[1] He puts his trust in God and hopes that by the combined efforts of
Christendom these Tartars will be driven finally down to their Tartarus,
ad sua Tartara Tartari detrudentur. The pun was likewise perpetrated by
Matthew Paris, Innocent IV, and St. Louis ! *The Journey of William
of Rubruck,* ed. W. W. Rockhill (Hakluyt Soc., 1900), p. xix.

it is essential to remember that Europe was no longer shrinking in terror from the Tartars, but on the contrary was looking upon them as potential converts and allies. Embassies were continually setting out to one or other of the centres of their power, Sarai on the Volga, the new Persian capital of Tabriz, or distant Cathay, from the Pope, or the King of France, or the King of England, with invitations to embrace Christianity and projects of alliance.[1] Merchants also began to go thither to trade and Franciscan friars to preach, and by degrees a busy intercourse sprang up between East and West.[2] But before describing this intercourse at its height, some description must be given of the pioneers of Eastward travel, the two friars who first made the journey to Mongolia and brought back the first description of Tartar power in Asia to Europe, and the greatest traveller of all the Middle Ages, the merchant Marco Polo, who with his father and uncle first reached Cathay itself, abode there for eighteen years and finally came back to Europe by sea.

The first travellers of whom we have record were Franciscan friars, sent on diplomatic missions to the Great Khan, the one by Pope Innocent IV, the other by King Louis IX of France. They came and went, and sojourned only long enough to deliver their letters and receive the Great Khan's very haughty reply. But they are particularly interesting, because they give a view of the manners and customs of the Tartars at an early stage, and are the first Europeans to make the land journey across the deserts and mountains of Central Asia and the distant Mongolian plain. The first to set out was John of Pian de Carpine, an Italian and Provincial of the Franciscan Order at Cologne. He started in 1245, and went by way of Bohemia, Silesia, and Kiev to the Tartar horde on the Volga, and then, with a Polish companion, on across Central Asia in the midst of hardships so terrible that he afterwards died from their effects. He

---

[1] One of the best statements of the scheme occurs in Marino Sanuto's *Secreta* (written 1306–7 and finally revised 1321). The conquest of the Turks is to be carried out by the aid of the Tartars, beginning with Egypt. He gives a sketch of the history and customs of the Tartars and of European intercourse with them up to that date, and mentions that many Christian traders have gone to the East by way of the Tartar lands.

[2] See C. R. Beazley, *Dawn of Mod. Geog.* (1906), iii, pp. 309–499.

was received by the Great Khan elect, Kuyuk, at a place half a day's journey from Karakorum in Mongolia, where a host of Mongol notables and envoys had gathered for the election, and returned with letters from 'Kuyuk, the strength of God, God in Heaven and Kuyuk Khan on earth, the seal of the Lord of all men', reaching the papal court in 1247. Imbued though he was with a profound hatred for the Tartars, he was a remarkable observer, who has left the best description of Tartar manners and customs written in the Middle Ages, and an excellent account of the ceremonies at the election of a great khan.[1]

Meanwhile in 1248-9 a Mongol embassy came to St. Louis of France, just when he was in the midst of a crusade at Cyprus, from the Tartar general in Persia, offering alliance against the Muslims. This stimulated the dispatch of an unsuccessful mission under another friar, Andrew of Longjumeau, to the same Khan whose election Pian de Carpine had seen, but who died before it reached him, and it was not until 1251 that there set out the second great friar traveller of the Middle Ages, William of Rubruck, a native of French Flanders, who carried letters from St. Louis to the new Khan. He went by sea to the Crimea and on to the Don and the Volga, and then pressed on across Central Asia by forced marches which tried him terribly, for he was very fat, often so hungry that he was reduced to eating the biscuits which he had brought as a delicacy for the Tartar nobles, and sometimes so cold that he had to turn his sheepskin coat with the wool inside, and his bare toes were frost bitten in their sandals. He leaves us a very good account (addressed to St. Louis) of the Tartars, with their cart-borne tents, their wandering herds, and their drink of kumiss, or fermented mares' milk, for which he conceived a liking, though among the Christians dwelling with the Tartars it was held equivalent to a denial of their faith to drink it. He gives a particularly graphic description of the hordes of the Don and Volga on the move ; and also of the Court of Mangu Khan near Karakorum. Here he

[1] For Pian de Carpine's narrative of his journey and an account by his companion, Benedict the Pole, see *The Journey of William of Rubruck . . . with two accounts of the Earlier Journey of John of Pian de Carpine*, ed. W. W. Rockhill (Hakluyt Soc., 1900), pp. 1-39.

met embassies from many parts and priests of all sorts of religions—Catholics, Nestorians, Armenians, Manicheans, Buddhists, and Muslims—all disputing with each other and all trying to establish their claims over the soul of the Khan, who, like Gallio, cared for none of these things, but made use of them as it suited him. ' We Moal,' said Mangu to the friar, who spoke with him through an interpreter, ' believe that there is only one God, by whom we live and by whom we die, and for whom we have an upright heart . . . But as God gives us the different fingers of the hand, so he gives to men divers ways. God gives you the Scriptures and you Christians keep them not. You do not find in them, for example, that one should find fault with another, do you ? ' ' No, my lord,' said William, ' but I told you from the first that I did not want to wrangle with anyone.' ' I do not intend to say it for you,' he said, ' Likewise you do not find that a man should depart from justice for money.' ' No, my lord,' said William, ' And truly I came not to these parts to obtain money ; on the contrary I have refused what has been offered me ' ; and a secretary present bore witness that he had refused silver and silken cloths. ' I do not say it for you,' again replied the Khan. ' God gave you, therefore, the Scriptures and you do not keep them. He gave us diviners, we do what they tell us and we live in peace.' [1] If this was a barbarian it was a barbarian of insight.

William's own description of his difficulties with rival Christians, such as the Armenian monk Sergius and the Nestorians, somewhat bears out the Great Khan's palpable hit. Of the Nestorians, like all Christian travellers to the East, he gives a very hostile account, on the principle, not unfamiliar among some modern missionaries, that a heathen is greatly to be preferred to a rival Christian sectary. His story of the monk Sergius (who subsequently turned out to be an impostor who had never taken orders at all, but was a cloth weaver in his own country) is one of the most amusing passages in medieval travel literature. This man was in the habit of working miracles upon the persons of the Tartars, by giving them draughts of holy water, in which he had placed a little cross ; previously, however, he took the precaution

---

[1] Op. cit., pp. 235-6.

of mixing a good dose of rhubarb with the holy water, the effect of which was naturally regarded by the ignorant Tartars as a great miracle. William, though shocked, bore this without protest, until the monk happened to visit one Master William Buchier, of Paris, a skilled goldsmith who had been captured in the Hungarian raids and was employed in various important works at Karakorum, and who was then convalescing from a serious illness. Master Buchier consumed two bowls of the concoction, thinking it to be holy water, and it nearly killed him. This at last moved William to protest. ' Either,' said he to the monk, ' go as an apostle doing real miracles by the grace of the Word and the Holy Ghost, or do as a physician in accordance with the medical art. You give to drink to men not in a condition for it a strong medicinal potion, as if it were something holy ; and in so doing you would incur great shame should it become known among men.' [1] Our good friar had plenty of sense, but he lacked the instincts of the medical missionary.

William of Rubruck set out again for Europe in July, 1254, leaving behind a companion, Bartholomew of Cremona, to preach to the Tartars, and returned to the Volga and then by way of the Caucasus and Armenia to Cyprus. He is not only a very valuable writer from a geographical, ethnological, and philological point of view (he picked up the Mongol tongue and gives a good account of the languages with which he met), but also a very entertaining one. Where John of Pian de Carpine is impersonally accurate, William's personality emerges clearly from his narrative, which is full of conversations and of those small intimate details which make a story live. He deserves, indeed, to be more widely popular than he is.

To these two friars belongs the imperishable glory of pioneers, for they were the first Europeans to make the land journey to Mongolia and return. But the next adventurers of whom we know went further and saw and did far more, and, by making the return journey by sea, encircled the whole of the then known world. They were not friars or ambassadors, but belonged to a class which was to provide the main impetus to travel in the period which was now opening, merchants going upon their own initiative and at

[1] Ibid., pp. 192–3, 216.

their own cost and risk, moved by no motive save love of adventure and that *auri sacra fames* to which in the history of mankind it has so often been allied. Marco Polo was incomparably the greatest traveller and the most magnificent observer of the whole Middle Ages, shining among the others— good as they are—like Apollo among the hinds of Admetus.

The story of the Polos is well known.[1] About the same time that William of Rubruck was setting forth on his journey, two Venetian jewel merchants, Nicolo and Maffeo Polo, trading to Constantinople, decided to take ship from that city to the Crimea, where they had a counting house at Soldaia (the modern Sudak), and to go on a trading expedition to the Khan of the Golden Horde on the Volga. They soon disposed of their jewels and spent a year at his camp, and then war broke out between this Khan and the Ilkhan of Persia and cut off their road back. But no Venetian was ever at a loss or averse from seeing new lands, and so the Polos decided to go on and visit the Khan of Central Asia or Chagatai, and perhaps make their way back to Constantinople by some unfrequented route. They struggled over the great steppes which lie beween the Volga and the Aral, and coming by Khiva followed the line of the Oxus down to the city of Bokhara, one of the richest and most crowded marts of Asia, lying upon the great silk-route. Here they remained for three years and learned the Tartar tongue, until one day an embassy came to the city on its way back from Persia to the Great Khan in China, and the envoys, amazed to find Italians in this distant spot, persuaded the brothers to accompany them. So for a year the Polos journeyed with the Tartar embassy across the heart of Asia, until at last they stood in the presence of Kublai Khan himself. He gave them the warm welcome which his envoys had promised, and listened to all that they had to tell him about the West, for they were the first Europeans that he had seen. Finally he decided to send them back on a mission to the Pope, asking for a hundred men of learning to preach to

---

[1] The standard English edition of Marco Polo's book is *The Book of Ser Marco Polo the Venetian concerning the Kingdoms and Marvels of the East*, ed. Sir Henry Yule (3rd edit., revised by H. Cordier, Hakluyt Soc., 1903, 2 vols.). See also H. Cordier, *Ser Marco Polo, Notes and Addenda* (1920).

his Tartars and some oil from the sacred lamp on the Sepulchre
at Jerusalem. The return journey across central Asia
was slow and hazardous and took the brothers three years,
but they reached Acre at last in 1269.

They set out to go back to the Great Khan in November,
1271, bearing with them letters from Pope Gregory X and
the holy oil; but the only men of learning who accompanied
them were two Dominicans, who deserted in a panic at
Lajazzo. However, they took with them no mean substitute
for the hundred men of learning asked for by the Great Khan
in the person of Nicolo's son Marco Polo, a lad of seventeen.
Landing at Lajazzo in the Gulf of Alexandretta, the Polos
travelled by way of Mosul and Baghdad to Ormuz on the
Persian Gulf, where they possibly intended to take ship
and make the long sea journey to one of the Chinese ports.
They did not, however, do this, but instead turned north
through the salt desert of Kerman, through Balkh and
Khorasan and Badakhshan (where they halted for a year
to allow Marco Polo to recover from an illness), over the
icy highlands of Pamir, the 'roof of the world', where Marco
saw and noted the long horned mountain sheep, the *ovis Poli*,
which now bears his name, though indeed William of
Rubruck saw and described it before him. They followed
the old southern caravan route, on which no European
was ever seen again until the nineteenth century, passing
through Kashgar, Yarkand and Khotan until they reached
the edge of the Gobi desert. Here they halted to load their
camels with provisions and then set out on the terrible
three days' journey across the desert, beset with nightmare
fears and the sound of ghostly drums and gongs, tempting
the unwary traveller from the road at night. At last they
came safely to Tangut on the extreme north-west of China,
skirted the frontier across the Mongolian steppes, and reached
the court of the Great Khan in May, 1275, having journeyed
for three and a half years.

The Khan received them with high honour, and instantly
took the young Marco into his service. It was the beginning
of a long and close association, for Kublai Khan soon found
him very intelligent, discreet, and observant, and began to
employ him on various missions. Everywhere Marco Polo
went, readily picking up several of the languages current

in the Great Khan's dominions, he observed and made notes of what he saw, and the Khan was wont to say that alone among his envoys this man used his eyes and could bring back with him not merely an account of the rendering of his mission but a hundred interesting and entertaining details about the lands through which he passed and the people whom he saw. How much do we not owe to the noble curiosity of Kublai Khan, which stimulated Marco Polo to see and to enquire, and to make such careful notes concerning the marvellous empire which he was the first European to see ! The extent of his travel was immense. He journeyed through the provinces of Shansi, Shensi and Szechuan, and even skirted the edge of Tibet to Yunnan and penetrated to Northern Burma. He was for three years Governor of the Chinese city of Yangchow. He went by sea on a mission to Cochin-China and on to India. He describes the Great Khan's capital of Cambaluc, or Peking, in the North, and his summer palace at Shandu with its woods and gardens, its marble palace and bamboo pavilion, its magicians, and its stud of white mares ; indeed, he gave Shandu immortality in a misty Western island, destined one day to rule a sea empire wider even than the land empire of Kublai Khan, for it was from his description of it that Coleridge drew his dream picture of Xanadu :

> In Xanadu did Kubla Khan
> A stately pleasure dome decree,
> Where Alph the sacred river ran
> Past caverns measureless to man
> Down to a sunless sea.
> And there were gardens bright with sinuous rills
> Where blossomed many an incense-bearing tree,
> And here were forests, ancient as the hills,
> Enfolding sunny spots of greenery.

He describes also Manzi, or Southern China, with its capital, the beautiful Kinsai (Hangchow), which later European travellers always described (as indeed he did himself) in terms almost of rapture, declaring it to be the greatest, richest and loveliest city in the world ; Kinsai, which stood like Venice upon innumerable canals, with its twelve great gates and the twelve thousand bridges which spanned its

waterways, its wide streets lined by houses and shops and
gardens, the stone warehouses of merchants from India
reflected all along its great canal, and hard by the city
that Western Lake, which generations of Chinese poets
have so incomparably sung; Kinsai, with its silk clad
population of lords and merchants, and its ladies, of whom
even a Franciscan friar could not refrain from noting that
they were the most beautiful in the world.[1] Marco Polo
tells also of Zaiton (Ts'üenchow), the great port of the province
and plainly, from the accounts which survive of it, one of the
greatest ports of the world,[2] to which there came a hundred
times more pepper every year than reached the whole of
Christendom through Alexandria and the harbours of
the Levant. At Zaiton the big junks laded spices and aloes,
ebony and sandal wood from Indo-China, together with
Tibetan musk and the unmatched silks of China, and
sailed with them to India, there to trade them for pearls
and precious stones from Ceylon, pepper and ginger and
muslins ' like tissue of spiders' webs ' from Southern India.
Marco Polo describes, indeed, the whole of that splendid empire,
full of wealth and commerce, with its canal and river traffic,
its system of posts and caravanserais, its paper money,
and its great ruler Kublai Khan, who was worthy of the
ancient civilization which he thus inherited. He describes
also the strange and half barbarous people of Tibet and
Central Asia, and is the first European to speak of Burma,
Siam, Java, Sumatra and Ceylon. It is almost impossible
to speak too highly either of the extent of his observation
or of its accuracy. It is true that he repeats some of the
usual travellers' tales, and that where he reports from
hearsay he not infrequently makes mistakes; but where
he had observed with his own eyes he was almost always
accurate; he had a great opportunity, and he was great
enough to take it.

Marco Polo had, indeed, ample time to make these

[1] Oderic of Pordenone. See below, p. 149.

[2] Ibn Baṭṭūṭah said of it later : ' The harbour of Zaiton is one of the
greatest in the world—I am wrong, it is the greatest. I have seen
there about a hundred first class junks together; as for the small ones,
they were past counting ' (*Cathay and the Way Thither*, ed. Yule (1916 ed.),
iv, p. 118). He had seen Alexandria, Constantinople, and the great ports
of Southern India ; and Marco Polo and the other Italians knew Venice
and Genoa, the greatest European trading cities of the Mediterranean.

observations, for he remained in China from 1275 to 1292. Then the old Khan was very unwillingly persuaded to allow the three Polos to return to Europe as escorts of a Tartar princess who was being sent as a bride to the Ilkhan of Persia. They set sail from Zaiton and spent over two years on the journey, but finally reached Persia, handed over the lady, and came back by Tabriz, Trebizond, and Constantinople to Venice at last in the winter of 1295.

There is no need to labour the effect of the tremendous mass of exact knowledge which the reports of Marco Polo brought to the enterprising mercantile world of Venice and Genoa, and to the hardly less enterprising ecclesiastical world which was still cherishing its great scheme of converting the Tartars. The two friars who first penetrated to Mongolia and the three merchants who first made the great tour to Cathay by land and back to Europe by sea were only pioneers of a widespread movement. For it was by now plain that the Tartar Empire had wrought one of the most startling revolutions in the history of the world up to that date by bringing into contact for the first time the two ends of the earth, Europe and the Far East. For the next fifty years or so, roughly between 1290 and 1340, a steady stream of travellers took the Eastern road. They had need, indeed, to find new trade routes, for the collapse of the Latin power in Palestine, culminating in the loss of Acre in 1291, was seriously interrupting the old. The term 'trade routes' is used advisedly, for although some of the best travel books belonging to this period were written by missionaries, the real impetus to travel was given by trade, and the most frequent journeys to Persia, India and Cathay were made by merchants. These merchants now found themselves no longer mere clients at the closed gates of the East, loading their ships with goods brought to those termini by Muslim middlemen ; they found that they could pass through the gates and themselves follow the trade routes. Direct access to the East was at last open to them, and it has been said with truth that ' the unification of Asia by the Mongols was as important a fact for the commerce of the Middle Ages as the discovery of America for the men of the Renaissance. It was equivalent to the discovery of Asia.' [1]

[1] R. Grousset, *Hist. de l'Asie* (Paris, 1922), iii, p. 130.

What the Tartars in effect did was to throw open two out of the three great trade routes between East and West. One, the Egyptian road, remained in the hands of the Muslims and closed to Europeans, though the Venetian galleys still brought back their cargoes of spices and silk from the great terminus port of Alexandria. But the other two, the Persian-Syrian and long sea route and the Transasiatic land route were in the hands of the Tartars and were now thrown open. Marco Polo went by the latter and returned by the former.

Consider first the sea route to India, reached through the new Ilkhanate of Persia. During the Tartar period Persia resumed her historic rôle of antechamber to the East, which she had not played since the days of Alexander. The capital of Tartar Persia, Tabriz, or Tauris, soon outshone Baghdad as the chief mart of the district, and was visited and admired by all the great travellers of the age. ' It is the best city in the world for merchandise,' said Oderic of Pordenone, ' and is worth more to the emperor than his whole kingdom is to the King of France.' It had the initial advantage that it could be reached by caravan routes from two ports which were in Christian hands and thus did not incur, like Alexandria, the papal ban against trading with the infidel (not that Christian merchants took the ban very seriously). One of these ports was Lajazzo or Ayas, on the Gulf of Alexandretta in the kingdom of Little Armenia, from which Marco Polo started on his outward journey, and the other was Trebizond, on the southern shore of the Black Sea, the capital of an independent Greek state, from which he took ship on his way home. Coming from either of these ports to Tabriz, merchants could then follow the caravan route down to Ormuz at the mouth of the Persian Gulf, which was the chief port for the Indian trade at this period, and of which Marco Polo and other travellers have left admirable descriptions.

Very soon this Persian route almost ousted the Egyptian route as the vestibule between the Mediterranean and the Indian Ocean. The Mamluk sultans of Egypt imposed such heavy tolls at Alexandria that Indian merchandise increased 300% in price by the time it got to Europe; also they were apt to molest the Christian merchants and strictly forbade them the interior. But in Persia the Ilkhans pursued an enlightened policy, imposing low customs, protecting traders, policing the roads, establishing a regular system of posts, and allowing free passage everywhere. The Europeans were not slow to take advantage of the new facilities ; we hear of an Italian merchant in Tabriz as early as 1264 (his will, made there in that year, survives and sets forth his stock of cloth from Venice, Germany and Flanders, pearls and sugar and chessmen from the East, saddles, cups, candlesticks and drinking glasses).[1] At first the trade of the district fell mainly to the Genoese, and to this day the Turks of Asia Minor are wont to attribute to that enterprising people any ancient stone building whose origin is unknown.[2] Marco Polo found them all powerful at Tabriz in 1294 and mentions that a Genoese company was already navigating the great inland Caspian Sea. But the Venetians began to compete with them early in the fourteenth century, and had an advantageous commercial treaty with the Ilkhan in 1320 and a Consul in Tabriz in 1324.

At first, too, Christian missionaries had a considerable success. The great Khan Hulagu, who first made himself master of Persia, had a Nestorian wife,[3] and they both treated their Christian subjects with a favour which contrasted strongly with their severity towards the Muslims, so that the Armenian writers celebrate them ' as a new Constantine and Helena, the hope and solace of Christians, the torches and protectors of religion.' [4] This favour was even more marked under Arghun Khan (1284–91), who also had a Nestorian wife, and rumours of whose conversion to Christianity were constantly coming West. It was the deliberate policy of this prince to bring about a general crusade against the Mamluks of Egypt by a combination between himself and the Latin Powers, and constant embassies passed between him and the Pope and other Christian monarchs. In 1287 the famous Rabban Bar Sauma, a Nestorian Uigur from Cathay, who had come to Armenia on his way to make a

---

[1] W. Heyd, *Hist. du Commerce du Levant*, ed. Furcy Raynaud, (2nd ed. Leipzig, 1923), ii, p. 110. His name was Pietro Viglioni.

[2] Ibid., ii, p. 121.

[3] Similarly William of Rubruck found that many royal and high-born Tartar ladies at Karakorum were Christians.

[4] Grousset, op. cit., iii, pp. 102–3.

pilgrimage to Jerusalem, was sent by Arghun on an embassy to Europe to rouse its rulers to common action against Islam. He visited Constantinople and Rome, delivered to Philip the Fair at Paris a letter from Arghun, written in Uigur characters, which may still be seen in the *Archives Nationales*, and interviewed Edward I of England in Guyenne. In 1289 the Ilkhan sent another embassy to Paris and London, promising the king of France that he would give him Jerusalem when it was taken, and in 1290 yet another envoy came from him to the Pope. It is of some interest that among the return embassies which were sent to Arghun one went from England in 1291, under the leadership of Geoffrey de Langele, and the account of its expenses has survived; moreover, two Mongol ambassadors actually presented themselves before Edward II at Northampton in 1307, and took back with them a letter to the Ilkhan Uljaytu.[1] It is not surprising, in view of these exchanges, that Christian missions flourished in Persia, that churches and houses of friars sprang up in various parts, and that one of the most interesting mission writers of this age (which abounds in them) should be Ricold of Monte Croce, the Dominican friar who laboured in Asia Minor, Mesopotamia and Persia from about 1286. But the fair hopes of the Christian missions were slain by the final conversion of the Ilkhans to Islam in 1316, and though a great missionary effort took place between 1318 and 1336, and Catholic bishoprics continued to be founded in these parts and maintained a wonderful vitality, we hear little of them after about 1340.[2]

But it was not for the sake of Persia alone that the opening of the land route was epoch making. Persia was only the ante-chamber; what was more important was that at Ormuz Europeans could now take ship and bear their gospel and their trade to India itself. In 1315 agents of the Genoese bank of Vivaldi (the same enterprising family which a quarter of

[1] For these diplomatic missions, see Abel-Rémusat, ' Mémoires sur les Rélations politiques des Princes chrétiens et particulièrement les Rois de France, avec les Empereurs Mongols ' (*Mem. de l'Acad. Royale des Inscriptions et Belles-Lettres*, T. iv and v, 1821–2). Short accounts are given by Grousset, op. cit., iii, pp. 107–9, and by Beazley, op. cit., iii, pp. 492–3, 539–47.

[2] For Ricold of Monte Croce and the Persian mission, see Beazley, op. cit., iii, pp. 187–215.

a century before had sailed forth to find the road to India down the African coast and disappeared for ever)[1] had trading stations on the Gujerat and Malabar coasts. European merchants regularly visited the great ports of the Gulf of Cambay and of Malabar and Coromandel, which were crowded with a mixed population of Christians, Hindus, Muslims and Chinese; for, as Heyd points out, the great age of the Tartars corresponds with the period of greatest activity in the political and commercial relations between India and China, and these ports, especially Calicut and Quilon, were among the richest in the world. Missionary activity was no less active here than in Persia. A Latin mission visited the Malabar region under John of Monte Corvino in 1291–2, and was indeed there when Marco Polo passed on his way home; and we hear of four Franciscans who were martyred at Tannah on the Gulf of Cambay in 1321, in circumstances which made a great impression upon contemporaries, for the episode is mentioned by almost every mission writer of the time. In 1329 John XXII made Quilon a bishopric and sent there as bishop the Dominican Jordanus of Séverac, one of the best travel writers of this period.[2] He was replaced later by John Marignolli, on the latter's return from China in 1348–9. There was a Catholic church called St. George of the Latins there, and the Latin mission found an indigenous Nestorian population of great antiquity, the reputed descendants of St. Thomas' converts, and the shrine of St. Thomas at Quilon was held in great veneration. Descriptions of India are given by Marco Polo, Jordanus, Oderic of Pordenone and Marignolli. We hear of the fabulous riches, the splendid bazaars, the great manufactures of muslin and cottons, the pearl fisheries of Ceylon, the pepper gardens and world famous ginger of Quilon, and the huge ocean-going ships which crowded the harbours. They describe the natural features of the country, the tremendous heat, the dark rice-eating population, the delicious fruits, jack and mango and coco-nut, the palmyra palm, the brilliant parrots, the many elephants and

---

[1] On this enterprise of Ugolino and Guido Vivaldi and two Franciscan friars and on the traditional explorations of Ugolino's son Sorleone in search of them, see Beazley, op. cit., iii, pp. 413–18.

[2] For Jordanus and the Indian mission, see ibid., iii, pp. 215–35.

crocodiles. They tell also of the religion of the Hindus, with their sacred oxen, their enormous idols, their ascetic fakirs, their sacred caste of Brahmans and the practice of suttee. Jordanus speaks of a prophecy, handed down among the Indians, that the Latin races were destined to conquer all the world ; in how dramatic a manner it was to receive fulfilment later he could not foresee ; but he declares that the King of France could easily, by his own force alone, subdue this fair land to Christianity, he deplores the success of the Muslim missionaries, who had the effrontery to travel about the East for all the world like ourselves (*sicut nos*),[1] and declares that if the Pope would but send two galleys to the Indian seas, and so catch the Sultan of Egypt in a noose, marvels might be accomplished.

Moreover, although all travellers touched at an Indian port all did not stay there. For they could now take ship on one of the Chinese junks which came to Quilon and Malabar. Ibn Baṭṭūṭah at one time saw thirteen large junks lying ready to sail in the port of Malabar, and admirable descriptions of them are given by Marco Polo, Oderic, Ibn Baṭṭūṭah and Jordanus. They were made of fir and single decked, with fifty or sixty cabins and four (sometimes six) masts, double planked and furnished with water-tight compartments. They used both sails and oars and their crews numbered some 300 or 400 men ; Ibn Baṭṭūṭah tells how the sailors had pots of herbs and ginger growing aboard, and sang 'La, la ! La, la !' as they pulled the oars. On the junk on which Oderic of Pordenone embarked at Quilon there were 'a good 700 souls, what with sailors and merchants'. Aboard one of these European travellers could sail on past Java and Sumatra and Indo-China to Cynkalan (Canton), or Zaiton by the route which Marco Polo took on his return journey, and many European travellers after 1290 came to China by this long sea route. Its disadvantage was that it was very slow (it took two years), and it was because the land route was much shorter and reputed to be safer that medieval

---

[1] Professor Beazley notes : ' It was at this very time, as a matter of history, that Moslem *perfida* began its permanent conquest of the Malay world, began successfully to compass the seas and lands of the Archipelago in search of proselytes, began to penetrate even to the interior of Java and Sumatra.' Ibid., iii, p. 234.

opinion preferred the second of the two roads which the Tartars opened to the West.

This was the great caravan route across Central Asia, and it may be said with truth that if the Tartar conquest of Persia opened the road to India the Tartar conquest of Russia opened the road to China.[1]   The great overland silk route across Asia is one of the oldest and one of the most romantic trade routes in the world and its immense importance at this period can hardly be overestimated. Travellers could get by it to China in five or six months, travelling with the imperial posts, though caravans naturally took longer. It could be reached from Trebizond or Lajazzo via Tabriz by making the golden journey to Merv, Bokhara and Samarcand along a caravan route which joined them ; [2] but from the beginning of the fourteenth century another route became much more important and that was the road which went from the Crimea by land or sea to Tana (Azov), then across the steppes to Astrakhan or to Sarai on the Volga, and by camel across the desert to Urgenje (near Khiva) on the Oxus, and so on to the Bokhara-Samarcand route, and straight across central Asia by one of the three great roads, the north Thian Shan (Pe-lu), the south Thian Shan (Nan-lu) or the north Kuenlun into China.[3]

This road again meant direct access for Europe to the Far East. In 1266 the Mongol Khan of Kipchak authorized the Genoese to establish a colony at Kaffa on the shores of the Crimea, and the Venetians had one at Soldaia. Later they were allowed to establish themselves in Tana, too. These two towns are immensely interesting and deserve each a monograph.[4] Tana was the great focus for the corn and furs and other products of Russia, the silks and spices of the Far East and the merchandise of India, coming up by the Khyber Pass or through Persia. Kaffa was a curious cosmopolitan city, crowded with mosques and churches, Tartars and Muslims and Christians, an inveterate centre for the slave trade. This Crimean district grew

[1] Grousset, op. cit., iii, p. 137.
[2] There was also a more southern route which went via Kashgar, Yarkand, and Khotan, and which Marco Polo followed.
[3] See Beazley, op. cit., iii, p. 462.
[4] See an excellent short account of them in Heyd, op. cit., ii, pp. 156–215.

steadily in importance as a great mart for the Eastern trade, and here again the Genoese played the most important part. They had a special branch of the Government, the *officium Gazarie*, or Crimean Office, to look after their Black Sea trade, and when in 1343 the Kipchak Khan quarrelled with the Italians, seized Tana, and laid siege to Kaffa, there was a dearth of corn and foodstuffs throughout the Byzantine Empire and the price of Eastern silks and spices forthwith *doubled* in Italy, which shows how the overland route had by this time outstripped the others in importance. Kaffa was to be brought even more disastrously to the notice of Europe in 1348, for it was through it that the Black Death, which originated in China, reached the West. Some say that it broke out among the Tartars who were once again besieging Kaffa, and that they threw the infected corpses into the town by means of their siege instruments in order to achieve a more rapid victory. Others say that it broke out among the defenders, the merchants who were gathered in the town having brought it with them from China rolled up in their bales of silk.[1] At all events the siege was raised owing to the plague, and it seems certain that it was in a Black Sea ship that the Black Death got to Italy.

What direct access from Azov to Peking meant to the merchants of the day is best witnessed not so much in the journeys of missionary travellers as in the account of the overland silk trade left by Francesco Balducci Pegolotti, an agent of the great Florentine house of Bardi, who about 1340 wrote an admirable merchants' handbook concerning chiefly the trade of the Levant and the East. He gives full information for a merchant starting from Tana and proceeding to Peking, returning again with £12,000 worth of silk (reckoned in modern money). The stages of the journey, the mode of conveyance appropriate to each stage, whether horses, camel wagons or pack asses, the time to be allowed for each stage, the provisions to be taken, and the estimated cost are all set forth, together with a careful comparison

[1] It is noticeable that a number of Chinese silks which still survive in medieval church treasuries or in museums in Europe belong to this period of the Yuan or Tartar dynasty. See some examples reproduced in *Chinese Art* (*Burlington Magazine Monographs*, 1925), Textiles, Plates 1 and 2.

of the weights and measures in use in Tana and in Cathay. His general instructions are full of interest. " In the first place you must let your beard grow long and not shave. And at Tana you should furnish yourself with a dragoman, and you must not try to save money in the matter of dragomen by taking a bad one instead of a good one, for the additional wages of the good one will not cost you so much as you will save by having him. And besides the dragoman it will be well to take at least two good men servants who are acquainted with the Cumanian tongue, and if the merchant likes to take a woman with him from Tana he can do so ; if he does not like to take one there is no obligation, only if he does take one he will be kept much more comfortably than if he does not . . . . The road you travel from Tana to Cathay is perfectly safe, whether by day or by night, according to what the merchants say who have used it . . . You may reckon that from Tana to Sarai the road is less safe than on any other part of the journey, and yet even when this part of the road is at its worst, if you are some sixty men in the company, you will go as safely as if you were in your own house. Anyone from Genoa or from Venice wishing to go to the places above named and to make the journey to Cathay should carry linens with him and if he visit Organci (Urgenje) he will dispose of these well. In Organci he should purchase *somni*[1] of silver and with these he should proceed . . . Whatever silver the merchants carry with them as far as Cathay the lord of Cathay will take from them and put in his treasury, and to merchants who thus bring silver they give that paper money of theirs in exchange. This is of yellow paper, stamped with the seal of the lord aforesaid, and this money is called *balishi* and with this money you can readily buy silk and all other merchandise that you have a desire to buy, and all the people of the country are bound to receive it, and yet you shall not pay a higher price for your goods because your money is of paper. And of the said paper money there are three kinds, one being worth more than another, according to the value which has been established

[1] The *somno* was a silver ingot weighing 8½ Genoese lb., the Genoese lb. being equal to about 5/7 of the London lb. ; it was reckoned as worth five golden florins.

for each by that lord.[1] And you may reckon that you
can buy for one *somno* of silver 19 or 20 lb. of Cathay
silk. You may reckon also that in Cathay you should get
3 or 3½ pieces of damask silk for a *somno* and from 3½ to 5
pieces of *nachetti* of silk and gold likewise for a *somno* of
silver." [2]

There can be no more striking commentary on the effect
of the Tartar conquests than that casual remark, dropped
by Pegolotti in passing, that ' the road you travel from
Tana to Cathay is perfectly safe, whether by day or night,
according to what merchants say who have used it.' Traders,
indeed, seem to have used it regularly, and so did some of the
friar travellers of the fourteenth century. There were
mission stations all along the route, at Kaffa and Tana,
at Bolgar, at Sarai, at Astrakhan, at Urgenje, at
Almalik (Kulja). ' Even more than in China or Persia,'
says Professor Beazley, ' these Latin outposts from the
Euxine to Kazan, from the Caucasus to Kulja, represent
the exploring spirit of the Roman Church in its highest
form. For where could the enmity of Nature and Man
be defied more recklessly ? Where in all the known world
could distance, barbarism, sterility and fanaticism present
a more formidable combination of obstacles ? ' [3] The
flourishing Christian mission at Almalik was the seat of a
Franciscan bishop, Richard of Burgundy, and it was here
that there laboured Friar Pascal of Vittoria, whose admirable
letter upon his travels, written in 1338, has fortunately
survived. The advent of a Muslim khan caused his massacre
and that of the whole mission, which included the Bishop,
Pascal, two other Franciscan priests, two Franciscan lay
brethren, a ' black ' interpreter named ' John of India ',
and a Genoese trader, who was in Almalik at the time.
This was in 1339, and although the church at Almalik was
rebuilt again by Marignolli in 1340, and the Latin mission
maintained a precarious existence until 1362, it is clear that
Pegolotti, had he but known it, when he described the road

[1] Paper money first began to be used in China as early as
c. A.D. 806–21.
[2] See extracts from Pegolotti's *Della Pratica della Mercatura* in
Cathay and the Way Thither, ed. Yule (Hakluyt Soc., 2nd ed., 1914),
iii, pp. 137–73 passim.
[3] Beazley, op. cit., iii, pp. 238–9.

as *sichurissimo*, was speaking of an age which was already passing away.[1]

These, then, were the different routes by which European travellers found their way to the Far East at the beginning of the fourteenth century. It remains to consider some of the most distinguished of those who went.[2] The most numerous travellers were undoubtedly the merchants, but although they have left traces of their activity in such practical forms as Pegolotti's handbook and a lexicon of Latin, Persian and Cuman, compiled in 1303 by an anonymous merchant of Northern Italy,[3] and although they are, from time to time, mentioned incidentally in the narratives of other travellers, these traders have for the most part left no written account of their adventures. Marco Polo's is the one great travel book written by a merchant in this period, and (with the exception of the extremely amusing book of the Moor Ibn Baṭṭūṭah) our accounts of the East occur in the letters, reports and books of Christian missionaries, and above all of the intrepid and indefatigable friars of St. Francis. Truly might Ricold of Montecroce remark,[4] ' 'Tis worthy of the grateful remembrance of all Christian people that just at the time when God sent forth into the Eastern parts of the world the Tartars to slay and to be slain, He also sent forth into the West His faithful and blessed servants Dominic and Francis, to enlighten, instruct and build up the Faith.' [5]

Of these friars one of the most intrepid and attractive is John of Monte Corvino, first papal legate to, and afterwards Archbishop of, Peking, who, when nearly fifty years of age, set out to take the gospel into India and China, the first Latin Christian to leave us a picture of India and St. Thomas' shrine, where he spent a year, and the true founder of the

---

[1] On Pascal of Vittoria and the Central Asian Mission see Beazley, op. cit., iii, pp. 235–50. There was also a Dominican Bishop of Samarcand in 1330.

[2] The most important accounts of Cathay by European travellers during this period are collected and translated in *Cathay and the Way Thither*, ed. Sir Henry Yule (2nd ed. revised by H. Cordier, Hakluyt Soc., 1913–16), 4 vols.

[3] See Beazley, op. cit., iii, p. 480, and Heyd, op. cit., ii, p. 242.

[4] For a list of such references see Yule's introduction to *Cathay and the Way Thither*, i, pp. 170–1.

[5] Quoted by Yule, ibid., i, p. 155.

Latin Church in China. Of his labours in Cathay we know from two letters, written in 1305 and 1306 respectively, which he sent home by some of the many Tartar envoys, who were continually passing to and fro between the Great Khan in Cathay and the Ilkhan of Persia ; and his second letter is addressed to the friars of the Persian mission. In the first he describes how he had laboured alone in Cathay for eleven years, until two years previously a German friar from Cologne had joined him ; how he had failed to convert the Great Khan himself, but had won over a great Nestorian prince named George, of whose son he was godfather, and who had built him a new church twenty days' journey from Peking. He himself had built in Peking a church with a bell tower and three bells ; moreover, he had bought 150 pagan boys, between seven and eleven years of age, had baptised them and taught them Greek and Latin, and had trained a number of them as a choir, so that the Great Khan himself delighted to hear them chanting. He had translated the New Testament and the Psalter into the language and character most generally used among the Tartars. He begs for news of home, for service books and above all for comrades to be sent to help him by the land road across Asia, where they could travel with the imperial letter carriers. ' I myself am grown old and grey, more with toil and trouble than with years, for I am not more than 58.'

The next year he sent another letter to the Persian friars, reporting the progress of his new church. The land had been bought for him by Master Peter of Lucolongo, ' a faithful Christian man and a great merchant,' who had joined him in Tabriz at the very beginning of his journey and had dwelt with him all these years in India and Peking ; a mute inglorious Marco Polo, whose own story we would fain have heard. The site was but the width of the street from the Khan's own palace, and on it had already sprung up a chapel and courts, offices and houses, ' and I tell you,' says the good friar, ' it is thought a perfect marvel by all the people who came from the city and elsewhere . . . and when they see our new building and the red cross planted aloft, and us in our chapel with all decorum chanting the service, they wonder more than ever. When we are singing, his Majesty the Cham can hear our voices in his chamber, and this wonderful fact is spread far and wide among the heathen . . . And I have a place in the Cham's court and a regular entrance and seat assigned me as legate of our lord the Pope, and the Cham honours me above all other prelates, whatever be their titles. And although his Majesty the Cham has heard much of the Court of Rome and the state of the Latin world, he desires greatly to see envoys arriving from that region.' [1]

This letter also reached the West safely and came to the knowledge of the Pope, who in 1307 created Monte Corvino Archbishop of Cambaluc and sent out to him three suffragans, followed by three more in 1312, all of them Franciscans from Italy. The first three became successively bishops of Zaiton, and one of them, Andrew of Perugia, wrote a letter in 1326 to his mother-house, which gives an interesting picture of the Latin Church in that city. A fine cathedral had been built there by a rich Armenian lady, and Andrew himself had built a handsome church and convent in a grove outside the city, with a fine lodging ' fit for any prelate'. ' I know none among all the convents of our province,' he says, ' to be compared with it in elegance and other amenities.' He was supported by an imperial dole, the value of which amounted to 100 golden florins a year, ' according to the estimate of the Genoese merchants ' (an interesting reference).[2]

But two years before he wrote the letter in which he records these things there arrived in China a far more important traveller from our point of view, to wit, Friar Oderic of Pordenone, who has left us what is perhaps the second best travel book of the period, second only to Marco Polo, and superior to Marco Polo in its personal note. Oderic went by the long sea route from Ormuz to Canton, stopping en route in India, Ceylon, Sumatra, Java, and Borneo. From Canton he went by land to Zaiton and on to Kinsai, Jamzai (Yangchow) and Menzu (Ningpo), and by the Grand Canal to Cambaluc, his companion during a part of his journey being an Irish friar named James. He spent three years in Cambaluc and returned home by a land route, which apparently included a visit to Tibet and Lhassa, of which

---

[1] For his letter see *Cathay and the Way Thither*, iii, pp. 45–58.
[2] See ibid., pp. 71–5.

he gives a vague but interesting account. He describes
Canton, ' a city as big as three Venices and all Italy has not
the amount of craft that this one city hath,' and speaks also
of the immense number of junks in the other cities of Southern
China, adding ' indeed it is something hard to believe when
you hear of, or even see, the vast scale of the shipping in these
parts'. Of this ' noble province of Manzi ' he says, ' I made
diligent inquiry from Christians, Saracens, idolaters and from
all the Great Khan's officers, and they all told me, with
one consent, as it were, that the province of Manzi hath
2,000 great cities, cities, I mean, of such magnitude that neither
Treviso nor Vicenza would be entitled to be numbered
among them. Indeed in that country the number of people
is so great that among us here it would be deemed incredible ;
and in many parts I have seen the population more dense
than the crowds you see at Venice on Ascension day. And
the land hath great store of bread, of wine, of rice, of flesh
and of fish of sorts, and of all manner of victuals whatever
that are used by mankind. And all the people of this
country are traders and artificers, and no man ever seeketh
alms, however poor he be, as long as he can do anything
with his own hands to help himself ; but those who are fallen
into indigence and infirmity are well looked after and
provided with necessities. The men, as to their bodily
aspect, are comely enough, but colourless, having beards
of long straggling hairs like mousers (cats, I mean). And
as for the women, they are the most beautiful in the world.'

He describes Zaiton, a city ' twice as great as Bologna ' ;
and the two houses of Franciscan friars there, and also the
beautiful Kinsai, of which he says : ' If anyone should desire
to tell of all the vastness and great marvels of this city,
a good quire of stationery (*bonus quaternus stationis*) would
not hold the matter, I trow, for 'tis the greatest and noblest
city and the finest for merchandise that the world
containeth.' [1] He gives a delightful picture also of Cambaluc

---

[1] In Ramusio's edition (1583) his account includes the interesting
phrase : ' 'Tis the greatest city in the whole world, so great, indeed,
that I should scarcely venture to tell of it, but that I have met at Venice
people in plenty who have been there.' It is not improbable that Oderic
should have met Venetian merchants who had visited Kinsai, but it is
impossible to say whether Ramusio invented the phrase or took it from
a lost early MS.

and the Great Khan's court there, and he materially contributes to our knowledge in several directions by noting things left unnoticed by Marco Polo, for instance the Chinese custom of binding the feet of their women, the wearing of long finger-nails by the men, and the practice of fishing with cormorants. It is plain enough that he left his heart behind him in China, for he ends his book with the words, ' As for me, from day to day I prepare myself to return to those countries, in which I am content to die, if it pleaseth Him from whom all good things do come.' But this good thing was not to come to him and he died in Italy.

His tales were written down by a brother friar (' just as he told his story, so friar William wrote it '), and they are followed by a testimony to the accuracy of the transcript by a third friar, who adds such a charming anecdote that it is impossible to refrain from quoting it, more especially as it possibly gives us our last picture of the saintly Archbishop John of Monte Corvino : [1] ' I, friar Marchesino of Bassano of the Order of Minorites, desire to say that I heard the preceding relation from the aforesaid Friar Oderic when he was still living ; and I heard a good deal more, which he has not set down. Among other stories which he told, this was one. He related that once upon a time, when the Great Khan was on his journey from Sandu to Cambalech, he with four other Minor friars was sitting under the shade of a tree by the side of the road, along which the Khan was about to pass, and one of the brethren was a bishop. So when the Khan began to draw near, the bishop put on his episcopal robes and took a cross and fastened it to the end of a staff, so as to raise it aloft ; and then those four began to chant with a loud voice the hymn ' *Veni Creator Spiritus !* ' And then the Great Khan, hearing the sound thereof, asked what it meant, and those four barons who go beside him replied that it was four of the Frank Rabbans. So the Khan called them to him and the Bishop thereupon, taking the cross from the staff, presented it to the Khan to kiss. Now, at the time he was lying down, but as soon as he saw the cross he sat up, and doffing the cap that he wore, kissed the cross in most reverent and humble manner. Now, the rule

[1] But the Bishop referred to may be Andrew of Perugia or one of the other friars who became Bishop of Zaiton.

and custom of that court is that no one shall venture to come into the Khan's presence empty-handed; so Friar Oderic, having with him a small dish full of apples, presented that as their offering to the Great Khan, and he took two of the apples and ate a piece of one of them, whilst he kept the other in his hand, and so he went his way. Now, it is clear enough from this that the Khan himself had some savour of the Catholic faith, as he well might, through the Minor friars who dwelt at his court continually. And as for the cap which he doffed so reverently before the cross, I have heard Friar Oderic say that it was a mass of pearl and gems and was worth more than the whole march of Treviso.' [1]

Europe was not to have much further news of Cathay. In 1328 John of Monte Corvino died, and ten years later an embassy from the Great Khan and from a group of Christian Alan princes appeared at the papal court, asking for the appointment of a new legate. It was accompanied by one Andrew the Frank, who is possibly the Andrew of Perugia, whom we met as Bishop of Zaiton. In reply an important papal embassy was sent out in charge of John Marignolli, an aristrocratic Franciscan of Florence, who has left us the last European account of the Far East at this period, inappropriately embedded in a history of Bohemia, which he wrote after his return. He took the overland route and spent four years in China, returning by sea from Zaiton and spending some time in Southern India on the way. He found the Tartars and Alans venerating the dead Archbishop as a saint in Peking and the Latin mission flourishing exceedingly. At Zaiton, too, he describes the three great churches of the Franciscans, and adds the interesting information that they had founded there a *fondaco* and bath house for the use of European merchants, an amazing testimony to the frequency with which Western traders (mainly no doubt Genoese) visited the great Chinese port.[2] After his departure no more is heard of the Latin mission; the Pope appointed Archbishops to it from time to time in later years, but, so far as the active cure of souls was concerned, to be made Archbishop of Peking

[1] For these passages and the rest of Oderic's account, see *Cathay and the Way Thither* (1913 ed.), vol. ii, *passim*.
[2] See ibid., iii, pp. 209–69.

must have been analagous to applying for the Chiltern Hundreds, since it was no longer possible for the Archbishop to reach his See.

There are surely few episodes in history more remarkable and more interesting than these years, when an Italian archbishop held sway in Peking, when Genoese merchants had a *fondaco* at Zaiton and chaffered in the ports of India, when Franciscan friars set up convents in the towns of Persia and China, and mission stations in Turkestan, and when merchants and missionaries regularly took the caravan roads across Central Asia, or sailed in junks through the Indian Ocean and among the Spice Islands.

It was indeed remarkable, but the reason that it is remarked less than it would seem to deserve lies in the fact that it was strictly an episode. For the gallant missions and the direct trade came to an end by the middle of the fourteenth century, and the great black curtain rolled down again, cutting all Europe from Asia and confining Europeans once again to the termini of the trade routes. In the battle of Islam and the Cross for the soul of Tartary it was Islam which won, as Islam to this day so often wins in dealing with less civilized peoples. Gradually the whole of Kipchak and Central Asia became converted, and shut off the land route which had been so *sichurissimo* in Pegolotti's day. So, too, the Ilkhans of Persia (having tried in vain for half a century to galvanize Europe into doing something more than talk about a common crusade against the Mamluks) finally embraced Islam in 1316, and though they at first retained their old Mongol tolerance, the Persian vestibule was all but closed again by the middle of the fourteenth century, and the Tartar dynasty itself fell before the end.[1] Finally, in 1368–70, a revolution drove out the Tartar dynasty in China and replaced it by a native dynasty, the Mings, who resumed the indigenous anti-foreign policy of the Chinese, so that even had Europeans been able to get to Peking and the port towns, they would not

---

[1] It should be observed, however, that occasional Europeans continued to reach India by this route during the fifteenth century. Towards 1440 the Venetian Nicolo Conti visited Malabar and may even have gone to China, of which he gives several accurate particulars, and in 1483 another Venetian and a Milanese crossed Persia and sailed from Ormuz to Cambay. Grousset, op. cit., iii, p. 137.

have been received there.   The conquests of Timur completed a process already almost complete before he came.

That great conqueror might, indeed, had he lived to complete his project of subduing China, have re-established something analagous to the empire of Kublai Khan, though it would have been an ardently Muslim empire and thus probably unfriendly to direct access by Christian merchants to the East.   But he pillaged Baghdad and Shiraz and in his campaigns, to render safe his own Trans-Oxianian realm and to make Samarcand the greatest trading centre of the East, he ravaged the country to the North and destroyed Tana, Sarai, Astrakhan, Urgenje and Almalik, and fatally interrupted the caravan route on which they were stages, while his death threw Higher Asia into an anarchy which still further cut off West from East.   Two European travellers have, indeed, left us accounts of Eastern journeys in the time of Timur. One, the Spaniard Clavijo, was sent on a mission to the conqueror's court by Henry of Castile in 1403, and travelled by way of Trebizond, Tabriz, Sultaniyah (a splendid mart, to which he notes that the traders of the West, 'aye, of Venice and of Genoa,' were still able to make their way from Kaffa, Trebizond or Syria), Nishapur, Meshed and the Oxus to Samarcand.   He has left an extraordinarily vivid picture of Timur and his court and of the prosperity of Samarcand, and from a camel driver, who had come with the Peking caravan of 800 camels to the city, he learned something of Cathay. The other traveller of this age is Schiltberger, a German taken captive and enslaved first by the Ottoman Sultan Bajazet, then by Bajazet's conqueror Timur, and then by other Tartar princes, whose *Reisebuch* recounts his enforced wanderings (1396–1425) in the lands of the Levant and Black Sea and Trans-Oxiana, leaving among other things a very good picture of Kaffa, and having a peculiar interest of its own because, alone among the medieval travel books, it is the work of an under-dog, a poor slave who picked up his knowledge from under-dogs like himself.[1]

But Clavijo and Schiltberger are truly, as Professor Beazley calls them, anachronisms.   They are writing the sad epilogue to a splendid age of travel which has passed away ;

[1] For Clavijo and Schiltberger see Beazley, op. cit., iii, pp. 332–81. The works of both have been published by the Hakluyt Society.

China and India were hid from them; they penetrated no
further than Samarcand along the once open trade route
and must pick up from camel drivers and the dregs of Timur's
camp their knowledge of the great worlds which lay beyond.
After Timur's death fanaticism ruled in Persia, anarchy in
Central Asia, an anti-foreign dynasty in China. So the East
was hidden once more from European eyes, and the teeming
peoples, the crowding junks, the rich civilization, were no
more than a legend to incite the adventurers of a later age,
when they sought the road to India and Cathay again.
For the closing of the routes and the triumph of the Turks
threw Europeans into an increasing dependence upon the
Egyptian road and the terminus at Alexandria, beyond
which they might never pass. Useless now to dream of taking
the road for Ormuz at Lajazzo or Trebizond; useless to
gather dragomen and set out from Kaffa or Tana. If they
would reach the lands of which Marco Polo wrote, they must
seek a new road, not by the East but by the West, not by
land but by sea. The failure of the great Tartar epic is
intimately connected with the epics of Vasco da Gama and
Columbus.

But looking back upon this episode, so marvellous, even
if it was so brief, does it not bear witness to the injustice of
many commonly received historical judgments? History
gives to the fifteenth century the name of the 'Age of
Discovery', because its discoveries were never lost. But
are Vasco da Gama and Columbus himself more remarkable
than Marco Polo, or than those half forgotten friars and wholly
forgotten merchants, who took the land and sea roads to
India and Cathay in the century between 1245 and 1345?
History, again, commonly represents the Tartars as mere
barbarians, unintelligent and savage ravagers like the Huns,
seeking to tear down the painfully reared civilization of Islam
and the West, and the man in the street has gone even further
than history; the phrase 'to catch a Tartar' has become
proverbial.

The truth is that popular opinion persists in remembering
only the early onslaughts of the Tartars, the first period of
destruction under the four Great Khans, Chinghiz, Ogotay,
Kuyuk and Mangu (1206–57), and erects into an historical
verdict the objurgations of Muslim or Christian writers like

Ibnu'l-Athir and Matthew Paris, writing under the stress of the first invasions, and often enough writing from hearsay.[1] The honest Matthew never saw a Tartar in his life, nor was Ibnu'l-Athir a witness of the horrors which he so vividly describes. It is true that the early invasions were orgies of the most barbarous slaughter, but is it fair to pass judgment on the Tartars on the witness of these alone ? After all what were the Europeans of the day but descendants of those Germanic barbarians, whose first invasions were described, and deserved to be described, in precisely the same terms by the Roman provincials upon whom they fell? No conquering people can fairly be condemned on the period of its conquests and by the mouths of the conquered. It is in the subsequent period of settled government that it proves its true greatness or baseness, and few imperial nations of to-day would care for any other criterion. The Tartars deserve to be judged, not in their nomad state and in the first age of the invasions, but as they were when settled in their four great Khanates. They deserve to be judged as a people so tolerant that they welcomed the representatives of all religions, Christian friar, Buddhist lama, Jewish rabbi, Muslim doctor and Mongol medicine-man, equally at their courts, and were regarded by Christians not as ' the worst enemies of human civilization ' but as potential allies against Islam. The fact that the alliance did not eventuate was due not to the Tartars but to the internecine bickering of Christian Popes and monarchs. They deserve to be judged as the one political power under whom the Armenians, always from that day to this persecuted by the Turks and never from that day to this helped by the Christians, enjoyed a momentary tranquillity, a respite in the long crucifixion of their history. They deserve to be judged as the power whose policy towards commercial intercourse between nations was so enlightened that they welcomed traders, lowered dues and protected caravans and roads throughout their dominions, maintaining free intercourse over the length and breadth of Asia, so that Professor

[1] Matthew Paris' famous account of the Tartars in the Chronicle, under the year 1240, may be found conveniently translated in *Matthew Paris' English History*, trans. J. A. Giles (Bohn's Antiq. Lib., 1852), i, pp. 312–14. Ibnu'l-Athir's account, under the years 1220–1 and 1230–1 is translated in E. G. Browne, *A Literary History of Persia* (1906), ii, pp. 427–31.

Beazley can with justice call this period ' the age of the nomad peace ' and Sir Henry Howorth, speaking of this marvellous bringing together of the peoples of West and East can write ' I have no doubt myself . . . that the art of printing, the mariner's compass, firearms and a great many details of social life, were not discovered in Europe, but imported by means of Mongol influence from the furthest East '.

Indeed, the question whether the Tartars were, or were not, the mere enemies of civilization is most properly answered by the consideration of what befel the old civilizations of Persia and China after the establishment of their rule, and it is a remarkable fact that, once the destruction of the first age of conquest was over, both countries were able not only to preserve their characteristic civilizations but to create new wisdom and beauty under Tartar domination. The great scholar and lover of Islam, Professor Browne, describes the Mongol invasion as ' one of the most dreadful calamities which ever befel the human race ' [1]; but he has to devote a whole volume to Persian literature alone under Tartar dominion, and his final judgment is that, allowing for the sufferings of Persia during the invasions, ' the period of Mongol ascendency (1265–1337) . . . was wonderfully rich in literary achievements.' Nor is it after all so wonderful, for the Ilkhans encouraged the study of the natural sciences and of history and were by no means indifferent to poetry. ' Even Hulagu Khan, the destroyer of Baghdad and deadly foe of Islam,' says Professor Browne ' was the patron of two of the greatest Persian writers of this period, the astronomer Nasiru'd-Din of Tus and the historian 'Ata Malik of Juwayn, author of the " History of the Conqueror of the World " i.e. Chingiz Khan. Two other historians, 'Abdu'llah b. Fadlu 'llah of Shiraz, better known as *Wassaf-i-Hadrat* and the Wazir Rashidu'd-Din Fadlu'llah, both of whom flourished in the reign of Ghazan Khan (1295–1304) must certainly be ranked among the greatest of those who have written in the Persian language on this important branch of knowledge. Persian literature, indeed, in the narrower sense, can hardly be said to have suffered permanently from the Mongol invasion,

[1] E. G. Browne, *Hist. of Persian Literature under Tartar Dominion*, 1265–1502 (Cambridge, 1920), p. 4.
[2] Ibid., p. 17.

since three of the greatest and most famous poets of
Persia, Sa'di of Shiraz, Faridu'd-Din 'Attar, and Jalalu'd-Din
Rumi were contemporary with it, and many other most
famous poets were subsequent to it '.[1] Moreover, not only
literature but also art and architecture flourished under the
Tartars. It was during their period that the first illustrated
books appeared in Persia, and the influence of the close
relations which existed between China and Persia under their
rule is shown in the blue and shining tiles of the Persian
mosques of this period, and the carpets in which clouds and
golden pheasants and dragons of China are mingled with
purely Persian designs.[2] Similarly under the Tartar or
Yüan dynasty in China, literature and the arts flourished
with a brilliance worthy of the great Chinese dynasties which
had gone before. In literature the novel and the drama both
date from this period, and in art a galaxy of famous painters,
among whom the most eminent was Chao Meng-fu, adorned
the age, many of them rising to high office under the Yüan
emperors.[3] Moreover, just as Chinese influences appear in the
Persian art of the period, Persian influences are manifest in
Yüan potteries, which are justly prized for their beauty, and
the art of enamelling was introduced into China by Persians.

But the adaptability which the Tartars showed to the older
and more advanced civilizations which fell under their sway
is perhaps most remarkably manifested in the rulers whom
they produced. Who is not conscious of ' that humane
great monarch's golden look ' which seems to shed a glow
over Marco Polo's page ? Kublai Khan was a king
worthy to rank among the wisest of his age, not merely a
great conqueror but a great ruler. In Persia the Tartars,
but three generations after the conquest, produced the great
Ilkhan Ghazan, reformer of administration and justice,

---

[1] E. G. Browne, *Literary History of Persia* (1906), ii, p. 443. He adds,
however, that the destruction of Baghdad as the metropolis of Islam
struck a fatal blow at the semblance of unity among the Muhammadan
nations and also at the prestige and status in Persia of the Arabic
language.

[2] See some suggestive remarks on this subject in Grousset, op. cit.,
iii, pp. 146–52.

[3] Among others were Li K'an, Kao K'o-kung, Huang Kung-wang,
Wang Mêng, Ni Tsan, Wu Chên and Yen Hui. See Giles, *Introd. to
the Hist. of Chinese Pictorial Art* (2nd. ed., Shanghai, 1918), ch. vi,
passim.

protector of the peasantry, promoter of science, learning, and architecture, who made Rashidu'd-Din his chief minister, received envoys from China, India, Egypt, Spain, England, and many other nations at his court, and was mourned throughout Persia when he died. To crown all, the Tartars had a share in producing one of the greatest lines of monarchs who have ruled in the world's history, the Great Mughals of India, for Baber's mother was a Tartar princess, the last descendant of the Chagatai Khans, and his father, the King of Ferghana, was descended from the third son of Timur. If we would seek a European parallel to the Tartars, both in their early barbarity and in their subsequent power of adapting themselves to higher civilizations, it is perhaps to be found in the Northmen, against whom men prayed, when first they appeared as Viking raiders, ' From the fury of the Northmen good Lord deliver us ! ' and who subsequently, as Normans, built up great civilizations in Normandy, England and Sicily. But the Normans were more fortunate ; they were not an episode ; they survived, and in history nothing succeeds like success.

The century 1245 to 1345 was indeed an heroic age in the history of travel and an epoch in the relations of East and West. But while we give our wonder and admiration to William of Rubruck, Marco Polo, John of Monte Corvino and the other travellers who first made Asia known to Europe in this brief and marvellous episode, let us not forget that it was solely and entirely due to the Tartars that they were able to do so, and let us modify in our own minds, if not indeed reverse, the unjust verdict by which history has too often ungratefully condemned them. For if the world had not caught a Tartar in the thirteenth century, it would have been the poorer for a legacy of imperishable courage and romance.

CHAPTER VIII

i. " TRAVELLERS' TALES OF WONDER AND
IMAGINATION "

ii. EUROPEAN TRAVELLERS IN AFRICA IN THE
MIDDLE AGES

By Professor ARTHUR PERCIVAL NEWTON

AS one surveys the world of the earlier middle ages, one
cannot fail to note the comparatively narrow area that
was clear and familiar to Latin Christendom and how it was
hemmed in on all sides by the mists of the unknown. Its
western shores were bounded by the dangers of the
unnavigable ocean, the north was closed with ice and the
regions of perpetual darkness, to the east there lay the vast
spaces of the steppes, dreaded as the lands whence again and
again for 1,000 years there had surged forth devastating
hordes of Scyths and Alans, Huns and Tartars to sweep down
upon the peoples of Christendom with fire and sword. Only
southward could men look out upon dangers that they understood from the lands of the infidel, but even there only the
fringe of the Muslim lands was seen clearly, and beyond them
again the haze closed down once more upon the torrid sands
of the unknown desert. Civilized men seemed to live in the
one bright spot in a shrouded world and, lacking knowledge,
they imagined around them wonders of all kinds.

Our concern in these pages is mainly with the authentic
travels of the time, but these cannot appear in their true
setting unless we say something also of the marvels that
abound in the " travellers' tales " of the thirteenth and
fourteenth centuries and that had a compelling influence
upon the explorers of the Great Age. In an earlier chapter
reference was made to the *Travels* of " Sir John de Mandeville "

as illustrating the general equipment of geographical ideas of the late fourteenth century, but the extracts there given were so reasonable in character as to fail to do justice to the extraordinary character of the work. Though achieving great popularity in its own day and long accepted as an authentic and valuable record of travel, we now know that it was a spurious compilation of a citizen of Liège, one Jehan d'Outremuse, fathered upon a fictitious English knight " Sire Jehan de Mandeville " much as Swift invented the imaginary Lemuel Gulliver to convey his satires. The stories with which the book is filled were culled from every kind of source from the authentic narratives of Friar Oderic of Pordenone or John de Piano Carpine to the ancient fables of Pliny and Solinus collected from the encyclopædic works of Vincent of Beauvais. The result is hopelessly inconsistent with any clear system of geography, but it peopled the mists surrounding Christendom with astonishing wonders such as the average reader in any age loves, and there were no means available for the disentangling of the true wonders from the false. Both made an equal appeal and had an equal aspect of reality.

Let us compare for example the accounts of some real and some unreal beasts. " In the isle of Taprobane be great hills of gold that pissemyres [i.e. ants] keep full diligently, and they fine the pured gold and cast away the unpured. And these pissemyres be great as hounds so that no man dare come to those hills, for the pissemyres would assail him and devour him anon, so that no man may get of that gold but by great sleight. And, therefore, when it is great heat, the pissemyres rest them from prime of the day unto noon. And then the folk of the country take camels, dromedaries and horses, and other beasts, and go thither, and charge them in all haste that they may . . . In that desert be many wild men that be hideous to look on, for they be horned and they speak nought, but they grunt as pigs. And there be many popinjays that they yclepe psitakes [1] in their language. And they speak of their proper nature and salute men that go through the deserts, and speak to them as pertly as though it were a man. And they that speak well have a large tongue and have five toes upon a foot. And there be also of other

[1] psittaci = parrots.

manner, that have but three toes upon a foot, and they speak not or but little, for they cannot but cry. In that country and by all Ind be great plenty of ' cokodrilles', that is a manner of a long serpent, and in the night they dwell in the water and on the day upon the land in rocks and in caves. And they eat no meat in all the winter, but they lie as in a dream, as do the serpents. These serpents slay men and they eat them weeping. And when they eat, they move the overjaw and nought the nether jaw, and they have no tongue. There also be many beasts that be yclept ' orafles ',[1] in Araby they be yclept ' gerfaunts ' that is a beast pomely or spotted, that is little more high than a steed. But he hath a neck a twenty cubits long. And his crupper and his tail is as of a hart and he may look over a great high house. And there be also in that country many ' camles ',[2] and he liveth by the air and he eateth nought nor drinketh nought at no time. And he changeth his colour oftentime. For men see him often now in one colour and now in another colour, and he may change him into all manner colours that him list, save only into red and white . . . And here be also of other beasts as great or more greater than is a destrier,[3] and men yclept them ' loeranez ' and some yclept them ' odenthos '. And they have a black head and three long horns trenchant in the front, sharp as a sword and the body is slender ; and he is a full felonous beast, and he chaseth and slayeth the ' oliphant ' ".[4]

It was as impossible for the medieval reader to distinguish the true from the false in such tales as these, as it would be for ourselves unless by experience we had learned to do so. The " odenthos " is no more incredible and " pissemyres " very little more than are the giraffe and the chameleon, but others of Mandeville's tales must have been a hard test for even the most credulous medieval reader. As an example we may quote the story of the growing diamonds, a hardy survival from the fables of antiquity. " Men find many time hard diamonds in a mass that cometh out of gold when they pure it and fine it out of the mine when men break

---

[1] Giraffes.
[2] Chameleons.
[3] War horse.
[4] *Mandeville's Travels*, ed. Hamelius, i, pp. 192, 193, 200.

M

that mass in small pieces. And sometime it happeneth that men find some as great as a pea and some less and they be all as hard as those of Ind. And albeit that men find good diamonds in Ind, yet natheless men find them more commonly upon the rocks in the sea and upon hills where the mine of gold is. And they grow many together, one little, another great . . . and they be square and pointed of their own kind both above and beneath without working of man's hand. And they grow together male and female, and they be nourished with the dew of heaven; and they engender children commonly and bring forth small children that multiply and grow all the year. I have often times assayed that if a man keep them with a little of the rock, and with the May dew oft sithes they shall grow every year and the small will wax great. For right as the fine pearl congealeth and waxeth great of the dew of heaven, so doeth the very diamond. And right as the pearl of his own kind taketh roundness, right so the diamond by virtue of God taketh squareness." [1]

In the mists of the Western Ocean, too, the middle ages imagined marvels. There lay islands that eluded those who sought them, but none of the stories of the geographers were more persistent or more generally accepted. The most celebrated of these islands were those of Saint Brandan, the Seven Cities, Brasil and Antilia, and again and again during the fifteenth and even the sixteenth centuries grants for their discoveries were sought and obtained from the Portuguese monarchs. It was said that in the year 565 after Christ the Irish Saint Brandan came with his ship to a certain island in the Atlantic where he beheld many marvels, and after living there for seven years he returned to his own country. Though it could never be found again, its existence was firmly believed, and it was marked on even the most scientific maps for centuries. As late as 1755 St. Brandan's Isle was placed 5° to the west of the Canaries, and maps even of the nineteenth century can be found recording it. Honorius of Autun in his geographical treatise of A.D. 1130 described it thus : "There is in the Ocean a certain isle agreeable and fertile beyond all others, unknown to men but discovered by chance and then sought for without anyone being able to find it again and so called the "Lost Isle". It was, so

[1] Ibid., i, 105.

they say, the island whither once upon a time St. Brandan came." [1]

The story of the island of the Seven Cities was told by medieval writers with great wealth of detail and even more firmly believed. At the time of the conquest of Spain by the Moors—it was said—after the defeat and disappearance of King Roderick, seven bishops took ship with their followers and sailed out into the ocean. After a long voyage they landed on an unknown island and there, having burned their ships, they settled. Each of them built himself a dwelling place for himself and his flock, and so the island came to be called the " Island of the Seven Cities ". Even in the time of Prince Henry the Navigator the tradition was fully credited and a Portuguese captain came to the Prince with a story that he had found the island, but had been forced by its inhabitants to flee because they refused to have any communication with the ancient fatherland. " The prince " says Ferdinand Columbus, " blamed [the captain and his sailors] severely, and ordered them to return to the island, to stay there for a time and to come again and report to him what they had seen. The men, struck with terror, betook them to their ship and sailed away and never appeared again in Portugal. Among other details [of their adventure] they related that their cabin boys who had brought away from the beach of the island some sand to clean their cooking pots, found that that sand was two-thirds composed of fine gold." [2]

Among the islands said to be situated in the far Western Ocean many medieval writers placed the Terrestrial Paradise, and this legend had so much influence on the minds of the first explorers of the new lands that it is of some importance. The idea of such a region is constant in Christian writers from the time of the early fathers Tertullian and St. Ambrose through Isidore of Seville down to Bonaventura and Thomas Aquinas, but though they agree upon many of the aspects of such a paradise they differ widely as to its situation. Cosmas, writing in the sixth century, tells us that

---

[1] P. Gaffarel, *Histoire de la découverte de l'Amérique avant Colomb* (Paris, 1892), i, 205.

[2] *History of the Life and Actions of Adm. Christopher Columbus written by his son T. Ferdinand Columbus* in Churchill's *Voyages*, (London, 1732).

" The earth is divided into two parts by the sea that is called Ocean ; the one is the part that we live in and the other beyond the Ocean is that which is joined to heaven. Men lived in that land before the Deluge ; there also Paradise is situated ".[1]

The writer of Mandeville places the Terrestrial Paradise so far in the east that it is also at the extremest end of the west, for, as he says, " The Lord God made the earth all round in the mid place of the firmament." He does not claim to have been there, but professes to describe it as he has heard say of wise men of old. " Paradise terrestre, as wise men say, is the highest place of earth that is in all the world, and it is so high that it toucheth nigh to the circle of the moon, there as the moon maketh her turn. For she is so high that the flood of Noë might not come to her that would have covered all the earth of the world all about and above and beneath save paradise alone . . . In the most high place of paradise, even in the middle place, is a well that casteth out the four floods that run by divers lands . . . And by the rivers may no man go, for the water runneth so rudely and so sharply because that it cometh down so outrageously from the high places above, that it runneth in so great waves that no ship may not row nor sail against it. And the water roareth so and maketh so huge noise and so great tempest that no man hear other in the ship, though he cried with all the craft that he could with the highest voice that he might." [2]   Again the pseudo-Mandeville tells us in another passage [3] that the Fountain of Eternal Youth springs from the Terrestial Paradise. " There is a fair well and a great that hath odour and savour of all spices ; and at every hour of the day he changeth his odour and his savour diversely. And whoso drinketh three times fasting of that water of that well, he is whole of all manner sickness that he hath, and they that dwell there and drink often of that well they never have sickness, and they seem always young . . . Some men yclepe it the well of youth . . . and men say that that well cometh out of paradise and therefore it is so virtuous."

It would be of great interest to explore the persistence

---

[1] *Cosmas*, ed. McCrindle (Hakluyt Society, 1897), p. 33.
[2] *Mandeville's Travels*, i, 202–3.
[3] Ibid., i, 113.

of the ideas of the Terrestrial Paradise and the Fountain
of Eternal Youth in the minds of explorers like Ponce de Leon
who sought the fountain in Florida at the beginning of the
sixteenth century, and the sailors of the mid-eighteenth who
poetically spoke of the island of Otaheite as *Le Paradis
Terrestre*. But it would be beyond our scope and the
quotation of a characteristic passage representing the typical
medieval cosmogony of Columbus must suffice. His third
voyage having resulted in his discovery of continental land
he wrote to King Ferdinand and Queen Isabella on his return
to Hispaniola in October, 1498, to tell them of what he had
found. In the course of this letter from which we have
already quoted,[1] occurs the following remarkable passage :—

"I have come to [the] conclusion respecting the earth,
that it is not round as they describe, but of the form of a pear,
which is very round except where the stalk grows, at which
part it is most prominent, or like a round ball, upon one part
of which is a prominence like a woman's nipple, this protrusion
being the highest and nearest the sky, situated under the
equinoctial line, and at the eastern extremity of this sea
[i.e. the Caribbean] . . . I do not suppose that the
earthly paradise is in the form of a rugged mountain, as the
descriptions of it have made it appear, but that it is on the
summit of the spot, which I have described as being in the
form of the stalk of a pear ; the approach to it from a distance
must be by a constant and gradual ascent ; but I believe
that no one could ever reach the top . . . From the gulf
to which I gave the name of the Gulf of Pearls [2] the water
runs constantly with great impetuosity towards the east,
and this is the cause why there is so fierce a turmoil from the
fresh water encountering the water of the sea . . . I
think that the water may proceed from the paradise, though
it be far off, and that stopping at the place which I have just
left, it forms a lake. There are great indications of this being
the terrestrial paradise, for its site coincides with the opinion
of the holy and wise theologians St. Isidore, Bede, Strabus,
the master of scholastic history, St. Ambrose and Scotus,
all of whom agree that the earthly paradise is in the east.
And, moreover, the other evidences agree with the supposition,

---

[1] Chapter I, p. 16.
[2] The modern Gulf of Paria.

for I have never either read or heard of fresh water coming in so large a quantity, in close conjunction with the water of the sea ; the idea is also corroborated by the blandness of the temperature . . . That the islands [in the seas] should possess the most costly productions is to be accounted for by the mild temperature, which comes to them from heaven, since these are the most elevated parts of the world." [1]

To the men of the middle ages as to the ancients the continent most abounding in marvels was Africa, and a problem of perennial interest was to account satisfactorily for the regular waxing and waning of the waters of the Nile. Mandeville connects the river with the earthly paradise and gives to it a most extraordinary course, showing how little sure knowledge there was in his time of the lands of the Moors. " This river cometh running from Paradys terrestre between the deserts of Ind and after it sinks into land and runneth long time many great countries under earth. And after it goeth out under an high hill that men yclepe Aloth that is between Ind and Ethiope . . . and after it environeth all Ethiope and Morekane and goeth all along from the land of Egypt into the city of Alisandre to the end of Egypt and there it falleth into the sea." [2]

Libya and Mauretania, the country of desert Africa, were above all to most Europeans the land of marvels, though we shall show later that some men in the Mediterranean cities held a real knowledge of those countries. To quote the fictions of Mandeville again. " Between the Red Sea and Ocean sea toward the south is the kingdom of Ethiope and of Libya the higher, the which land of Libya, that is to say Libya the low, that beginneth at the sea of Spain from thence where the pillars of Hercules be, and dureth unto anenst Egypt and toward Ethiope. In that country of Libya is the sea more high than the land, and it seemeth that it would cover the earth, and natheless yet it passeth not his marks . . . In that sea of Libya is no fish, for they may not live nor endure for the great heat of the sun, because that the water is evermore boiling for the great heat [3] . . .

---

[1] *Select letters of Columbus*, ed. R. H. Major (Hakluyt Society, 1870), pp. 134, 141–2, 144.
[2] *Mandeville's Travels*, i, 28.
[3] Cf. the ideas of Lambert as discussed in Chap. I *supra*.

The whole party meridional [of Africa] is yclept Moritania and the folk of that country be black . . . and they be yclept Moors. In that part is a well that in the day it is so cold that no man may drink thereof, and in the night it is so hot that no man may suffer his hand therein . . . In that country be folk that have but one foot and they go so blue that it is marvellous. And the foot is so large that it shadoweth all the body against the sun when they would lie and rest them." [1]

Mandeville abounds in descriptions of anatomical freaks, and much of his popularity may have been due to such strange fables, but he does not always commit himself to their exact geographical situation. " In [a certain] isle towards the south dwell folk of foul stature and of cursed kind that have no heads, and their eyes be in their shoulders. And their mouth is crooked as an horse shoe, and that is in the midst of their breast. And in another isle be folk that have the face all flat, all plain without nose and without mouth, but they have two small holes all round instead of their eyes, and their mouth is flat also without lips. And in another isle be folk of foul fashion and shape that have the lip above the mouth so great that when they sleep in the sun, they cover all the face with that lip." [2] Marvels such as these were the common stock in trade of popular medieval writers on geography, and ridiculous though they may be, they should not be entirely neglected in attempting to realize something of the attitude of mind of the travellers of the time, half critical and half credulous, but not wholly different from that of a later age which, having refused to accept the authentic pygmies and gorillas of Du Chaillu, accepted with hardly a qualm the " travellers tales " of Louis de Rougemont.

ii. European Travellers in Africa in the Middle Ages

When we turn from amusing fictions to examine whether Europeans had authentic knowledge of the interior of the lands beyond the Moors in the Middle Ages, we find that although it left little trace in literature and has only recently been recovered, some real information had been obtained.

[1] *Mandeville's Travels*, i, 96, 104.
[2] Ibid., i, 133–4.

Just as in the east political circumstances in the latter half of the thirteenth century threw open Central Asia to European travellers, especially Franciscan and Dominican friars, so about the same period, owing to Muslim toleration, they were able to penetrate for a time into North Africa. Under the dynasty of the Almohade emirs, who ruled over Morocco and Southern Spain in the twelfth century, many Christians were permitted to cross the Straits and settle in cities like Fez, Marrakesh, and Salli. Many Christian contingents served in the Moroccan armies and took part in the almost incessant civil wars. When the Almohades were defeated by the Berber tribe of the Beni Marin and the new dynasty of the Marinides was established, this policy of toleration was continued, especially under the enlightened Emir Yakub II. From 1225 onwards Franciscans and Dominicans co-operated in establishing Christian bishoprics in Morocco, and in 1256 we learn from the works of the missionary Humbert de Romans that the friars for several years, had been preaching in Arabic to the Moors.[1] There was some commerce also, and the dates and alum of the south of Morocco on the borders of the desert were carried in the thirteenth century as far north as the fairs of Bruges there to be exchanged for cloth and leather.

It was from the town of Sigilmessa beyond the main mass of the Atlas Mountains that the caravan routes passed out across the desert to the oases of the Sahara and the more fertile country of the Sudan far to the south. The first European who seems to have penetrated to these regions was an unnamed envoy of a certain cardinal of whom we learn from the writings of Raymond Lully at the end of the thirteenth century. The philosopher travelled much in North Africa in his efforts to convert the Moors and must have been familiar with many merchants engaged in the desert trade : though the *Blanquerna*, from which we derive our information, is an Utopian romance, M. de la Roncière believes that it contains passages describing events that actually occurred. Lully tells us that :—

[1] M. Ch. de la Roncière, the learned librarian of the Bibliotheque Nationale, has summed up the knowledge of Africa in the Middle Ages in his work *La Découverte de l'Afrique au Moyen Age*, 2 vols., (Cairo, 1924–5).

" It chanced that [one of the cardinal's messengers]
travelling to the south found a caravan of 6,000 camels
loaded with salt which left a town named Tabelbert [1] for the
country where the river of Damietta [i.e. the Nile] takes its
rise. The richness of that country was so great that he saw
all the loads of salt sold in fifteen days. The people there were
negroes and idolaters, leading a merry life and severely just.
Lying was punished with death. All their goods were held
in common. There was then an island in the middle of the
lake, and in the island a dragon [2] honoured by the sacrifices of
the natives and adored as god. The messenger went through
those lands, inquiring about the local customs and the density
of the population to the great astonishment of the people,
for he was a white man and a Christian; and in the memory
of man no Christian had ever before come into their country.
The messenger sent word by one of his squires and in writing
to the cardinal who had sent him forth, of all that has here been
said and many other things. The cardinal reported it to the
Pope and to his colleagues. Great was their disappointment
to learn that the dragon was adored as a god, and they devised
means to destroy the error in which those peoples lived." The
place where the caravan disposed of its salt " was in the
country of the south, in a region situated in the middle of the
sands near to a town named Gana. There there are numerous
idolatrous kings and princes who worship the sun and the stars
and birds and beasts. The inhabitants of those lands are
numerous ; they are of great stature and are negroes ". [3]

In an inscription attached to the map or portolan of
Giovanni di Carignano which was drawn about 1320 there is
further information about the Sahara that bears the stamp of
accuracy. The Berbers of the desert, it says, " go with their
mouths always covered. They pay no toll to the Saracens.
They are loyal merchants and receive the merchandise and
money of Sigilmessa to carry them on camel-back to Oualata [4]
and into Guinea. It takes them forty days to reach Oualata
through the desert. They carry water and victuals on their

[1] The oasis of Tabelbala.

[2] Probably a sacred crocodile.

[3] Raymond Lully. *Blanquerna*, chaps. 88 and 91. Quoted by
de la Roncière, op. cit., i, 111–12.

[4] A town in the Western Sudan near the headwaters of the Senegal
River.

camels, for they find neither dwellings of men nor water between those towns. Sometimes they are wrapped in the dust of the sands when they are surprised by a furious wind. Sometimes the heat is so great, when the sun is at its zenith, that they pass blood. I [i.e. the cartographer] have learned all that from a Genoese merchant worthy of belief who lived at Sigilmessa and traded with them.''

Only the most valuable commodities could repay the terrible risks and toils of the desert journey, but the lands beyond the Sahara had access to supplies both of gold dust and ivory, that would yield sufficient profit in the markets of the Mediterranean amply to recoup those who sought them. The land from which the gold dust came was the kingdom of Ghana lying beyond what the ancients called the Western Nile from a vague knowledge of the Senegal and the upper course of the Niger. John Leo Africanus, a Muslim of Spanish origin who wrote an elaborate description of Africa in Arabic at the beginning of the sixteenth century tells us that this land is " called by us [i.e. the Moors] *Gheneoa*, but by the men of Genoa, Portugal and Europe who have no exact knowledge of it, *Ghinea*. This kingdom extends along the Niger about 250 miles, of which a part is on the ocean shore. It is called Gualata towards the west, Tombut [1] on the eastern side and Melli in the part towards the south ".[2] Each of these regions is to be found marked in the beautiful maps that have come down to us from the Jewish cartographers who made Majorca famous in the fourteenth century. Those maps contain much more accurate detail of the geography of Africa than any other European source before the nineteenth century, and this information was available because of the large share that Jews took in the gold trade across the Sahara and their community of interest with their co-religionists on the other side of the Mediterranean.

Tolerance of Christian residents and travellers among the Moors was only a passing phase, but Jews had lived and flourished in North Africa for centuries without molestation. The Genoese and Venetians made considerable use of Jewish

---

[1] i.e. Timbuktu.

[2] Leo Africanus' work has often been translated into European languages. Translated into English by John Pory as *A geographical historie of Africa written in Arabike and Italian by John Leo a More* (London, 1600). See also Purchas (Maclehose's edn.), vols. v and vi.

intermediaries in their attempts to secure a share of the valuable trade, but though we know that they achieved some measure of success, the traces that have been left are tantalizingly few. M. de la Roncière has, however, recently brought to light a narrative of travel into the Sahara in the middle of the fifteenth century which shows what strenuous efforts the Genoese were making to cultivate new fields of commerce to replace those of the Black Sea that were being ruined by the Turks.

Antonio Malfante, the author, was probably a Genoese in the employ of a merchant house that desired to find opportunities for trade in Africa, and in 1447 having travelled further into the heart of the desert than any Christian before him, he wrote from the large oasis of Touat to inform his employers of the knowledge he had gained concerning the caravan trade and the rich countries along the Niger whence came the gold and ivory. The letter is long and full of interesting details,[1] but only a few extracts can here be summarized. "After we were come from the sea that is to say from Honeïn [to Sigilmessa]," Malfante begins, " we travelled for twelve days always towards the south in mounted caravan. . . . So we came after that stage into the Touat. The place where we are [2] comprises eighteen quarters enclosed within a single wall, and governed by the power of an oligarchy [composed of the chiefs of the various quarters]. Travellers are taken under the protection of one of these chiefs, and so merchants find themselves in complete security. For I am a Christian and yet no one has ever said an unfriendly word to me. They have never before seen a Christian here . . . Jews abound here, living peaceably in dependence on different masters who defend them. Business is carried on through their agency and there are many in whom one may have great confidence . . . The gold that is brought here is bought of those who come from the coast. . . . In the country of the negroes here there live the Philistines,[3] who camp in tents like the Arabs and reign as masters over all the lands from

---

[1] It is printed in the original Latin with a translation and a facsimile of certain pages in Ch. de la Roncière, *Découverte de l'Afrique*, i, 151–8. See also de la Roncière, *Découverte d'une relation de voyage, décrivant en 1447 le bassin du Niger* (Paris, 1919).

[2] Tamentit, the capital of the oasis.

[3] i.e. Touaregs.

the confines of Egypt to the Ocean. . . . These white men
are of a superb race and high countenance, and are
incomparable horsemen who ride without saddles and with
simple spurs. They have their mouths and noses covered
with a veil. . . . The lands that are under their dominion
are on the borders of the lands of the negroes and the
inhabitants follow the religion of Mahomet. The greater part
of these people are negroes, but a small number are white
men." [1] Among other Mahometan states are Thambet
[i.e. Timbuktu], Mali, Sagoto [Sokoto], and Bamba, and these
are enumerated from east to west ascending the course of the
river.

" To the south of the states there are many states and
territories solely inhabited by idolatrous negroes, incessantly
at war one with another to sustain their beliefs and their
fetishes. . . . They worship tufted trees, the dwelling-place
of a spirit whom they honour with sacrifices ; others worship
wooden and stone images to whom, they say, their incantations
give speech. My lord here who is sheik of this land . . . is
brother of a great merchant in Thambet and very worthy of
belief. He relates that he lived in that place thirty years ;
and my protector, as he says, stayed in the lands of the
negroes for fourteen years, and every day he tells me marvels
about those people. He says that those lands and peoples
have no end towards the south. They all go naked only
covering themselves with a little apron. They have
abundance of flesh, milk and rice, but no wheat or barley.

" A very great river flows through those lands and at a
certain time of the year it pours its floods over the lands,
that river passes at the gates of Tambet and runs through
Egypt, and it is the river which passes through Cairo.[2]
They have upon it many barks in which they carry on their
commerce. . . . Because battles are incessant among them
they sell men into slavery at a maximum rate of two
doubloons per head. . . . The place where I am is good, for
Egyptians and other merchants come hither from the lands
of the negroes bringing gold which they exchange for copper
and other merchandise . . . I have often asked where the

---

[1] Men of Moorish, i.e., Berber stock.
[2] This confusion of the Niger and the Nile was constant until the
discoveries of the nineteenth century.

gold is found and collected, but my protector says ' I have stayed fourteen years in the lands of the negroes, and I have never heard of nor seen any one who could speak of it with certain knowledge. Wherefore it must be thought that it comes from a far-off land, and according to my belief from one particular place '. Nevertheless, he said that once he was in a place where silver was worth as much as gold."

The whole of Malfante's letter bears the stamp of accuracy and is of absorbing interest, but its importance arises especially from the date at which it was written, for the years immediately following 1447, as we shall see in a later chapter, are an important epoch in the work of exploration of the African coast by the Portuguese under the leadership of Prince Henry the Navigator. Many Genoese sailors and merchants took part in that work, and though we have no proof that Malfante's information was accessible or known to the Infante, there can be no doubt that in the middle of the fifteenth century much more accurate information was coming to the Peninsula concerning the lands beyond the Moors than had been available at an earlier date. Through the Jews of Aragon and Majorca, the Moors of the captured cities of the Barbary Coast and possibly through Genoese and Venetian merchants who had traded in the interior, knowledge about the gold trade was brought, and the veil that covered the Dark Continent was lifted higher than it was ever to be again until centuries later.

CITY OF ST. ALBANS PUBLIC LIBRARY

CHAPTER IX

PRESTER JOHN AND THE EMPIRE OF ETHIOPIA

By Sir E. DENISON ROSS, C.I.E., Ph.D.

THE documentary history of the legend of a great Christian priest-king ruling far away beyond the lands usually visited by Western travellers dates only from the twelfth century, though it is probable that the story was current in oral tradition much earlier. In the Chronicle of Otto von Freisingen,[1] written before 1158, there is a story that a few years before the capture of the Crusaders' citadel of Edessa by the Moslems in 1144, a certain " Johannes Presbyter " had won a great victory over the Persians and the Medes. This victory has long ago been identified as that won over the Saljuq Sultan Sanjar in 1141 by the Turkish Khan Ye-lu-ta-shih,[2] and there were good excuses for the report that this Khan was a Christian. Von Freisingen had heard of this victory from the Syrian Bishop of Gabala on the coast of Syria whom he happened to meet in Viterbo in 1144. The bishop also told him that " Prester John " was the Nestorian king of a country situated in the Far East ; that he was descended from the Magian kings ; and that he possessed fabulous wealth. News of the defeat of Sultan Sanjar may quite easily have reached Europe soon after the event, but we do not hear of any attempt to take advantage of this triumph of supposedly Christian arms.

About 1165 there was circulated the famous forged letter from Prester John, which represented this monarch as ruling over the three Indias, and described his powers and possessions in the most exaggerated terms.

" John, Priest by the Almighty power of God and the

[1] *Monumenta Germaniae Historica Scriptores*, XX, p. 266.
[2] The actual date of this victory, 1141, is given by Albericus—who made use of Otto—but we do not know on what authority. See *Mon. Germ. Hist. Scriptores* IX, p. 580.

strength of Our Lord Jesus Christ, King of Kings and Lord of Lords, to his friend Emmanuel, Prince of Constantinople, greeting, wishing him health and the continued enjoyment of the Divine Favour.

" It hath been reported to our Majesty that thou holdest our Excellency in esteem, and that the knowledge of our highness has reached thee.

" Furthermore we have heard through our secretary that it was thy desire to send us some objects of art and interest, to gratify our righteous disposition.   Being but human we take it in good part, and through our secretary we transmit to thee some of our articles.   Now it is our desire and we will to know if thou holdest the true faith, and in all things adherest to our Lord Jesus Christ, for while we know that we are mortal, people regard thee as a god ; still we know that thou art mortal, and subject to human infirmities.

" If thou shouldst have any desire to come into the kingdom of our majesty, we will place thee in the highest and most dignified position in our household, and thou mayest abundantly partake of all that pertains to us.   Shouldst thou desire to return, thou shalt go laden with treasures. If indeed thou desirest to know wherein consists our great power, then believe without hesitation, that I, Prester John, who reign supreme, surpass in virtue, riches and power all creatures under heaven.   Seventy kings are our tributaries. I am a zealous Christian and universally protect the Christians of our empire, supporting them by our alms. We have determined to visit the sepulchre of our Lord with a very large army, in accordance with the glory of our majesty to humble and chastise the enemies of the cross of Christ and to exalt his blessed name.

" Honey flows in our land, and milk everywhere abounds. In one region there no poison exists and no noisy frog croaks, no scorpions are there, and no serpents creeping in the grass.

" No venomous reptiles can exist there or use there their deadly power.   In one of the heathen provinces flows a river called the Indus, which, issuing from Paradise, extends its windings by various channels through all the province ; and in it are found emeralds, sapphires, carbuncles, topazes, chrysolites, onyxes, beryls, sardonyxes, and many other precious stones.

" Between the sandy sea and the aforesaid mountains, is a stone in a plain, of incredible medical virtue which cures Christians or Christian candidates of whatever infirmities afflict them, in this manner. There is in the stone a mussel-shaped cavity, in which the water is always four inches deep, and this is kept by two holy and reverend old men. These ask the new-comers whether they are Christians, or do desire to be so, and then if they desire the healing of the whole body, and if the answer is satisfactory, having laid aside their clothes they get into the shell ; then if their profession is sincere, the water begins to increase and rises over their heads ; this having taken place three times, the water returns to its usual height. Thus every one who enters, leaves it cured of whatsoever disease he had.

" For gold, silver, precious stones, animals of every kind and the number of our people, we believe there is not our equal under heaven. There are no poor among us ; we receive all strangers and wayfarers ; thieves and robbers find no place among us, neither adultery nor avarice. When we go to war, we have carried before us fourteen golden crosses ornamented with precious jewels, in the place of banners, and each of these is followed by ten thousand mounted troopers and a hundred thousand infantry ; besides those who are charged with the care of the baggage, carriages and provisions.

" Flattery finds no place ; there is no division among us ; our people have abundance of wealth ; our horses are few and wretched. We believe we have no equal in the abundance of riches and numbers of people. When we go out at ordinary times on horseback, our Majesty is preceded by a wooden cross, without decoration or gold or jewels, in order that we may always bear in mind the passion of our Lord Jesus Christ. Also a golden vase full of earth to remind us that our body must return to its original substance—the earth. There is also a silver vase filled with gold borne before us, that all may understand that we are Lord of Lords. Our magnificence abounds in all wealth, and surpasses that of India.

" The palace in which our sublimity dwells, is after the pattern of that which the holy Thomas erected for the king Gundoforo, and resembles it in its various offices, and everything in the other parts of the edifice. The ceilings,

THE GREAT MAGNIFICENCE OF PRESTER JOHN, LORD OF GREATER INDIA
AND OF ETHIOPIA.

Frontispiece to a popular Italian poem on Prester John written by Giuliano Dati (1445-1524),
Bishop of Saint-Léon in Calabria.
This poem, containing fifty-nine verses of eight lines, was printed in Florence at the end of the
Fifteenth Century—but bears no date.

The Copy in the British Museum is numbered C.20. C.23.

CLagran Magnificentia del Prete Ianni Signore dellindia
Maggiore & della Ethiopia

pillars and architraves are of rarest wood. The roof of the same palace indeed is of ebony, lest by any means it might be destroyed by fire or otherwise. At the extremities over the gables, are two golden apples in each of which are two carbuncles, that the gold may shine by day, and the carbuncles sparkle by night. The larger palace gates are of sardonyxes, inlaid with snakes' horn, so that nothing poisonous may enter. The others indeed are also of ebony. The windows are of crystal. The tables on which our courtiers eat are of gold and some of amethyst. The standards supporting the tables are some of ebony and some of amethyst. In front of the palace is the court in which our justice is accustomed to watch the combatants. The pavement is of onyx, in order that by virtue of the stones the courage of the combatants may be increased. In the aforesaid palace no light is used at night, but what is fed by balsam. The chamber in which our sublimity reposes is marvellously decorated with gold and stones of every kind.

" At our table, thirty thousand men, besides occasional visitors are daily entertained ; and all there partake of our bounty whether it be for horses or other expenses. The table made of the most precious emeralds is supported by four amethyst pillars ; by virtue of which stone, no person sitting at the table can become inebriated.

" Every month we are served in rotation by seven kings, sixty-two dukes, and two hundred and sixty-five counts and marquises, besides those who are sent on various missions in our interest.

" Twelve archbishops sit on our right at table to meals every day, and twenty bishops on our left. The Patriarch of St. Thomas, the Metropolitan of Samarcand, and the Bishop of Susa, where our glory resides and our imperial palace is, each in his turn is ever present with us.

" If again thou askest how it is that the Creator of all having made us the most superpotential and most glorious over all mortals—does not give us a higher dignity or more excellent name than that of Priest (Prester), let not thy wisdom be surprised on this account, for this is the reason. We have many ecclesiastics in our retinue of more dignified name and office in the Church, and of more considerable standing than ours in the divine service. For our house-steward is a patriarch and king; our cup-bearer is an archbishop and king; our chamberlain is a bishop and king; our archimandrite, that is chief pastor or master of the horse, is a king and abbot. Whereof our highness has not seen it repugnant to call himself by the same name and to distinguish himself by the order of which our court is full. And if we have chosen to be called by a lower name and inferior rank, it springs from humility. If indeed you can number the stars of heaven and sands of the sea, then you may calculate the extent of our dominion and power."

This forged letter, which purports to have been written by Prester John, was in the first instance addressed to Manuel I, Emperor of Byzantium, who in his turn forwarded it to the Emperor Frederick Barbarossa.[1] That such a letter should ever have been regarded as genuine is hard for us to believe to-day. But if it was believed, one can easily picture the anxiety of Europeans to discover this monarch, if only on account of his great wealth. The popular legends of *Alexander the Great* lay at the root of all the amazing statements of the forgery. Up to this stage in the documentary legend of Prester John, we are led to look for him in what is vaguely known as " India ". And if the view is correct that the verbal legend originally referred to the King of Ethiopia, we may explain the transference of Prester John's habitat to Asia first to the fact that Ethiopia was regarded in the Middle Ages as one of the Three Indias, though it was not known exactly where it was ; and secondly to the fact that reports of the conversion of the Turks to Christianity had reached Europe.

If we imagine that in the twelfth century, if not earlier, travellers' tales were current in Italy and France regarding a mighty Christian Emperor living somewhere in India, probably ruling over all the Indies when the famous forgery was spread about Europe between 1165 and 1177, numbers of people would be prepared to accept it as genuine, if only because it confirmed these travellers' tales. The report contained in the Chronicle of Otto von Freisingen and the continuation, may very well have been known only to a few scholars, but it was certainly known to the writer who perpetrated the forgery, which must be regarded as one of

[1] The earliest French versions are addressed direct to Frederick.

the biggest literary hoaxes ever attempted. On the sole ground that he is said to have translated it from Greek into Latin, the letter has been attributed to Christian, Archbishop of Mainz, who was a partisan of Frederick Barbarossa in his opposition to Pope Alexander III. Seeing that no Greek original has ever been found, the Archbishop must be regarded at least as suspect. But he must have kept his secret very close, and have been overjoyed at the popularity of his invention. Some idea may be formed of the wide currency the letter obtained from the fact that there are more than a hundred manuscripts of the letter preserved in the Libraries of Europe. The British Museum alone possesses ten in the original Latin, one in French and two in English, and there are also a number of versions in German.

In the meantime Pope Alexander III had learnt from his private doctor Philipus, and from others, that " Prester John, king of India " was anxious to be instructed in the true Catholic faith; that he wished to have a church in Rome and an altar in the Church of the Holy Sepulchre at Jerusalem. The Pope therefore dispatched Philipus to discover this king, bearing a letter, of which various texts—differing very much in length—have been preserved. It is dated 27th September, 1177. This letter does not appear to have been suggested so much by the forged letter, as by the story brought to the knowledge of the Pope by his own doctor Philipus. We know nothing of this doctor beyond what we are told in the Pope's letter, but it is quite likely that he made a pilgrimage to Jerusalem and had encountered pilgrims from the actually existing Christian kingdom of Abyssinia, who had charged him to convey the message he brought to the Pope regarding the pious ambitions of their king, and there is every reason to believe that we have here the first documentary allusion to the King of Ethiopia.

One can imagine the Pope being convinced of the *bona fides* of the Doctor Philipus, and thereupon sending him on a mission and entrusting him with a letter couched in sympathetic terms. It may be recalled that Alexander III had been engaged in a continual struggle with Frederick Barbarossa from 1159 down to 1177, when the latter, by the Peace of Venice, at last recognized the claims of Alexander III to the Papacy.[1] Doctor Philipus, we may presume, set out with this letter, and for all we know to the contrary, may have delivered it to the Negus of Abyssinia. But we never hear of the Doctor again, and the first stage in the Prester John inquiry thus ends in 1177.

It must be remembered that during the period of the Crusades the only known road to Abyssinia was blocked by the Mamluk rulers of Egypt. The Ethiopians themselves were hemmed in all round by the Muslims, and even had they wished, could not have effectively come to the aid of the Crusaders. An instructive example of this state of affairs is to be found in the Arabic History of the Mamluk Sultans by Mufazzal ibn Abu'l-Faza'il [2] which tells us that in the year A.H. 677 (A.D. 1273) the Sultan received a letter from the king of Abyssinia, which had been sent under cover of a letter addressed to the king of Yemen, asking the Sultan to order the Patriarch of Alexandria to appoint a Bishop for Ethiopia. From this we may judge how strict was the watch kept on Prester John by the Sultan of Egypt, and consequently how difficult it would be for Europeans to enter Abyssinia. It is indeed remarkable that during the first six Crusades we hear of no definite effort being made to discover the whereabouts of this potential Christian ally. It was not the Crusades, but the invasion of Europe by the Mongols in the middle of the thirteenth century that led to the dispatch of the first mission to find Prester John in Central Asia. In 1241 the Mongols reached Silesia, and it seemed that nothing could stay their relentless onward march, when suddenly the news of the death of the great Khan Ogodai caused them all to return to Tartary. It seems almost incredible that Europe should have been saved from further devastation simply by the circumstance that a new Khan had to be elected.

The Western nations now set about discovering who these strange nomads really were, where they came from, and how

---

[1] In Hastings' *Encyclopaedia of Religion and Ethics* (under " Prester John ") it is stated, but not upon what authority, that this treaty was signed in July, 1177, and that Alexander III remained in Venice until October, and in the interval received an Embassy from Prester John.

[2] Edited and translated by E. Blochet. *Patrologia Orientalis*, Tom. *XIV*.

to keep them off in future. In 1245 Innocent IV sent a
letter to the Khan of the Tartars by the hand of Pian de
Carpine, the Dominican. Pian de Carpine set out from Lyons
in April, 1245, and took nearly ten months to cross Europe,
only leaving Kiev in February of the following year. Twenty
days later he encountered the first Mongols, by whom he was
sent on to the Volga where he met Batu, the grandson of
Chingiz Khan. Batu, having examined the Pope's letter
which he caused to be translated into Mongolian, decided to
send Pian de Carpine on to the Grand Khan. The Dominican
reached the Imperial camp, near Karakorum, in July, and
there witnessed the enthronement of Kuyuk, who had
succeeded Ogodai. Pian de Carpine was well received, and
returned safely to Lyons at the end of 1247 bringing the reply
of the Grand Khan to Innocent IV. This reply was drawn
up in three languages. First a version was written in
Mongolian, and this was translated into Latin, and finally,
at the last moment a *Sarasin* version was prepared. The
Latin version has long been known in Europe, but the
Sarasin version has only quite recently been discovered
in the Vatican, and turns out to be written in Persian. This
important discovery, made known to us by Monsieur Paul
Pelliot,[1] has thrown a flood of new light on the history of the
missions which passed between the Pope and the Mongols.

A few years later Saint Louis sent William of Rubruck on a
similar mission to that of Pian de Carpine. At this juncture
the Christians and the Mongols found themselves opposed
to a common enemy, the Mamluks of Egypt. Numerous
embassies passed between the Christians and the Mongols,
which were all abortive, and intercourse finally came to an
end with the formal adoption of Islam by the Mongols of
Persia at the beginning of the fourteenth century.

The story of the European travellers into China in the
thirteenth century forms the subject of another chapter in
this book, and it is therefore needless here to discuss at any
length the adventures of Pian de Carpine, Rubruck, Marco
Polo or Oderic de Pordenone. There can be little doubt
that these travellers all cherished a hope that they might
discover Prester John in Tartary. As Yule says : " When

---

[1] *Les Mongols et la Papauté* in *La Revue de l'Orient Chrétien*, 3ième
Série, T. iii (xxiii), 1922–3, pp. 3–30.

the Mongol conquests threw Asia open to the Frank travellers in the middle of the thirteenth century, their minds were full of Prester John ; they sought in vain for an adequate representative and they found *several* . . . and the honour of identification with Prester John, after hovering over one head and another, settled finally upon that of the king of the Keraits."

No trace has yet been found of the presence of Christians in China prior to the year A.D. 636. What we know of the earliest Nestorian missions is due to the discovery of the famous inscription in Chinese and Syriac which was erected in Si-an-fu in A.D. 781. By the year 1000 there probably did not remain a single Nestorian church in China proper, but long after this date the Nestorians continued to flourish in Central Asia. The two principal tribes who carried on the faith were the Keraits and the Onguts. These Turkish tribes had been converted to Christianity by the influence of Nestorian merchants, and priests were sent to them by the Metropolitan of Merv. The Great Khan Ye-lu-ta-shih who defeated Sanjar in 1141, was not a Kerait Turk but a Kitan, and it was probably the mistaken notion that he was a Christian Kerait that led to the rumour that this conqueror of the Moslem Seljuqs was a Nestorian. Pian de Carpine and William Rubruck both hoped that they had found some trace of Prester John, but the only identification which gained any popularity was made by Marco Polo, who thought he had discovered him in the person of a certain Ong Khan or more correctly Wang Khan, a Christian Turk of the Kerait family, who, after a long period of friendly relations with Chingiz Khan, was finally attacked and slain by the Mongol Khan, at the beginning of the fourteenth century. The Christian prince whom Marco Polo himself saw was named George. He imagined this man to be a descendant of Ong Khan, but modern research has proved him to belong not to the Keraits, but to the other tribe of Christian Turks known as the " Ongut ". It was in the country of the Onguts that Oderic of Pordenone, writing in 1330, thought that he had discovered the land of Prester John. He was the last traveller to place the priest-king in Central Asia, but Marco Polo's work had so much influence and was so widely read that the legend of a Central Asian Prester John long survived among scholars and educated men in Western Europe.

Let us now turn to a different line of approach which has hitherto been somewhat neglected, and examine how it came about that among the Portuguese of the fifteenth century it was the Emperor of Ethiopia who was uniformly spoken of as " Prester John ". Our first consideration must be directed rather to some little-known Portuguese historians than to Prester John himself.

The fate of the works of the great Jesuit missionaries to Abyssinia is as romantic as the adventures of the missionaries themselves ; for although during the sixteenth century half a dozen really fine histories of Ethiopia were written in Portuguese, it was not until the beginning of the present century that the best of them saw the light of print. Though the histories reached Lisbon in safety, they were wholly disregarded, and it was not until the year 1660 that a certain Balsazar Tellez published an epitome of two of them, those of Almeida and Paez.[1] Tellez' work was only an abridgment, but the next step is represented by further abridgment in the shape of Latin, French and English adaptations of the epitome. The only important works of the group that became generally known more or less in their complete form were those of Father Lobo and of Affonso Alvarez. But the works of Father Lobo and Affonso Alvarez are chiefly narratives of travel and adventure and contain very little regarding the history of Ethiopia. Paez, Almeida and others made a profound study of the language and history of Ethiopia, but there seems to have been some rooted objection in Portugal to making known the results of their researches. Thanks to the untiring labours of Father Beccari, and the liberality of the Jesuits in Rome, all these unpublished chronicles have now been carefully printed.[2]

It thus came about that the views held by the real historians of Ethiopia regarding the name of Prester John were only known to the world through the abridged accounts given by Tellez and later writers ; and an examination of the

[1] The *Historia de Ethiopia a alta*, of Tellez, printed in Coimbra in 1660, is so rare that only a few copies are known to exist to-day.

[2] P.C. Beccari. *Rerum Aethiopicarum scriptores occidentales inediti a saeculo XVI ad saeculum XIX.* Roma, 1905, etc.

original sources reveals a considerable distortion of the facts on the part of the compilers.

The following considerations may be advanced ; first, that the origin of the name John as applied to a priest-king is to be found in the Amharic language ; secondly, that Marco Polo, as known to the Portuguese, did possibly locate part of Prester John's kingdom in Ethiopia ; thirdly, that Abyssinian envoys in the fifteenth century tried to invent an etymology in order to please the Portuguese ; and fourthly, that the Portuguese were never able to reconcile the name with the generally accepted legend, except by supposing Ethiopia to be all that remained of Prester John's vast empire.

There have been, as it were, two schools of thought among recent writers, (1) those who hold that Prester John must be sought in Tartary, and (2) those who think he belongs to Africa.   Yet a third theory was put forward by the Russian scholar Bruun in 1876, who suggested that Prester John might be found among the kings of Georgia, but this theory, though regarded with some indulgence by Sir H. Yule, is summarily dismissed by Zarncke, who declares that it does not furnish an atom of probability.   Apart from the well-known researches of Yule, the principal monographs are those of Gustav Oppert [1] and Zarncke.[2]   Quite recently a valuable resumé of the whole question has been published by the Rumanian scholar Constantin Marinescu,[3] but the real pioneers in the field, like Kircher, Mosheim and d'Avezac are forgotten.

It must be remembered that from the middle of the fifteenth century the name " Prester John " invariably means Emperor of Abyssinia, for by that time this title had been universally adopted by the Portuguese, and was used as much as we use the titles Shah, Tsar, Kaiser and Sultan.   My own impression is that it was as a *general title* that it first reached Europe ; that from the outset it referred to the King of Ethiopia, and that the confusion which arose

---

[1] G. Oppert. *Der Presbyter Johannes in Sage und Geschichte.* Berlin, 1864.

[2] Fr. Zarncke. *Der Priester Johannes,* in the *Abhandlungen der phi'.-hist. Classe der K. Sächsischen Gesell. d. Wissenschaften,* § VII (1879) § VIII (1883).

[3] *Bulletin de l'Academie Roumaine,* vol. x, Bucharest, 1923.

in the twelfth century was partly due to the wide application
of the term " India ", and partly to the inaccessibility of
Ethiopia. In order to explain how the name came to be
applied to the emperor of Ethiopia, we must go back to the
early history of the Abyssinian Church. Christianity is said
to have been introduced into Abyssinia about the middle
of the fourth century by a certain Frumentius, a commercial
traveller, who was eventually appointed first Bishop of Axum
by Athanasius, the patriarch of Alexandria. It was this
conversion which first brought the Abyssinians out of their
own country, notably for the purpose of making the
pilgrimage to Jerusalem ; and it was the dependence of the
Abyssinian Church on the Patriarch of Alexandria which
brought them into further contact with the European
merchants in Egypt. After the rise of Islam, when
pilgrimages to Jerusalem became a difficult matter, Abyssinia
—though spared until the sixteenth century from Muslim
invasion—was more or less isolated, but the practice of
importing their " Abuna ", or chief prelate from Alexandria
continued ; and thus foreigners in Alexandria no doubt often
heard of the Christian Emperor in Africa. It is highly
probable that it was the Italian merchants and sailors who
first brought home stories of the great Christian Emperor
who lived in a country beyond Egypt, and whose subjects, as
far as they knew, were all priests. The Emperor must
therefore also be a priest, and thus one of his titles became
" Presbyter " or " Prester ".

The earliest conception of the kingdom of Prester John
was no doubt a sort of immense Indian Empire corresponding
somewhat to the Roman Empire, and there is written
evidence to show that when a Prester John was at last
thought to have been discovered in Ethiopia, this country
was supposed to be the section of India to which his once
vast kingdom had been reduced by the conquests of the
Tartars. In support of this view we may cite an Italian
writer of the fifteenth century and a Portuguese historian
of the sixteenth century. A certain Genoese traveller
named Antonio Uso di Mare wrote as follows in 1455 :—

" The Emperor and Christian Patriarch of Nubia and
Ethiopia, Prester John, is called *Abet Selip*, that is ' Hundred
Men '." This of course is an error, for the title is obviously

a corruption of *Abdus-Salib*, or "Servant of the Cross", a name given to him by his Muslim enemies. "These countries are all that is left to Prester John, since the great Khan of Cathay, named Castigan, gave battle to him in 1187 in the beautiful plain of Tenduch in Cathay. Crushed by the innumerable multitude of his adversaries, Prester John lost all the territories he possessed in Asia. He only kept the provinces of Ethiopia and Nubia, which abound in gold and silver." [1]

The other passage comes from the famous *History of King Manoel of Portugal* by Damião Goes, first published in 1567. In chapters 58, 59, and 60 of Book III we read that King John II of Portugal sent Pedro de Covilham and Antonio de Payva on a mission chiefly in order to discover the heretical Christian Emperor " in India " and to convert him to the true religion. Goes goes on to say that " Covilham did not of course find Prester John in India, as according to Paul the Venetian [i.e. Marco Polo] this monarch had been defeated and killed by the Emperor of China, *and there were never any more Prester Johns* in that part of the world, although there were still many Nestorians in the interior of India ".

How ignorant the Portuguese were of the actual extent of Prester John's realms, even in 1520 when a mission was sent under da Lima, is shown by the instructions issued to the mission to ascertain whether these realms extended as far as the Cape of Good Hope. Another Portuguese writer, Paez,[2] whose account of Abyssinia, though written in the sixteenth century, has only recently been published in the original Portuguese, gives the following information regarding Prester John :—

"Authors hold many and various opinions concerning the extent and position of the kingdoms and provinces which are comprehended under the name of Ethiopia ; but I shall not attempt either to approve or refute their views, for my object here is only to discuss that region which is governed by the Emperor we usually call Prester John. Now although many and serious authors affirm that this Emperor is not Prester John but quite another king, who is contiguous with

---

[1] See Ch. de la Roncière, *La Découverte de l'Afrique au moyen âge* (Cairo, 1925), vol. ii, p. 122.
[2] See Beccari, op. cit., vol. ii, p. 13.

the Tartars, where there are still Christians, as I was recently
assured by a *mancebo, natural de Tartaria*, who landed in
this country : nevertheless in this history I shall call him
Prester John, as he is better known in Europe by this name
than by any other."

The earliest discussion of the name from the point of view
of Ethiopia occurs in another work by Damião Goes which
first appeared in Latin in 1540. The explanation given to
him by certain Abyssinian envoys may be translated as
follows :—

" Our Emperor is always called Preciosus Ioannes, and
not Presbyter Ioannes, as is everywhere mooted. This
name (*agnomem*) is written in our language with the
characters ዣን: ብሉል: which is pronounced Ioannes Belul,
that is John the Precious or High, and in Chaldee [i.e. Geëz]
it is written ዣን: -ዐንቀአ that is, Iannes Encoe, which if
you translate it also means John the Precious or High. He
is called Emperor of Ethiopia and not of Abyssinia as Mathew
(the envoy) wrongly stated. For Mathew was an Armenian
and could not know our affairs thoroughly, more especially
those respecting our religion." [1]

These statements contain a number of errors, as later
Portuguese writers discovered for themselves. The Amharic
characters as printed in the Paris edition of 1541, have been
specially cut out by someone ignorant of the alphabet,
but as here printed the letters are what they were originally
intended for. It was unfair of the Abyssinians to say that ዣን:
(more correctly ዣን:) *žan* is pronounced Ioannes ; and the
letter ዣ Ž does not exist in the Chaldee (Geëz) language at
all. It is, however, the case that the correct title of their
ruler is Emperor of Ethiopia [*ya Etiopia Negus*].

There is a very curious passage in the Ethiopian History
of Tellez which deserves quotation as it may possibly be of
some importance to the bibliography of Marco Polo.
Although this passage has been preserved in the English
translation, it has apparently never attracted the attention
it deserves. It runs as follows :—

" Marcus Paulus Venetus, in his *Itinerary*, very much
strengthened the vulgar error, writing that the great King
called Prester John used to reside in Archico, which is the

[1] D. Goes, *Fides, religio, moresque, Aethiopum sub imperio Pretiosi
Joannis* (second edition, Paris, 1541), pp. 88, 89.

first known town belonging to Ethiopia within the Red Sea."
Now there is no allusion either to this fact, nor any mention
of Archico [Arkiko], in Yule's exhaustive edition of Marco
Polo or in Pauthier's.   It is also remarkable that in Tellez'
rare allusions to Marco Polo his book of travel is always
called *Itinerario*, a title which appears, as far as I am aware,
only in the Latin version printed in Amsterdam in 1585.
Tellez gives the reference as Chapter 52.

The fullest discussion of the name Prester John is, however,
to be found in the first chapter of Almeida's " History of
Abyssinia ",[1] which as it has only recently been published
in the original is perhaps worth translating in full :—

" This name is so generally used in Portugal and Europe
in speaking of the Emperor of the Abyssinians that of
necessity some explanation of it must be given by anyone
undertaking to write a history of Ethiopia and of this
Abyssinian Empire.

"But, as nearly all historians writing on the things of this
world dispute this point, investigating and giving different
reasons for and versions of this name, I have no intention
of delaying in order to repeat that which can easily be found
in their works ; I will only state that among them Father
Nicolao Godinho,[2] of our society, in Book I, Chapter V of his
work on matters relating to Abyssinia, treats this point with
the greatest erudition, and establishes in this work with mature
judgment and the greatest erudition two assured and well
founded facts.   First, that the name Prester or Presbyter
John was originally given to a Christian Emperor, although
a Nestorian, who reigned in the desert of Asia, whose ordinary
name was Joanam, taken from Jonas the Prophet (this name
has been erroneously changed by Europeans into João).
This name was as common among the rulers of that monarchy
as was that of " Pharaoh " among the kings of Egypt ; the
term " Presbyter " was taken from the cross which was
always carried before him, as among our own people it is
carried before Archbishops and Primates ; it is said that when
he made war two crosses were carried, one of gold and one of
precious stones, testifying to the Christian religion which he
professed, and by the richness of the material of which they

---

[1] See Beccari : op. cit., vol. v, pp. 3–6.
[2] *De Abassinorum Rebus*, Lugduni, 1615.

were made in the same degree as precious stones and gold surpass silver, copper, iron or any other metal, so does the Christian religion surpass all the monarchs of the world in power and nobility.

"The second fact established by Father Nicholao Godinho is that the application of this name of Emperor of Asia to the ruler of Ethiopia arose from the mistake made by Pedro de Covilhão, who had been sent with another companion (as we shall explain in detail below) by the King Dom João II of enlightened memory to discover India and the Christian Emperor commonly known as Prester John, whose fame at that time was very widespread in Europe. In Cairo, Suakim and Aden, where he landed on returning from India, he heard many things of the Emperor of Abyssinia, amongst others that he was a Christian, master of many large kingdoms, that he was in holy orders, and carried a cross. Being convinced that his search had been successful, and that this was Prester John whom his king had sent him to seek, he wrote to him from Cairo to this effect. The news, welcomed in Portugal, spread throughout Europe, and caused the Emperor of Abyssinia from that day to this to be commonly called by all Prester John; a contributory factor in the extinction of the monarchy of Joanam in Asia was that no Christian Emperor having been heard of there for so many years, the rising fame of the African ruler confirmed the latter in the title of Prester John due to the Asiatic king.

"The truth of the matter has never, up to to-day, been doubted, nor will it be so by anyone in Ethiopia, for either they are ignorant that their Emperor is known by this name, or if we mention it they become alarmed and seek information, but are *unable to find anything corresponding to the term or title in their language.* Nevertheless there are some in Europe influenced by Caga Za Ab (whom Domião de Goez, in the third part of the Chronicle of King Dom Manoel, Chap. 60, calls Zagazabo), an ambassador who, commanded by King David, went there to visit His Excellency Dom João III of Portugal, and also by that of Pedro, likewise an Abyssinian, who accompanied Father Francisco Alvarez of Ethiopia to Portugal, and thence to Italy when he took the letters of the Emperor David to Pope Clement VII, and both one and the other, Caga Za Ab and Pedro, wished to devise versions of this

name in their language; they did this easily among people
unacquainted with it, feigning that they acted by authority,
and saying that the name Prester John was derived from
Belul and *Jan*, that this was the same as Precious Gian,
and that we ourselves in saying João were merely corrupting
the name Jan. All this is fiction without foundation in
fact, although someone in Valencia [1] had an idea that we
ought to say *Beldigian*, and that Belul Jan was not two but
one word only.

"*There is no doubt that the Abyssinians call their Emperor
Jan*, and sometimes Belul as well, but both names are never
used together; it would be considered a great solecism and
vulgarity among them if anyone said "Belul Jan" or "Jan
Belul"; after each of these names the word "qhoj" is usually
added, it is synonymous with our word "my" when used
to signify affection and tenderness; as an expression of
endearment we say to a child, "my dear," "my prince,"
"my king"; and this is approximately what the Abyssinians
wished to convey when addressing their king. They say
"Janqhoj", "Ianqhoj" or "Belulqhoj", although this second
name is less used among them than the first. The root of the
matter is this: Jan, in the ancient Ethiopian language is said
to mean elephant, and because this animal is the most
powerful and the most alarming of all, his name is given to the
king as a title of honour and majesty. Therefore those who
appeal at the court of the emperor that he may dismiss them
or command the complaints they bring to be heard, cry this
name loudly, if they are Amaras, "Janqhoj, Janqhoj," until
the Emperor commands a servant to listen to their requests.
I said if they are Amaras, because if they are Moors they cry
"Sidi, Sidi" and if Portuguese "Senhor, Senhor" which is
the same, if Tigres "Adarie, Adarie". Those belonging
to other nationalities with other languages make use of the
terms peculiar to them.

"The name Belul is less used; it really signifies a jewel or
ornament, which on the death of the reigning ruler and
election of a new Emperor, was entrusted to an official,
whose duty it was to go and communicate the news to the

---

[1] This refers to Luis de Urreta, who wrote a *Historia de la Etiopia*,
Valencia, 1610, which was very severely criticized by his contemporaries.

elected Emperor and place the ornament in his ear, the certain and infallible sign of his election ; hence some called the new Emperor after the name of the ornament " Belulqhoj ", which is equivalent to "my jewel " or "my chosen " as it is the sign of his election.

"But as I have already stated, the two words Jan and Belul are not in any case used together, neither are as a rule used without the addition of the word " qhoj " ; it is thus clear that there is no foundation whatever for the statement that the name Prester John is derived from them, especially as there is no doubt that before entering Ethiopia Pedro de Covilhão wrote from Cairo to the King Dom João II that he had found Prester John, whom his Majesty had ordered him to seek, he did not invent the name, but applied that mentioned to him by the King, which he first heard in Portugal, to the Emperor of Ethiopia on finding that he was a Christian, was in Holy Orders and carried a cross, which were more or less the particulars he had heard of Prester John of the Indias, whom he had come to seek.

" As we are treating the subject of the name Prester John, which has erroneously been given to the Emperor of the Abyssinians, it is advisable to state briefly that they call the King " Nugue " and the Emperor " Neguça Nagasta " which is equivalent to "King of Kings ", the Queen "Neguesta " and the Empress "Negesta neguestat ", "Queen of Queens ".

Another important passage on the same topic occurs in Paez [1] :—

" As for the reason why in Europe we usually call the Emperor of Ethiopia Prester John, it may possibly be due to the fact that as the Emperor is usually a *diacono*, some Greeks call him Presbyter, and then adding to this the title of *zan*, which, as I have said, is given to the Emperor, they came to say *Preste zan*, and foreigners, who are often wont to corrupt names, accommodating them to their own language, thus called him Prester Ioam. This name Zan is of ancient usage in Ethiopia, for, in order to describe some of the offices still held by the descendants of those officials whom Solomon gave to his son Menelik, it is still employed ; for they speak of the officials of *zan*, as we should say officials of the Emperor. Thus, the master-of-the-horse of the

[1] See Beccari : op. cit., vol. ii, p. 72.

Emperor is called *zan beleu*, and the chief armourer is called *zan xalami*."

Now none of these statements contains the whole truth, and it is curious that neither the missionaries nor the Abyssinian envoys should have attempted a still more obvious explanation of the origin of the name. Almeida himself tells us that the Abyssinians called their Emperor *jan*, and that to *jan*, was added *qhoj* (anglice *hoy*), he also knew that *žan hoy* was the phrase used by the Amharas when addressing their Emperor. He must also have known, though he does not say so, that this vocative was also used when speaking of the Emperor. The Amharic word *žan* ዣን: is probably derived from the Ethiopian *dayyānī* = a judge, and not from *jan* an elephant. In Ethiopic the common word for elephant is ፊል. I think Almeida must have had in mind the Amharic *zahhon*. *Žan hoy* was still in common use down to the death of the late Emperor Menelik.

Now it may be suggested that this king of Ethiopia was first spoken of by foreigners in Jerusalem and Alexandria as Presbyter, or Preste or Prete, that a need being felt for some fuller title, they inquired his title from the Abyssinians, and learned that they called him *žan hoy*. This they added to Preste, and in the process converted it into *Giannoi*, and finally into *Gianni*. He is also spoken of as *The Prester*, and even in Ariosto's day he was still known as *Presto* or *Pretianni*.[1] Even if this theory be incorrect, it is strange that it did not suggest itself to the Abyssinian envoys or to the Portuguese travellers and historians.

Not until the Crusades came to an end were missionaries sent to Nubia and Ethiopia, for the Mamluks had blocked the road through Egypt, and when it was at last discovered that the real Prester John was an African king in Ethiopia, neither very powerful nor very rich, but at least a Christian, it took a long time for the legendary stories attaching to this name to die out. In 1316, however, two years before the departure of Oderic of Pordenone on his travels into Asia, eight Dominicans, sent by Pope John XXII, arrived in Abyssinia, and made a number of converts to Catholicism. Abyssinians even entered the Dominican Order, the most

[1] See Orlando Furioso : Canto xxxiii, 106 : "*Gli diciam Presto o Pretianni noi.*"

notable being the famous Tekla Haymanot. Among the earliest true accounts of Prester John must be reckoned the story told in 1391 to King John I of Aragon by a priest who had spent several years at Prester John's court.[1] In 1402 an Ethiopian Embassy under the Florentine Antonio Bartoli arrived in Venice. In 1408 some Ethiopian pilgrims came via Jerusalem to Bologna to visit Padua and Rome, and in 1427 there came to the court of Alphonso V of Aragon two ambassadors from Prester John, one a Christian and the other an "infidel".[2] Friar Jordanus (fourteenth century) places Prester John in Africa, while Fra Mauro (middle of the fifteenth century) in his map expressly identifies him with the King of Abyssinia.

The Portuguese attempts to achieve the circumnavigation of Africa began in 1433, and in 1455 in a letter written in Portugal by the Genoese Uso Di Mare, who was mentioned above, we find the first allusion to the exact whereabouts of Prester John, which he declares to be about 300 leagues from Gambia, six days' journey from the shore. In 1452 we hear of Abyssinian ambassadors at Lisbon; in 1481 there is another embassy in Rome, and at length in 1487 Covilham is sent by the King of Portugal to look for Prester John. Martin Behaim of Nuremberg in his map of 1492 mentions an Emperor of Abessinie, but he places Prester John in Cathaia, an error that almost certainly arose from his close dependence upon Marco Polo for his geographical information regarding Eastern Asia.

The traditions regarding the sources of the Nile were already in the fifteenth century associated with the residence of Prester John. It was reported that the Nile came out of a great cavern, at the entrance of which Prester John had constructed two large towers joined by a large chain, so that no one might look into the cavern. There proceeded from within the cavern a very sweet song which made the hearer never wish to go away. If Prester John so desired, he could

---

[1] He first related his adventures to a certain Comte de Foix. See Antonio Rubió y Lluch. *Documents per l'historia de la cultura catalana mig-eval.* Barcelona, 1908.

[2] The interview with the King took place at Valencia in the presence of Cardinal de Foix, papal legate, who reported the circumstances to Pope Martin V in the presence of a certain William Fillastre. See *Bulletin de la Société de Géographie de Paris,* 1842, p. 148.

make the river flow in another direction, and when travellers at last discovered where Prester John resided, some went so far as to maintain that the Sultan of Cairo paid annual tribute to him so that he might not change the course of the Nile.   The Sultan, one writer tells us, allowed no Christian to proceed to India by the Red Sea, nor by the Nile towards Prester John lest these Christians should make a treaty with him by which the Nile should be diverted in its course away from Egypt.   Finally, he says, the reason why Prester John does not do so is because of the large number of . Christians who inhabit Egypt, who would as a consequence die of hunger.

Before leaving the subject of the African Prester John further brief reference must again be made to the first two missions that were sent to that country by the Portuguese, the one in 1487 and the other in 1520.   Pedro de Covilham after paying two visits to India eventually arrived in Abyssinia in 1490. Though he was never allowed to return to Portugal he sent many reports home to his king and the question of the Ethiopian Prester John was settled once and for all.   The second mission, under Dom Rodrigo da Lima, who reached Abyssinia in 1520, was actually in response to a mission sent by the Queen Regent of Ethiopia under a certain Matheus, an Armenian, who was, as we saw above, the complaisant informant of Damião Goes.   After a series of misadventures extending over two years, he finally reached Lisbon in 1514. The return mission took this same Matheus with it, but his ill-luck pursued him to the end, and he died a few days after he landed at Massowa.

One of the results of da Lima's mission, which spent five years in the suite of Prester John, was the compilation of those works on the History, Manners and Customs of Ethiopia from which we have so freely quoted.   By the middle of the sixteenth century such men as Alvarez, Almeida and Paez had written more about Abyssinia and its history than was known of almost any Asiatic country at the period ; but the lack of recognition that their labours received still left Western Europe in ignorance of the facts, and it was not until the visit of the British traveller Bruce in the eighteenth century that the curtain was fully lifted from Prester John's Ethiopian kingdom.

CHAPTER X

The Search for the Sea Route to India, A.D. 1415–1460.

By Professor Edgar Prestage, M.A., D.Litt.

A STUDY of the map of Portugal will suggest some of the causes that led her people to become navigators. The country possesses a long seaboard, a splendid natural harbour in Lisbon and a number of others, such as Oporto, Vianna and Setubal, which in the days of small ships proved adequate, while some of them could even shelter crusading fleets. On the north and east lies Spain, divided in the Middle Ages into three kingdoms, the largest of which, Castile, by her superior power prevented the Portuguese from expanding landward and obliged them to look to the ocean as a field of energy and profit. Though the Celts have never been seamen, the Celtic strain in the race provided the imagination necessary for the undertaking of great enterprises, while pluck and perseverance came from other sources, perhaps from the half-tamed Lusitanian stock and the Germanic invaders, for the Phœnician element was too small to have had much influence.

We know little of the early maritime history of Portugal. Trading relations with the Northern countries and those of the Mediterranean seem to have been active in the first reigns of the Christian rulers of the country and Lisbon and Oporto were important commercial centres, as they could hardly fail to be in view of their geographical position. At the same time a royal navy was gradually developing. In his Chronicle of the first King Afonso Henriques, Duarte Galvam tells us how Dom Fuas Roupinho captured a fleet of Moorish galleys off Cape Espichel, seized others at Ceuta and later on how he fell in with fifty-four Moorish boats in the Straits of Gibraltar and was defeated and killed. Sancho I could send forty galleys to join the Crusading armada which took Silves, capital of the Algarve in 1189, while Lisbon arsenal dates from the reign of Sancho II, and in that of Afonso III it built warships for the Crown. King Dinis had the extensive pine forest of Leiria planted, and when the post of admiral, which he had created in 1307, became vacant, he sought a substitute from Genoa, then a leading naval power. His choice fell upon Manoel Pezagno, who in February, 1317 became admiral of the Portuguese navy, and undertook that he and his successors would provide twenty Genoese skilled in navigation to command the galleys. Pezagno proved a competent organizer; he built ships, taught the Portuguese the art of warfare at sea, and freed the coast from Moorish pirates.

In 1326 Afonso IV sent him on a diplomatic mission to our Edward II of England, to negotiate a marriage between his daughter and the future Edward III, and in 1337 he commanded a large fleet which was defeated by the Castilians off Cape St. Vincent. The admiral had brought over to Portugal members of leading Genoese families to serve in the navy, and the first two Portuguese ocean voyages of which we have a record were probably carried out under their auspices. Their destination was the Canaries, which the Genoese Malocello had visited in 1270. The date of the first voyage is uncertain, but as we know that it preceded the wars with Castile and the Moors, it must have been in or before 1336. The second, related by the poet Boccaccio from letters written by Florentine merchants at Seville, took place in 1341. The expedition consisted of two vessels furnished by Afonso IV and a smaller ship manned by Portuguese, Italians and Castilians; they left Lisbon on July 1st, and returned in November, bringing with them four natives, skins, dyewood and a stone idol. Various islands were touched at; the first, probably Fuerteventura, estimated to be 150 miles in circumference, they found to be barren and inhabited by naked savages and goats; the next, perhaps Grand Canary, seemed even larger and was more populous; the natives lived in houses, possessed palm and fig-trees and cultivated vegetable gardens. Other islands were visited and more were seen; on one they saw a mountain, supposed to be 30,000 feet high. Strange to say, the islanders

appeared to have no boats.   The delineation of the Fortunate
Islands, as the Canaries were then called, on the Laurentian
Portolano of 1351 may be due to this last expedition, which
was not followed up, because the King of Portugal had
other commitments, and perhaps also because in the result
it only just paid its expenses.   It had, however, apparently
been undertaken for the purpose of exploration and not
merely as a mercantile venture.

According to the doctrine received in the Middle Ages,
the Popes had power to dispose of newly found lands, and
on November 15th, 1344, Don Luis de la Cerda, a great
grandson of Afonso X of Castile and Admiral of France,
obtained from Clement VI a grant of the Canaries in fief to
the Apostolic See under an annual tribute of 400 gold florins.
The Pontiff, while reserving the rights of third parties, wrote
to various monarchs, asking them to assist the Prince, among
them to Afonso IV.   In his reply, dated February 12th,
1345, the King of Portugal reminded Clement that his subjects
had been the first to discover the islands, which were nearer
to his realm than to any other and that he had arranged to
send a further expedition to conquer them before he was
prevented by wars with his neighbours.   It seemed, therefore,
that he, rather than any other king, ought to be allowed to
conclude the business he had began ; nevertheless he would
bow to the Pope's decision, but in view of his own needs the
only assistance he could give to his relative Don Luis would
be in the form of foodstuffs.   Various attempts to which I
shall refer later were made by the Portuguese in the fifteenth
century to obtain possession of the Canaries, but the claims
of Castile finally prevailed.

The last years of Afonso IV were disturbed by the revolt
of his son and heir Peter, in consequence of the execution
by royal order of the latter's mistress D. Ignez de Castro ;
internal questions occupied the attention of Peter during
his reign of ten years, while Ferdinand, who succeeded to the
throne in 1367, involved himself in three wars with Castile.
Though we have no record of ocean voyages during the last
half of the fourteenth century, it would be rash to conclude
that none took place.   If their results proved disappointing
the Chroniclers might well omit to register them, but unless
the voyages continued, it is difficult to explain the activity

displayed in that sphere from the second decade of the fifteenth century onwards, and the enthusiasm with which Prince Henry devoted himself to the work of discovery, as soon as he grew up, becomes even more remarkable. Though the naval operations undertaken by Ferdinand were as unsuccessful as the military, he did more by his legislation than any of his predecessors to develop Portuguese sea power.

Traders of various nations had then establishments in Lisbon, which was a free port, and according to the historian Fernam Lopes, as many as 400 or 500 merchant ships often lay before the city at one time, while 100 or 150 loaded salt and wine at Sacavem and Montijo in the outskirts. As many of these vessels, if not most, belonged to foreigners, the King decreed a series of protective measures to develop the mercantile marine. He encouraged shipbuilding by supplying wood gratis from the royal forests, and allowing other materials to be imported duty free ; he reduced the imposts on merchandise carried in the first voyage of a new vessel, he gave owners a partial exemption from military service ; lastly he instituted a register and statistics of shipping and a system of marine insurance on co-operative lines. These measures must have contributed in no small degree to render possible the voyages of exploration in the following century.

On 6th April, 1385 the Cortes of Coimbra bestowed the crown on John I, who thus became founder of the great dynasty of Aviz. On 9th May, 1386 the treaty of Windsor was signed between Portugal and England, and on 2nd February, 1387, the King married Philippa, daughter of John of Gaunt, Duke of Lancaster. From this marriage sprang five sons, justly called by Camões " altos Infantes " ; the third of them, Henry, named by us the Navigator,[1] half an Englishman by blood and more than half in character, though by physiognomy he strikes us as purely Portuguese,[2] was born on Ash Wednesday, 4th March, 1394.

His mother, God-fearing, determined and imbued with a high sense of duty, enforced strict morality on the Court and

[1] Notwithstanding this title bestowed on him in modern times by Englishmen, Henry's only personal voyages were to Ceuta and Tangier and Alcacer.

[2] See below, p. 200.

brought up her sons in accordance with her ideals ; she took care that in addition to bodily training they should receive a clerkly education, with the result that they became men of action and students at the same time, and two of them, like their father, wrote learned books. We do not know when Henry first turned his attention to the sea, but Barros gives us to understand that even before the conquest of Ceuta in 1415 he sent out ships to explore down the west coast of Africa, and Faria e Sousa says that the voyages began in 1412 and that in this year the Portuguese reached Cape Bojador, the " bulging " Cape, 60 leagues beyond Cape Non. The latter historian was only born in 1590 and cannot always be relied upon, but there is reason to think that in the course of the fourteenth century the Portuguese had found Madeira and some of the Azores, as well as the Canaries. According to Diogo Gomes, who belonged to Henry's household, a certain D. John de Castro was captain of a fleet that the Prince fitted out in 1415, and Zurara[1] says that from the time Ceuta was taken, the Prince always had ships at sea to guard against Moorish pirates, so that the fear of them kept in security the shores of the Peninsula and the merchants who traded between East and West.

Gomes adds that in 1416 Henry sent down the coast beyond the Canaries a noble kight Gonçalo Velho to find out the reason of the currents there, and that this man afterwards reached a spot called Terra Alta, but the best evidence shows that Cape Bojador was not passed until much later. The Prince's continuous exploring activities began after the capture of Ceuta at which he won his spurs. In that town, to the knowledge he had already acquired at home and from books about the lands to the South, he added information derived from men who had visited them. Moors told him of the journeys of traders from the Mediterranean coast to Timbuktu and Cantor on the Gambia, and of the regions as far as Guinea. The notices he received from one traveller and another were compared and checked with happy results, for having ascertained the existence of some tall palms near the mouth of the Senegal, he was able to guide the caravels he sent out to find that river many years after.

---

[1] *Chronicle of Guinea*, ed. Beazley and Prestage (Hakluyt Society, London, 1896), cap. 5.

In order the better to supervise the preparation of the expeditions which he resolved to dispatch regularly on a preconceived plan, he retired from Court and fixed his abode in the Algarve, of which he had been appointed Governor, and finally at Sagres near St. Vincent, where he built a small town called *Villa do Infante.* Its geographical position and the fact that ships put in to refit, made it an ideal base of operations ; there, immersed in the study of mathematics and cosmography, he passed his years, varied by occasional visits to Court and to other parts of the Kingdom ; there he selected his captains and had his mariners instructed.

Before we consider the motives that determined his life work and the results he achieved it will be well to have in mind the appearance and character of a man, one of the greatest Portugal has produced, and, as the founder of continuous modern discovery, a world figure. For the first we possess his portrait in one of the triptychs painted by Nuno Gonçalves about 1459 for the altar of St. Vincent in Lisbon Cathedral, and now in the Museum of Ancient Art in that city. Though very like the earlier miniature in the Paris copy of the *Chronicle of Guinea,* the expression of the face is different ; the Prince has a softer, even a dreamy look, as of one looking beyond the present ; we see no longer the practical man of business and the stern moralist, but the idealist who carried out the voyages for the spread of knowledge and of the Faith.[1] We learn something about his character from his friend Zurara and though the Chronicler wrote as a panegyrist, his substantial truthfulness has never been successfully impugned ; Oliveira Martins, Henry's hardest critic, fails to convince us that the Prince selfishly sacrificed his brothers in the pursuit of his ends, though as an idealist he seemed at times merciless. This is what Zurara says and Barros confirms : "The noble Prince was of a good height and broad frame, big and strong of limb, the hair of his head somewhat erect, his colour naturally fair, but by constant toil and exposure it had become dark. His expression at first sight inspired fear in those who did not know him and when wroth, though such times were

[1] See my article in *The Burlington Magazine* for September, 1910, with reproductions of the painting and Dr. José de Figueiredo, *O Pintor Nuno Gonçalves* (Lisbon, 1910), p. 15.

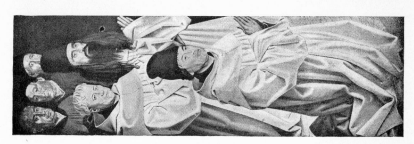

rare, his countenance was harsh. He possessed strength of heart and keenness of mind to a very excellent degree, and he was beyond comparison ambitious of achieving great and lofty deeds. Neither lewdness nor avarice ever found a home in his breast, for as to the former he was so restrained that he passed all his life in purest chastity, and as a virgin the earth received him again at his death to herself . . . [1] His palace was a school of hospitality for the good and high born of the realm and still more for strangers, and the fame of it caused him a great increase of expense, for commonly there were found in his presence men from various nations, so different from our own that it was a marvel to wellnigh all our people ; and none of that multitude could go away without some guerdon from the Prince. All his days he spent in the greatest toil, for of a surety among the nations of mankind no man existed who was a sterner master to himself. It would be hard to tell how many nights he passed in which his eyes knew no sleep ; and his body was so transformed by abstinence that it seemed as if Dom Henry had made its nature to be different from that of others. . . . The Prince was a man of great wisdom and authority, very discreet and of good memory, but in some matters a little tardy, whether it was from the influence of the phlegm in his nature [2] or from the choice of his will, directed to some certain end not known to men. His bearing was calm and dignified, his speech and address gentle. . . . Never was hatred known in him, nor ill-will towards any man, however great the wrong done him ; and so great was his benignity in this respect that wise-acres reproached him as wanting in distributive justice. And this they said because he left unpunished some of his servants who deserted him at the siege of Tangier . . . not only becoming reconciled to them, but even granting them honourable advancement over others who had served him well . . . and this is the only shortcoming of his I have to record. He ever showed great devotion to the public affairs of this Kingdom . . . and keenly enjoyed the labour of arms, especially against the enemies of the Holy Faith,

---

[1] This detail is registered by Diogo Gomes, who was with Henry when he died ; he says that a hair shirt was found on the Prince's body.

[2] Doubtless inherited from his English forbears.

while he desired peace with all Christians; . . . a base or unchaste word was never heard to issue from his mouth. . . . His heart never knew what fear was, save the fear of sin." [1]

Cadamosto, a Venetian and thus a foreigner, is no less eulogistic; he calls Henry the most accomplished Prince of his time, the least of whose virtues would suffice to immortalize another. He ascribes Henry's steadfastness in pursuing his objects under great difficulties to the confidence his great learning gave him. This was written in Venice after the Prince's death, and may fairly be considered an impartial testimony.

According to Zurara, the first object Henry set before himself was the discovery of Guinea, which explains the title bestowed on the Chronicle. Five reasons moved him thereto; he desired (1) to obtain knowledge of the lands beyond Cape Bojador, (2) to establish trading relations with any Christians who might live there, (3) to ascertain the extent of the Muhammadan power in Africa, (4) to find a Christian King who would help him to fight the Infidel, and (5) to spread the Christian Faith. His ends were thus scientific, commercial, political and religious; it is worthy of note that Zurara puts the scientific first. But if the religious comes last, it was not the least to weigh with Henry. In his *Chronicle of the capture of Ceuta* Zurara says that he learned to hate the Infidel in his mother's womb, moreover as governor of the Order of Christ he had a positive obligation to combat the foes of the Cross, and the traditions of his family and country impelled him thereto; he proved his crusading zeal at Ceuta and in the attempt on Tangier and he showed solicitude for the conversion of the captives that his men brought home.

The inception of the expeditions of discovery is described by Duarte Pacheco in *Esmeraldo* and by Barros in his *Asia*; one night the Prince lay sleepless in bed, pondering over his schemes, and at last, as if seized by a sudden fury, he leapt up, called his servants and ordered some ships to be made ready at once for a voyage southwards along the coast of Marocco. All were astonished and attributed this outburst to a divine revelation. Damião de Goes, a more critical

---

[1] V. *ut supra.*

historian than Pacheco or Barros,[1] refers to this story in
his *Chronicle of Prince John* but rejects it ; he explicitly states
that Henry had in view the finding of the Indies and sets out
the reasons for his belief in its feasibility.   The accounts of
Herodotus and other ancient writers convinced him that India
had been reached by the circumnavigation of Africa and this
certainty (the word Goes uses), together with the information
he derived from natives well up in African affairs, led him to
order the refinding of the forgotten route.

At least one expedition had gone out in the Middle Ages to
find a sea way to the East, that of the Genoese Doria and
Vivaldo in 1291, so that the attempt was no novelty, even
apart from the classical voyages known to the Prince.   He
had certainly studied the works of ancient and medieval
geographers cited by Zurara and from them and especially
from Marco Polo must have drawn inspiration.   The
abundance and precision of the data he had collected account
for the persistence he showed, and for his refusal to be
daunted by failures, heavy expense, and hostile criticism.

The enterprise may have seemed to him all the more
feasible because he could have no accurate idea of the distance,
since according to many cartographers Africa was a peninsula
about half its actual size, that is to say, the Southern coast
of Guinea continued directly to the Indian Ocean.   Even
in the Laurentian Portolano of 1351, the best medieval map
of the dark continent, the latter is shown with a short leg.
Henry knew that caravans going across the Sahara had long
traded with the Guinea coast, so that if his ships could
reach it, they would be well on the way to the East
and might hope to find Prester John and secure his
assistance.

In view of a discovery made some years ago, we can no
longer consider hyperbolical the passage in Cap. 2 of the
Chronicle of Guinea in which Zurara states that inhabitants
of the greater and lesser India, that is Indians proper and
Abyssinians,   visited   Portugal   and received   Henry's
hospitality, for a document published in part by Senhor

---

[1] Vignaud says that there are only three first hand authorities as to
the intentions and acts of Prince Henry, Zurara, Gomes and Barros ;
but he should add Goes, if he includes Barros, for they were
contemporaries.   *Histoire Critique de la grande enterprise de Christophe
Colomb* (Paris 1911), vol. i, cap. 4.

Pedro d' Azevedo shows that an ambassador of Prester John was in Lisbon in 1452.[1]

The presence of this man in Portugal suggests that the Prince had previously opened up relations with Abyssinia and perhaps had sent to fetch him from Italy. If so, this would explain Zurara's statement that Indians travelled in the Infant's ships.[2] M. de la Roncière records an embassy from the same country to the Pope and the King of Aragon in 1450.[3]

Before describing the maritime expeditions made under Henry's auspices, it is natural to enquire how far their results may have been anticipated. The undoubted pre-Henrician voyages down the coast of Africa are very few. The Phœnicians sent by Pharaoh Necho may have rounded the Cape of Good Hope, but Hanno probably got no further than Sierra Leone, while the Genoese Malocello only reached the Canaries. Doria and Vivaldo disappeared, so that it is impossible to fix their furthest south, while the voyages of the men of Dieppe in the fourteenth century are certainly not proven, the evidence for them being too late.

As has been already remarked, Henry's continued and systematic explorations began only after the capture of Ceuta, at which time he had attained the age of twenty-one. In 1419 João Gonçalves Zarco and Tristam Vaz Teixeira, knights of his household, seeing their master's longing to discover Guinea, offered their services and went as far south as possible, but were driven back by a storm and found the island of Porto Santo. In the following year they returned and in the words of Zurara " passed over to Madeira ", which strengthens the view that the islands were already known to the Portuguese as they were to others, for the group appears on fourteenth century maps. The story of the discovery by the Englishman Robert Machin, popularized by D. Franciseo Manuel in his *Epanaphoras*, has no foundation.

From 1422 at least and probably earlier, the Prince despatched yearly expeditions of one or two ships down the

---

[1] See his note in the *Boletim da Classe de Letras* of the Lisbon Academy of Sciences, vol. xiii, p. 525.

[2] In the English version of the *Chronicle of Guinea*, chapter 2, " passing " is a mis-translation for " passages " (vol. i, p. 7, bottom).

[3] Ch. de la Roncière, *La Découverte de l'Afrique au moyen âge* (Cairo, 1925), vol. ii, p. 119.

coast, for when Bojador was finally passed, we are told that twelve years had been spent in the attempt. The fact that it ran out far into the ocean, and the shoals and currents that surrounded it, terrified the mariners, who were accustomed to hug the shore and dared not sail far enough from land to get into deep water and avoid them. They were convinced that the ocean beyond the Cape was unnavigable ; moreover they shared the prevalent belief that life could not be sustained in the torrid zone.

Neither these fears, nor general condemnation of the business as dangerous and unprofitable, moved Henry, and in 1433 he sent out his squire Gil Eannes with orders to double Bojador. This man did no better than the others, but having been despatched again in the following year for the same purpose, he succeeded. Contemporaries regarded the feat as equal to one of the labours of Hercules, and a modern historian has pronounced it greater than that of Bartholomew Dias in passing the Cape of Storms. The glory of Gil Eannes lay not in penetrating some leagues further south, but in overcoming the obstacles which had daunted his predecessors and destroying the conviction that Bojador was the limit of possible navigation.

The French proverb—" the first step is the most difficult " —proved true once more, for now one voyage after another resulted in progress. Gil Eannes went out again the year following with Baldaya, Henry's cupbearer, and sailed 150 miles beyond the Cape, now shorn of its terrors, to the Angra dos Ruivos, while in a subsequent voyage the latter reached the Rio do Ouro, 240 miles to the south, and in 1436 he discovered the Porto do Galé, 50 miles further on.

So far the expeditions had been an exclusive venture of the Prince,[1] and financed by his own resources and those of the Order of Christ, so that when he was unable to attend to them, they ceased. This respite happened from 1437 to 1440, for in those years occurred his disastrous attempt against Tangier, the death of his brother King Edward, and political troubles which kept him fully occupied.

He was anxious to obtain from the natives information about the lands his caravels had been skirting, and when more

---

[1] Duarte Pacheco speaks of him as " the first inventor of this navigation and discovery." *Esmeraldo*, bk. iii, cap. 5.

peaceful conditions prevailed at home and the expeditions recommenced in 1441, he ordered his captains to try and take some captives. His wish was gratified by Antam Gonçalves who brought back ten Azenegues, among them a chief Adahu, while Nuno Tristam, who had assisted in the capture, went on to Cape Branco. Desirous of returning to his country, Adahu promised that five or six Moors would be given in exchange for him, and Gonçalves, sailing from Lisbon this time and accompanied by one Balthazar, a knight of the household of the Emperor, obtained ten negroes, gold dust and ostrich eggs. In 1443 Nuno Tristam made a further advance to Arguim Bay and took more natives. The Prince welcomed them because he hoped they would serve as guides and interpreters and assist in the propagation of Christianity, but to the people they meant cheap labour and profit, hence slave raids became a feature of succeeding expeditions. Public opinion now turned in Henry's favour, and private adventurers came forward and undertook voyages on their own account with his consent. The merchants and mariners of Lisbon and Lagos were foremost in this, and the latter formed a company for which Lançarote Pessanha, the receiver of customs, took out a fleet of six caravels and secured 235 natives. It is right to say that according to Zurara masters treated the captives like their other servants ; the younger were taught trades, freed and married to Portuguese women. Nearly all became Christians and were absorbed into the white population. The Portuguese had no repugnance to black blood, so that slavery with them rarely assumed the harsh aspect it wore when practised by the races of Northern Europe.

In 1444 Nuno Tristam and others reached the Senegal, in the next year Dinis Dias rounded Cape Verde, and John Fernandes spent seven months among the natives of the Arguim coast and brought back the first reliable account of part of the interior ; in 1446 he made a further advance, and in the opinion of the Visconde de Santarem passed Cape Verga, receiving the reward of 100 doubloons from Henry and the same amount from Peter, then Regent.[1] The sandy, sterile, almost uninhabited regions had been left far behind ; the navigators were now coasting a land covered with palm

[1] *Chronicle of Guinea,* vol. ii, p. 349.

trees and verdure and well peopled, whose products rewarded their efforts. But there was a dark side ; the raids had aroused the hostility of the natives, and in 1445 and 1446 three of the leaders perished at their hands. It is not surprising, for Zurara tells us that by 1448 the Portuguese had carried off 927 captives. In 1445 twenty-five caravels sailed to the West African Coast, including fourteen which left Lagos under Lançarote Pessanha to avenge the death of Gonçalo de Sintra the previous year ; and when passing the Magdalen Islands off Cape Verde they saw the arms of the Prince cut on trees, with his device *Talant de bien faire*.

By 1446 no less than 51 caravels had left Portugal, penetrating 450 leagues beyond Cape Bojador, and it was found that the coast went south-east with many promontories, and the Prince had it inserted in his charts. Zurara remarks that what had previously been shown on the *mappa mundi* with respect to this coast had only been depicted at hazard. The result of the expeditions are shown in the map of Andrea Bianco, dated London 1448. In 1447 one of the Prince's captains opened up relations with the city of Messa in Marocco, and obtained a lion, which he sent to an old servant of his, resident in Galway. The fame of the discoveries had spread over Europe, and men in search of adventure and honour came from various countries to take part in them. Among these was a Danish noble Vallarte, who in 1448 obtained from Henry a caravel to take him to " Blackland ", where he lost his life. This is the last expedition mentioned by Zurara, for though he wrote his Chronicle in 1453, he did not continue the record beyond 1448, because trade and peaceful inter-course with natives had less interest for him than deeds of arms. From that year to 1460 our information is meagre ; almost the only voyages we know of are two of Cadamosto, a Venetian seaman in Henry's service, already mentioned, who in 1455 and 1457 explored the course of the Gambia and Senegal, and discovered the Cape Verde islands, and two voyages of Diogo Gomes in 1458 and 1460. Sierra Leone had probably not been attained in the Prince's lifetime.[1]

---

[1] The southern limit of the Henrician explorations is an unsolved problem. His biographers have not discussed it adequately, nor have they presented us with a satisfactory map showing the places found with the respective dates.

For forty years of effort the result may appear small, but the impetus he had given was never lost, and though exploring expeditions became less frequent and regular, the advance that each made was incomparably greater.

Twenty-two years after his death Diogo Cão, who had been brought up in his household, discovered the Congo, five years later Bartholomew Dias, probably the son of Dinis Dias, one of his captains, reached the southernmost point of the African continent, and in 1498, after a voyage longer than man had hitherto achieved, Vasco da Gama anchored off Calicut, on the Malabar coast of India, thus realizing at length the union of West and East, for which the Prince had striven.

The coast voyages have been described; it remains to consider those in what Zurara calls the " ocean sea ". Some of the Azores are marked in the Medicean Portolano of 1351, and it is possible that the group was found by Portuguese vessels under Genoese pilots, but we have no record of any visit before Henry sent Gonçalo Velho to look for them in 1431 or 1432. By 1439 seven were known, and Afonso V gave the Prince leave to colonize them ; the first settlers were Portuguese and Flemings, hence they appear under the name of the " Flemish islands " in some maps.

It is impossible in the present state of our knowledge to make full, or even very definite, statements about the expeditions to the West in Henry's lifetime. After the discovery of the Azores, it was natural that mariners should seek for other lands in that direction, and in 1452, Diogo de Teive and Pedro Velasco sailed 150 leagues south-west of Fayal in search of Antilia. Legends of lost islands existed, and so fixed was the belief in them that men asked for and obtained grants of what they hoped to find, as witness the concession made in 1457 by King Afonso V to his brother Ferdinand.

Antonio Galvam mentions a voyage of 1447, and an inscription in the 1448 map of Andrea Bianco has convinced some geographers that the north-east corner of Brazil was found about that time, but though this is doubtful, the protest of King John II against the line of demarcation, established by Pope Alexander VI in 1493, and the consent of Spain to its removal westward by the Treaty of

Tordesillas in 1494,[1] so as in fact to include Brazil in the Portuguese sphere, suggest an earlier knowledge of that country.

In 1500 the pilots of Alvarez Cabral's expedition recognized the *Terra de Santa Cruz* (i.e. Northern Brazil) as the same land they had seen marked on an old map belonging to Pero Vaz Bisagudo,[2] and since only the Portuguese navigated the Western Atlantic, we may conclude that it had been reached many years before that date and previous to the expedition sent by King Manoel I to explore those seas in 1498, which is recorded by Duarte Pacheco. Robert Thorne, writing in 1527, dates the discovery of what we now call Brazil before 1494.[3] That the Western Continent was believed, if not actually known, to exist, is clear from a remarkable assertion of Las Casas; he declares that Columbus on his third voyage planned to sail south from the Cape Verde islands because he wanted to ascertain if the King of Portugal was wrong when he affirmed that there was *terra firma* in that direction.

It is possible that when Prince Henry found the African route to the East to be longer than he had anticipated, he thought of reaching it by the north-west passage; at any rate, as Dr. Sofus Larsen has recently sought to show, Christian I of Denmark seems to have sent out an expedition of Danes with Portuguese emissaries aboard in 1472-3, which coasted along a continental shore in the region of what we now know as the St. Lawrence. The suggestion of the expedition is said to have come from Afonso V of Portugal, but as he generally had little interest in the work of discovery, he may have inherited the idea from his uncle, who

---

[1] The Bull and Treaty are in *Alguns Documentos do Archivo nacional acerca das navigações e conquistas portuguesas* (Lisbon, 1892), pp. 65 and 69.   Translated in F. C. Davenport, *European Treaties bearing on U.S.A.* (Washington, 1917), i, 61 sqq.

[2] *Alguns Documentos*, p. 122.

[3] Thorne mentions this in connexion with the Tordesillas Agreement of 1494, " When this aforesaid consent of the division of the world was agreed of betweene them (i.e. the Kings of Spain and Portugal) the King of Portugal had already discovered certaine Islands that lie over against Cape Verde, and also certaine part of the maine land of India toward the South, from whence he fette Brasill, and called it the land of Brasil.   So that for all that should come in his terme and limites, he took 370 leagues beyond Cape Verde." Hakluyt's *Voyages* (Everyman edn.), i, 226.

P

certainly maintained relations with his kinsmen, the Danish Kings.[1]

From what has gone before, it will be seen that our information about the voyages of the fifteenth century, whether those made under Henry's auspices, or private ventures, is incomplete, and often confused. In a remarkable study in the review *Lusitania* for January, 1924, Dr. Jaime Cortesão, director of the Lisbon National Library, contends that the monopoly aimed at by the Portuguese led them to conceal facts which might provoke international complications or assist their rivals. In 1443, a royal decree provided that no one should sail beyond Cape Bojador without Henry's leave, and that those who infringed this law should suffer confiscation of their vessels and cargoes, but the Holy See alone could render the monopoly effective against foreigners, and the Prince in his capacity as Crusader and missionary of Christianity and Empire, obtained from successive Popes exclusive rights for Portugal over the lands already discovered or to be discovered to the South. Protests came from Castile, whose rulers considered North-West Africa as part of their inheritance by virtue of their descent from the old Gothic sovereigns, and in addition to the Canaries, we find them claiming Guinea after Henry's seamen had penetrated there. The dispute lasted half a century, and provoked incidents which, had Castile been in a position to undertake it, might have led to war with Portugal.

Reference has already been made to the Papal grant of the Canaries in 1344 to D. Luis de la Cerda; he seems to have made no attempt to act upon it, but in 1402 and the following years the Normans Jean de Bethencourt and Gadifer de la Salle established Christian colonies in some of the islands, doing homage for them to the King of Castile, who reserved his supreme dominion; thus when Henry initiated voyages down the African coast, he found a foreign power on the flank. It was necessary for the full success of his policy of Portuguese expansion at all costs to obtain possession of the islands, which his Castilian rivals might

---

[1] *Boletim da Classe das Letras* of the Lisbon Academy of Sciences, vol. xv, p. 214. This is a brief summary of Dr. Larsen's conclusions. His argument is fully set forth in Sofus Larsen, *The Discovery of North America twenty years before Columbus* (Copenhagen—London, 1925).

use as a base from which to push out towards the coveted goal of Guinea.

In the long and complicated struggle between the two powers that ensued, we have the first of the contests for possessions beyond the sea that have marked the succeeding centuries. Every weapon, naval, military and diplomatic was employed, and the story deserves study in much greater detail than it has yet received. In 1425 the Prince sent an expedition under D. Fernando de Castro to conquer the islands, but the effort failed, and in the following year King John of Castile despatched an embassy led by the Bishop of Burgos to Portugal to make formal assertion of his prior claims to the Archipelago. Henry endeavoured to induce the King to relinquish these, but meeting with a refusal, he determined to secure an overriding grant from the over-lord of the islands, Pope Eugenius IV. In 1435 he succeeded in this, but the day of papal pre-eminence in international affairs was past; the Great Schism with Popes and Anti-Popes bidding against one another for the support of rival powers was hardly healed, and Eugenius IV himself was already in danger of the summons to account for his actions before a Council of the Church that overtook him four years later. King John protested violently against the Pope's infringement of his rights, and by his orders the Bishop of Burgos raised the question of ownership at the Council of Basel. The Pope hesitated to decide definitely between the two powers, but admonished the King of Portugal to do nothing to the prejudice of the King of Castile. This did not satisfy Henry, and in 1437 he made his attack on Tangier, his object being, as Dr. Cortesão thinks, to anticipate Castile by securing this important base and to assert the rights of Portugal to the conquest of North Africa. Ill-success did not daunt him, it only led him to change his methods, and he made further attempts to obtain the Canaries by negotiation. Though his diplomatic efforts had no result, he obtained in 1446 from his brother, the Regent Peter, a decree that no ships were to go to the islands without his leave, and in 1447 he bestowed the captaincy of the Island of Lanzarote on Antam Gonçalves. Not content with thus asserting and exercising rights of ownership, he allowed and probably encouraged attacks in 1450, 1451, and

1453 on the islands which did not recognize Portuguese authority.

All this time the Castilians persisted in sending ships to trade down the African coast, and in 1452 some caravels of Seville returning from Guinea were met by Palenço, a celebrated Portuguese sea-rover, who captured one, and imprisoned the crew, while a Genoese merchant found on board had his hands cut off. King John addressed two letters to King Afonso V, dated May 25th, 1452, and April 10th, 1454, describing and protesting against these hostile acts and holding Henry responsible for them, and the long dispute was not settled until 1480. The Treaty of Alcaçovas, signed on March 6th of that year, allotted the Canaries to Castile and North Africa, Guinea and the islands in the ocean to the south to Portugal.[1] This secured the monopoly she had worked for, because so long as she held the seas and lands adjacent to the Canaries the possession of the latter by another power was immaterial, nevertheless she would not rely altogether on written agreements, and on April 6th, 1480, Afonso V signed a decree ordering that the crews of any foreign vessels found in the Portuguese zone of navigation should be thrown into the sea.[2] Moreover to remove from Castile the temptation to infringe the Treaty, a policy of secrecy was adopted, which included the suppression of information that might serve competitors, and at the same time measures were taken to find out foreign plans and the title deeds relating to the claims of rivals. It was King John II who fully developed the policy of secrecy, but even in Henry's lifetime Afonso V had a Castilian in his service who acted as " reader of the Chronicles and books of Castile ".

The strange silence preserved by Portuguese Chronicles of the fifteenth century about the discoveries is thus explicable. When Barros came to write of them, he could find no complete copy of Zurara's *Chronicle of Guinea*, and he declares that more discoveries were made in the reign of Afonso V than those

---

[1] As the Treaty says nothing of the East Indies, Vignaud argues that the Portuguese, even as late as this, had no intention of penetrating there. In fact the Treaty only dealt with disputed territories, and there was no reason why it should mention India.

[2] *Alguns Documentos*, p. 45.

CITY OF ST. ALBAN
PUBLIC
LIBRARY

he relates.[1] As Dr. Cortesão says, it is not likely that the King would forget to have the voyages after 1448 recorded, when he commissioned Zurara to write the achievements of the Menezes family in Africa. Damião de Goes states that in his time histories which formerly existed had vanished ; he notes that the *Chronicle of Afonso V* by Ruy de Pina contained only one chapter about the voyages, that of King Duarte by the same author said nothing on the subject, while there was no Chronicle at all covering the latter part of the reign of John I, the beginning of the period of discovery. Goes does not mention the work of Cerveira from which Zurara drew, so that it had evidently disappeared also.[2] Pina composed in the sixteenth century the Chronicles of the Kings of the preceding century, using the works of his predecessors, but he omitted to speak of the most important event and chief glory of the age, the voyages and discoveries. Nothing but the official policy of secrecy can account for his silence; as royal Chronicler he must have acted under orders, for otherwise he would not have dared to leave out notable achievements in the recording of which many persons then living had an interest. The disappearance of the earlier and more complete books can only be attributed to the policy of secrecy ; they were almost certainly destroyed.

Even the *Chronicle of Guinea* has been tampered with and truncated, as an examination of the two existing MSS. proves, and we have hardly any information about the Atlantic voyages to the West in the last half of the fifteenth century, though we know that some were made. Of this same Chronicle Pina only used enough to form one chapter. Now if, when the discoveries were in their infancy and their great development could not be foreseen, Zurara had been employed to record them, and if Cerveira had related them even more minutely, how came it that they were apparently treated as of less importance when they had transformed the face of the world ? There seems to be but one answer, that suggested by Dr. Cortesão. It is only by chance that we have lately learnt that an ambassador of Prester John

[1] *Asia.* Decad. i, bk. ii, cap. 2.

[2] Vignaud is mistaken in saying that Barros saw Cerveira's book; what he saw were letters of his written from Benin. Decad i, bk. ii, cap. I.

visited Lisbon eight years before Henry's death, and we cannot help wondering what other important finds may be awaiting students among the ancient Portuguese archives in the Torre do Tombo. Again, it was not until the eighteenth century that Caetano de Sousa printed a document by which two years after that embassy, on June 7th, 1454, Afonso V conceded to the Order of Christ the spiritual jurisdiction of Nubia and Ethiopia.

The policy of secrecy not only led to the suppression of historical works ; nautical guides, maps, instructions to navigators and their reports suffered the same fate.

In the Cortes of 1481 the representatives of the Third Estate petitioned King John II not to allow foreigners to establish themselves in his dominions, adding that, as regards Florentines and Genoese, they had brought no profit, but on the contrary had found out secrets about Mina,[1] and the islands. They spoke more truly than they could have known, for it is probable that it was during his residence in Portugal that Columbus obtained the information which enabled him to find his new islands in the West.

Though the traditional view of Henry's designs and achievements as set out here has been subscribed to by most modern scholars, two, Payne and Vignaud, sought to minimize them. The former considered Henry as mainly an organiser of slave-raids and entirely misunderstood his character ; through ignorance of Portuguese psychology and history he committed himself to baseless statements and indulged in unworthy ironical remarks. His distorted picture [2] will unfortunately be read by hundreds for one who can find time to go to the sources and learn the true facts.

Vignaud was better informed, more sober and less prejudiced than Payne, and he offered more solid arguments in support of his case ; influenced however by Zurara's lack of precise statement, he contended that the Prince never aimed at reaching the East Indies, but only endeavoured to open up relations with Prester John. Now though Goes, who has been quoted earlier, wrote nearly a century after Henry's death, D. Manoel I made an assertion similar to

---

[1] The fort of São Jorge da Mina, the centre of Portuguese power and commerce on the Guinea coast, the modern Elmina.

[2] *Cambridge Modern History*, vol. i, pp. 10–11.

that of the historian in the letters patent whereby the title of Admiral was granted to Vasco da Gama on January 10th, 1502; the King there said that his uncle began to discover Guinea with the purpose and will to find India by that coast.[1] As Dr. Cortesão remarks, the designation of " India " in a grant to the finder of the way thither, made only four years after the great voyage, cannot refer to the realm of Prester John. Besides this, actual contemporary evidence of Henry's intentions has been preserved. In cap. 16 of the *Chronicle of Guinea* Zurara reports the Prince as saying that he wished to get knowledge of the Indies as distinct from Abyssinia, and this was as early as 1442.[2] Account must also be taken of the Papal Bulls ; in one of January 8th, 1454, Pope Nicholas V bore witness to Henry's desire to make the ocean navigable as far as the Indians " who are said to worship the name of Christ " (i.e. the so-called " St. Thomas's Christians " of the Malabar Coast), while Pope Calixtus III in March, 1456, conceded to the Order of Christ spiritual jurisdiction in all the lands to be acquired by the Portuguese explorers beyond Cape Non, throughout all Guinea and beyond that Southern region " as far as the Indians ". In these " Indians " Vignaud merely saw Abyssinians, but he found himself unable to explain away the reference in cap. 16. In his voyage of 1456 Diogo Gomes had orders to reach India, if possible, and took an interpreter for use if he arrived there. By India Vignaud understood Abyssinia, but he made no reference to *Esmeraldo* where Duarte Pacheco describes the difference of opinion as to whether the voyages should be made down the coast, or across the ocean as a nearer way, until " some land of India was found ".[3] At the time this was written, India certainly meant what it does to us. Moreover, Barros reports that when Bartholomew Dias returned from his discovery of the Cape, King John II named the latter *Good Hope* " for the promise it gave of the finding of India, so desired and *for so many years sought after* ".

If contemporary chronicles are not more outspoken

---

[1] *Alguns Documentos*, p. 127.

[2] " He not only desired to have knowledge of that land, but also of the Indies and of the land of Prester John, if he could."

[3] Ibid., bk. iii, cap. 4.

regarding Henry's ultimate purpose, the reason lies to a great extent in the fear of arousing the jealousy and opposition of other powers, of Castile and especially of Venice, which controlled the lucrative trade between Europe and Asia. In any case, Zurara could hardly be expected to dilate on a point which had small importance when he wrote, since India was still a far off goal.

INDEX

Abyssinia, *see* Ethiopia ; histories of, *see* Almeida, Tellez
Adam of Bremen, 7, 81, 110, 121
Adamnan, 60 f.
Africa, Central, explored, 90, 100 ; East, ancient knowledge of, 22 ; Cosmas' knowledge of, 36 ; West, Castilians on, 211, 212 ; charts of, 207 ; Portuguese voyages to, 204–8, 210 ; Ptolemy's knowledge of, 22 ; voyage to, 204
Africa, Africanus' description of, 170 ; European travellers to, in Middle Ages, 167, 168 ; Jews in, 170, 171 ; Malfante's description of, 170 ; maps of, 203 ; Moslem toleration of Christianity in, 168 ; travellers' tales of, 166
Africanus, John Leo, 170
Agathemerus, Geographical treatise of, 26
Agricola, conquest of Britain by, 20
Ailly, Cardinal Pierre d', cosmogony of, 13–15 ; debt of to Bacon, 18 ; debt of to Ptolemy, 14, 17 ; influence of on Columbus, 15, 17
Albertus Magnus, cosmogony of, 10
Alcaçovas, Treaty of, 212
Alexandria, 3, 4, 33, 61, 137
Almalik, mission station at, 145
Almeida, history of Abyssinia by, 183, 188–92
al Muqaddasī, journeys of, 96
Alvarez, 183
America, discovery of by Vikings, 81
Antichthones, 7
Antipodes, discussed by Bede, 6 ; discussed by Lambert, 8, 9 ; discussed by Dante, 9 ; discussed by Albertus Magnus, 11 ; discussed by Roger Bacon, 11, 12
Antonine itinerary, 27, 28, 52–60, 64
Arab coins in Sweden, 82
Arab Empire, culture of, 88, 89 ; extent of, 88, 89, 113 ; geographical literature of, 91, 96–8 ; population of, 89 ; postal system of, 91
Arabian amber, 94 ; astronomical tables, 11 ; authors, 13 ; geography, 24 ; merchants, 110, 117 ; pilgrimages, 91 ; thought, 2, 3, 18, 89
Arabia, 14, 21, 33, 35, 100
Arculf, Bishop, 60–66
Aristotle, 14, 15, 17

Atlas of Medieval Geography, 109
Atlas Mountains, 20 ; caravans from, 168
Audomarensis, L., Liber Floridus of, 8
Autun, Honorius of, 162

Bacon, Roger, 3, 10–13, 18
Baghdad, 109, 125, 127, 133, 137
Baltic, amber route from, 20 ; German merchants on, 105 ; Mohammedan trade with, 94
Banks, *see* Vivaldi
Basil, St., 24–5
Baṭṭūṭah, Ibn, 90, 99–100, 135 (note), 141
Beazley, Professor C. R., quoted, 50–3, 56, 69, 105, 116, 153, 156
Beatus, maps, 5
Beauvais, Vincent of, 160
Bede, The Venerable, 2, 5–7, 18, 37, 69, 72, 165
Benjamin of Tudela, 105
Björkö, 73, 83
Black Death reaches Europe, 143
Black Sea, 10, 125, 137 ; Swedes on, 82 ; trade on, 142 ; trade ruined by Turks, 171
Blanquerna, 168
Bojador, Cape of, none to sail beyond, 210 ; reached by Portuguese, 199 ; rounded by Portuguese, 205
Bokhara, 132, 142
Bolgar, 111, 122
Boshüslan, 83
Brahmins, early age of, 27
Brazil, discovery of, 208, 209 ; Portuguese claims to, 209 ; Terra da Santa Cruz, 209
Breviarius, 50–2

Cabrul, Alvarez, 209
Canaries, allotted to Castile, 212 ; Castilian claims to, 210–11 ; dispute over, 211 ; granted to Luis de la Cerda, 197 ; Normans in, 210 ; Portuguese claims to, 197 ; Portuguese voyages to, 196
Carolingian Empire, fall of, 74 ; overthrows Frisian Empire, 72
Caspian Sea, shape of, 24 ; trade on, 111, 138 ; Vikings on, 83
Castile, 11 ; claims to Canaries,

CITY OF ST. ALBAN
PUBLIC
LIBRARY